Generative AI with La

Build large language model (LLM) apps with Python, ChatGPT, and other LLMs

Ben Auffarth

BIRMINGHAM—MUMBAI

2023

Generative AI with LangChain

Copyright © 2023 Packt Publishing

Senior Publishing Product Manager: Tushar Gupta

Acquisition Editor – Peer Reviews: Tejas Mhasvekar

Project Editor: Namrata Katare

Content Development Editors: Tanya D'cruz and Elliot Dallow

Copy Editor: Safis Editing

Technical Editor: Kushal Sharma

Proofreader: Safis Editing

Indexer: Manju Arasan

Presentation Designer: Ajay Patule

Developer Relations Marketing Executive: Monika Sangwan

First published: December 2023

Production reference: 1141223

Published by Packt Publishing Ltd.
Grosvenor House
11 St Paul's Square
Birmingham
B3 1RB, UK.

ISBN 978-1-83508-346-8

www.packt.com

To Diane and Nico

– Ben Auffarth

Contributors

About the author

Ben Auffarth is a seasoned data science leader with a background and Ph.D. in computational neuroscience. Ben has analyzed terabytes of data, simulated brain activity on supercomputers with up to 64k cores, designed and conducted wet lab experiments, built production systems processing underwriting applications, and trained neural networks on millions of documents. He's the author of the books *Machine Learning for Time Series* and *Artificial Intelligence with Python Cookbook*. He now works in insurance at Hastings Direct.

Creating this book has been a long and sometimes arduous journey, but also an exciting one. It has been enriched immeasurably by the contributions of several key individuals to whom I owe great thanks. Foremost, I extend my heartfelt gratitude to Leo, whose insightful feedback significantly refined this book. I am equally delighted with my astute editors — Tanya, Elliot, and Kushal. Their efforts went above and beyond expectations. Tanya, in particular, was instrumental in guiding me through the writing process, continually challenging me to clarify my thoughts and significantly shaping the final product.

About the reviewers

Leonid Ganeline is a machine learning engineer with extensive experience in natural language processing. He has worked in several start-ups, creating models and production systems. He is an active contributor to LangChain and several other open-source projects. His interest lies in model evaluation, especially in LLM evaluation

I would like to express my gratitude to my parents, for teaching me how to think rationally, and to my wife, for supporting me in this endeavor.

Ruchi Bhatia is a computer engineer with a Master's degree in information systems management from Carnegie Mellon University. Currently, she is leveraging her skills as a product marketing manager in the rapidly evolving field of data science and AI at HP. She takes pride in being the youngest triple Kaggle Grandmaster across the Notebooks, Datasets, and Discussion categories. Her previous role as the Leader of Data Science at OpenMined allowed her to steer a team of data scientists to create innovative and impactful solutions.

I want to take a moment to express my heartfelt thanks to my parents. Their unwavering support and encouragement throughout my journey have been invaluable. Without their belief in my abilities and their constant guidance, I wouldn't have achieved the milestones I have today. Thank you, Mom and Dad, for always being there for me.

Join our community on Discord

Join our community's Discord space for discussions with the authors and other readers:

https://packt.link/lang

Table of Contents

Preface

In the dynamic and rapidly advancing field of AI, generative AI stands out as a disruptive force poised to transform how we interact with technology. This book is an expedition into the intricate world of **large language models (LLMs)** – the powerful engines driving this transformation – designed to equip developers, researchers, and AI aficionados with the knowledge needed to harness these tools.

Venture into the depths of deep learning, where unstructured data comes alive, and discover how LLMs like GPT-4 and others are carving a path for AI's impact on businesses, societies, and individuals. With the tech industry and media abuzz with the capabilities and potential of these models, it's an opportune moment to explore how they function, thrive, and propel us toward future horizons.

This book serves as your compass, pointing you toward understanding the technical scaffolds that uphold LLMs. We provide a prelude to their vast applications, the elegance of their underlying architecture, and the powerful implications of their existence. Written for a diverse audience, from those taking their first steps in AI to seasoned developers, the text melds theoretical concepts with practical, code-rich examples, preparing you to not only grasp LLMs intellectually but to also apply them inventively and responsibly.

As we embark on this journey together, let us prime ourselves to shape and be shaped by the generative AI narrative that's unfolding at this very moment–a narrative where you, armed with knowledge and foresight, stand at the forefront of this exhilarating technological evolution.

Who this book is for

The book is intended for developers, researchers, and anyone else who is interested in learning more about LLMs. It is written in a clear and concise style, and it includes plenty of code examples to help you learn by doing.

Whether you are a beginner or an experienced developer, this book will be a valuable resource for anyone who wants to get the most out of LLMs and to stay ahead of the curve about LLMs and LangChain.

What this book covers

Chapter 1, What Is Generative AI?, explains how generative AI has revolutionized the processing of text, images, and video, with deep learning at its core. This chapter introduces generative models such as LLMs, detailing their technical underpinnings and transformative potential across various sectors. This chapter covers the theory behind these models, highlighting neural networks and training approaches, and the creation of human-like content. The chapter outlines the evolution of AI, Transformer architecture, text-to-image models like Stable Diffusion, and touches on sound and video applications.

Chapter 2, LangChain for LLM Apps, uncovers the need to expand beyond the stochastic parrots of LLMs–models that mimic language without true understanding–by harnessing LangChain's framework. Addressing limitations like outdated knowledge, action limitations, and hallucination risks, the chapter highlights how LangChain integrates external data and interventions for more coherent AI applications. The chapter critically engages with the concept of stochastic parrots, revealing the deficiencies in models that produce fluent but meaningless language, and explicates how prompting, chain-of-thought reasoning, and retrieval grounding augment LLMs to address issues of contextuality, bias, and intransparency.

Chapter 3, Getting Started with LangChain, provides foundational knowledge for you to set up your environment to run all examples in the book. It begins with installation guidance for Docker, Conda, Pip, and Poetry. The chapter then details integrating models from various providers like OpenAI's ChatGPT and Hugging Face, including obtaining necessary API keys. It also deals with running open-source models locally. The chapter culminates in constructing an LLM app to assist customer service agents, exemplifying how LangChain can streamline operations and enhance the accuracy of responses.

Chapter 4, Building Capable Assistants, tackles turning LLMs into reliable assistants by weaving in fact-checking to reduce misinformation, employing sophisticated prompting strategies for summarization, and integrating external tools for enhanced knowledge. It explores the Chain of Density for information extraction and discusses LangChain decorators and expression language for customizing behavior. The chapter introduces map-reduce in LangChain for handling long documents and discusses token monitoring to manage API usage costs.

It looks at implementing a Streamlit application to create interactive LLM applications and using function calling and tool usage to transcend basic text generation. Two distinct agent paradigms, plan-and-solve and zero-shot, are implemented to demonstrate decision-making strategies.

Chapter 5, Building a Chatbot like ChatGPT, delves into enhancing chatbot capabilities with **re-trieval-augmented generation (RAG)**, a method that provides LLMs with access to external knowledge, improving their accuracy and domain-specific proficiency. This chapter discusses document vectorization, efficient indexing, and the use of vector databases like Milvus and Pine-cone for semantic search. We implement a chatbot, incorporating moderation chains to ensure responsible communication. The chatbot, available on GitHub, serves as a basis for exploring advanced topics like dialogue memory and context management.

Chapter 6, Developing Software with Generative AI, examines the burgeoning role of LLMs in software development, highlighting the potential for AI to automate coding tasks and serve as dynamic coding assistants. It explores the current state of AI-driven software development, experiments with models to generate code snippets, and introduces a design for an automated software development agent using LangChain. Critical reflections on the agent's performance emphasize the importance of human oversight for error mitigation and high-level design, setting the stage for a future where AI and human developers work symbiotically.

Chapter 7, LLMs for Data Science, explores the intersection of generative AI and data science, spotlighting LLMs' potential to amplify productivity and drive scientific discovery. The chapter outlines the current scope of automation in data science through AutoML and extends this notion with the integration of LLMs for advanced tasks like augmenting datasets and generating executable code. It covers practical methods for LLMs to conduct exploratory data analysis, run SQL queries, and visualize statistical data. Finally, the use of agents and tools demonstrates how LLMs can address complex data-centric questions.

Chapter 8, Customizing LLMs and Their Output, delves into conditioning techniques like fine-tuning and prompting, essential for tailoring LLM performance to complex reasoning and specialized tasks. We unpack fine-tuning, where an LLM is further trained on task-specific data, and prompt engineering, which strategically guides the LLM to generate desired outputs. Advanced prompting strategies such as few-shot learning and chain-of-thought are implemented, enhancing the reasoning capabilities of LLMs. The chapter not only provides concrete examples of fine-tuning and prompting but also discusses the future of LLM advancements and their applications in the field.

Chapter 9, Generative AI in Production, addresses the complexities of deploying LLMs within real-world applications, covering best practices for ensuring performance, meeting regulatory requirements, robustness at scale, and effective monitoring. It underscores the importance of evaluation, observability, and systematic operation to make generative AI beneficial in customer engagement and decision-making with financial consequences. It also outlines practical strategies for deployment and ongoing monitoring of LLM apps using tools like Fast API, Ray, and newcomers such as LangServe and LangSmith. These tools can provide automated evaluation and metrics that support the responsible adoption of generative AI across sectors.

Chapter 10, The Future of Generative Models, ventures into the potential advancements and socio-technical challenges of generative AI. It examines the economic and societal impacts of these technologies, debating job displacement, misinformation, and ethical concerns like human value alignment. As various sectors brace for disruptive AI-induced changes, it reflects on the responsibility of corporations, lawmakers, and technologists to forge effective governance frameworks. This final chapter emphasizes the importance of steering AI development toward augmenting human potential while addressing risks such as deepfakes, bias, and the weaponization of AI. It highlights the urgency for transparency, ethical deployment, and equitable access to guide the generative AI revolution positively.

To get the most out of this book

To benefit from the value this book offers, it is essential to have a foundational understanding of Python. Additionally, possessing some basic knowledge of machine learning is recommended.

Download the example code files

The code bundle for the book is hosted on GitHub at https://github.com/benman1/generative_ai_with_langchain. We also have other code bundles from our rich catalog of books and videos available at https://github.com/PacktPublishing/. Check them out!

Download the color images

We also provide a PDF file that has color images of the screenshots/diagrams used in this book. You can download it here: https://packt.link/gbp/9781835083468.

Conventions used

There are a number of text conventions used throughout this book.

`CodeInText`: Indicates code words in text, database table names, folder names, filenames, file extensions, pathnames, dummy URLs, user input, and Twitter handles. For example: "Mount the downloaded `WebStorm-10*.dmg` disk image file as another disk in your system."

A block of code is set as follows:

```
from langchain.chains import LLMCheckerChain
from langchain.llms import OpenAI


llm = OpenAI(temperature=0.7)


text = "What type of mammal lays the biggest eggs?"
```

When we wish to draw your attention to a particular part of a code block, the relevant lines or items are set in bold:

```
from pandasai.llm.openai import OpenAI
llm = OpenAI(api_token="YOUR_API_TOKEN")


pandas_ai = PandasAI(llm)
```

Any command-line input or output is written as follows:

```
pip install -r requirements.txt
```

Bold: Indicates a new term, an important word, or words that you see on the screen. For instance, words in menus or dialog boxes appear in the text like this. For example: "Select **System info** from the **Administration** panel."

Warnings or important notes appear like this.

Tips and tricks appear like this.

Get in touch

Feedback from our readers is always welcome.

General feedback: Email feedback@packtpub.com and mention the book's title in the subject of your message. If you have questions about any aspect of this book, please email us at questions@packtpub.com.

Errata: Although we have taken every care to ensure the accuracy of our content, mistakes do happen. If you have found a mistake in this book, we would be grateful if you reported this to us. Please visit http://www.packtpub.com/submit-errata, click **Submit Errata**, and fill in the form.

Piracy: If you come across any illegal copies of our works in any form on the internet, we would be grateful if you would provide us with the location address or website name. Please contact us at copyright@packtpub.com with a link to the material.

If you are interested in becoming an author: If there is a topic that you have expertise in and you are interested in either writing or contributing to a book, please visit http://authors.packtpub.com.

Share your thoughts

Once you've read *Generative AI with LangChain*, we'd love to hear your thoughts! Scan the QR code below to go straight to the Amazon review page for this book and share your feedback.

https://packt.link/r/1835083463

Your review is important to us and the tech community and will help us make sure we're delivering excellent quality content.

Download a free PDF copy of this book

Thanks for purchasing this book!

Do you like to read on the go but are unable to carry your print books everywhere? Is your eBook purchase not compatible with the device of your choice?

Don't worry, now with every Packt book you get a DRM-free PDF version of that book at no cost.

Read anywhere, any place, on any device. Search, copy, and paste code from your favorite technical books directly into your application.

The perks don't stop there, you can get exclusive access to discounts, newsletters, and great free content in your inbox daily

Follow these simple steps to get the benefits:

1. Scan the QR code or visit the link below

https://packt.link/free-ebook/9781835083468

2. Submit your proof of purchase
3. That's it! We'll send your free PDF and other benefits to your email directly

1

What Is Generative AI?

Over the last decade, deep learning has evolved massively to process and generate unstructured data like text, images, and video. These advanced AI models have gained popularity in various industries, and include **large language models (LLMs)**. There is currently a significant level of fanfare in both the media and the industry surrounding AI, and there's a fair case to be made that **Artificial Intelligence (AI)**, with these advancements, is about to have a wide-ranging and major impact on businesses, societies, and individuals alike. This is driven by numerous factors, including advancements in technology, high-profile applications, and the potential for transformative impacts across multiple sectors.

In this chapter, we'll explore generative models and their application. We'll provide an overview of the technical concepts and training approaches that power these models' ability to produce novel content. While we won't be diving deep into generative models for sound or video, we aim to convey a high-level understanding of how techniques like neural networks, large datasets, and computational scale enable generative models to reach new capabilities in text and image generation. The goal is to demystify the underlying magic that allows these models to generate remarkably human-like content across various domains. With this foundation, readers will be better prepared to consider both the opportunities and challenges posed by this rapidly advancing technology.

We'll follow this structure:

- Introducing generative AI
- Understanding LLMs
- What are text-to-image models?
- What can AI do in other domains?

Let's start from the beginning – by introducing the terminology!

Introducing generative AI

In the media, there is substantial coverage of AI-related breakthroughs and their potential implications. These range from advancements in **Natural Language Processing (NLP)** and computer vision to the development of sophisticated language models like GPT-4. Particularly, generative models have received a lot of attention due to their ability to generate text, images, and other creative content that is often indistinguishable from human-generated content. These same models also provide wide functionality including semantic search, content manipulation, and classification. This allows cost savings with automation and allows humans to leverage their creativity to an unprecedented level.

 Generative AI refers to algorithms that can generate novel content, as opposed to analyzing or acting on existing data like more traditional, predictive machine learning or AI systems.

Benchmarks capturing task performance in different domains have been major drivers of the development of these models. The following graph, inspired by a blog post titled *GPT-4 Predictions* by Stephen McAleese on *LessWrong*, shows the improvements of LLMs in the **Massive Multitask Language Understanding (MMLU)** benchmark, which was designed to quantify knowledge and problem-solving ability in elementary mathematics, US history, computer science, law, and more:

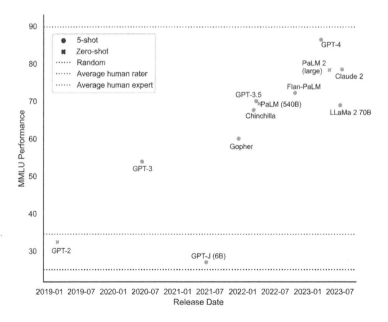

Figure 1.1: Average performance on the MMLU benchmark of LLMs

Please note that while most benchmark results come from 5-shot, a few, like the GPT-2, PaLM, and PaLM-2 results, refer to zero-shot conditioning.

You can see significant improvements in recent years in this benchmark. Particularly, it highlights the progress of the models provided through a public user interface by OpenAI, especially the improvements between releases, from GTP-2 to GPT-3 and GPT-3.5 to GPT-4, although the results should be taken with a grain of salt, since they are self-reported and are obtained either by 5-shot or zero-shot conditioning. Zero-shot means the models were prompted with the question, while in 5-shot settings, models were additionally given 5 question-answer examples. These added examples could naively account for about 20% of performance according to *Measuring Massive Multitask Language Understanding* (Hendrycks and colleagues, revised 2023).

There are a few differences between these models and their training that can account for these boosts in performance, such as scale, instruction-tuning, a tweak to the attention mechanisms, and more and different training data. First and foremost, the massive scaling in parameters from 1.5 billion (GPT-2) to 175 billion (GPT-3) to more than a trillion (GPT-4) enables models to learn more complex patterns; however, another major change in early 2022 was the post-training fine-tuning of models based on human instructions, which teaches the model how to perform a task by providing demonstrations and feedback.

Across benchmarks, a few models have recently started to perform better than an average human rater, but generally still haven't reached the performance of a human expert. These achievements of human engineering are impressive; however, it should be noted that the performance of these models depends on the field; most models are still performing poorly on the GSM8K benchmark of grade school math word problems.

Generative Pre-trained Transformer (GPT) models, like OpenAI's GPT-4, are prime examples of AI advancements in the sphere of LLMs. ChatGPT has been widely adopted by the general public, showing greatly improved chatbot capabilities enabled by being much bigger than previous models. These AI-based chatbots can generate human-like responses as real-time feedback to customers and can be applied to a wide range of use cases, from software development to writing poetry and business communications.

As AI models like OpenAI's GPT continue to improve, they could become indispensable assets to teams in need of diverse knowledge and skills.

For example, GPT-4 could be considered a polymath that works tirelessly without demanding compensation (beyond subscription or API fees), providing competent assistance in subjects like mathematics and statistics, macroeconomics, biology, and law (the model performs well on the Uniform Bar Exam). As these AI models become more proficient and easily accessible, they are likely to play a significant role in shaping the future of work and learning.

OpenAI is a US AI research company that aims to promote and develop friendly AI. It was established in 2015 with the support of several influential figures and companies, who pledged over \$1 billion to the venture. The organization initially committed to being non-profit, collaborating with other institutions and researchers by making its patents and research open to the public. In 2018, Elon Musk resigned from the board citing a potential conflict of interest with his role at Tesla. In 2019, OpenAI transitioned to become a for-profit organization, and subsequently Microsoft made significant investments in OpenAI, leading to the integration of OpenAI systems with Microsoft's Azure-based supercomputing platform and the Bing search engine. The most significant achievements of the company include OpenAI Gym for training reinforcement algorithms, and – more recently – the GPT-n models and the DALL-E generative models, which generate images from text.

By making knowledge more accessible and adaptable, these models have the potential to level the playing field and create new opportunities for people from all walks of life. These models have shown potential in areas that require higher levels of reasoning and understanding, although progress varies depending on the complexity of the tasks involved.

As for generative models with images, they have pushed the boundaries in their capabilities to assist in creating visual content, and their performance in computer vision tasks such as object detection, segmentation, captioning, and much more.

Let's clear up the terminology a bit and explain in more detail what is meant by generative model, artificial intelligence, deep learning, and machine learning.

What are generative models?

In popular media, the term artificial intelligence is used a lot when referring to these new models. In theoretical and applied research circles, it is often joked that AI is just a fancy word for ML, or AI is ML in a suit, as illustrated in this image:

Figure 1.2: ML in a suit. Generated by a model on replicate.com, Diffusers Stable Diffusion v2.1

It's worth distinguishing more clearly between the terms generative model, artificial intelligence, machine learning, deep learning, and language model:

- **Artificial Intelligence (AI)** is a broad field of computer science focused on creating intelligent agents that can reason, learn, and act autonomously.

- **Machine Learning (ML)** is a subset of AI focused on developing algorithms that can learn from data.

- **Deep Learning (DL)** uses deep neural networks, which have many layers, as a mechanism for ML algorithms to learn complex patterns from data.

- **Generative Models** are a type of ML model that can generate new data based on patterns learned from input data.

- **Language Models (LMs)** are statistical models used to predict words in a sequence of natural language. Some language models utilize deep learning and are trained on massive datasets, becoming **large language models (LLMs)**.

This class diagram illustrates how LLMs combine deep learning techniques like neural networks with sequence modeling objectives from language modeling, at a very large scale:

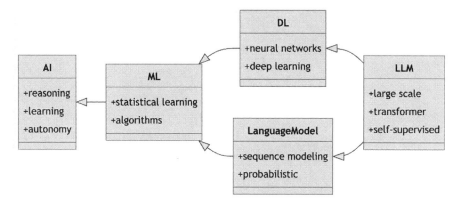

Figure 1.3: Class diagram of different models. LLMs represent the intersection of deep learning techniques with language modeling objectives.

Generative models are a powerful type of AI that can generate new data that resembles the training data. Generative AI models have come a long way, enabling the generation of new examples from scratch using patterns in data. These models can handle different data modalities and are employed across various domains, including text, image, music, and video.

The key distinction is that generative models synthesize new data rather than just making predictions or decisions. This enables applications like generating text, images, music, and video.

Some language models are generative, while some are not. Generative models facilitate the creation of synthetic data to train AI models when real data is scarce or restricted. This type of data generation reduces labeling costs and improves training efficiency. Microsoft Research took this approach (*Textbooks Are All You Need*, June 2023) to training their phi-1 model, where they used GPT-3.5 to create synthetic Python textbooks and exercises.

There are many types of generative models, handling different data modalities across various domains. They are:

- **Text-to-text**: Models that generate text from input text, like conversational agents. Examples: LLaMa 2, GPT-4, Claude, and PaLM 2.
- **Text-to-image**: Models that generate images from text captions. Examples: DALL-E 2, Stable Diffusion, and Imagen.
- **Text-to-audio**: Models that generate audio clips and music from text. Examples: Jukebox, AudioLM, and MusicGen.

- **Text-to-video**: Models that generate video content from text descriptions. Example: Phenaki and Emu Video.

- **Text-to-speech**: Models that synthesize speech audio from input text. Examples: WaveNet and Tacotron.

- **Speech-to-text**: Models that transcribe speech to text [also called **Automatic Speech Recognition (ASR)**]. Examples: Whisper and SpeechGPT.

- **Image-to-text**: Models that generate image captions from images. Examples: CLIP and DALL-E 3.

- **Image-to-image**: Applications for this type of model are data augmentation such as super-resolution, style transfer, and inpainting.

- **Text-to-code**: Models that generate programming code from text. Examples: Stable Diffusion and DALL-E 3.

- **Video-to-audio**: Models that analyze video and generate matching audio. Example: Soundify.

There are a lot more combinations of modalities to consider; these are just some that I have come across. Further, we could consider subcategories of text, such as text-to-math, which generates mathematical expressions from text, where some models such as ChatGPT and Claude shine, or text-to-code, which are models that generate programming code from text, such as AlphaCode or Codex. A few models are specialized in scientific text, such as Minerva or Galactica, or algorithm discovery, such as AlphaTensor.

A few models work with several modalities for input or output. An example of a model that demonstrates generative capabilities in multimodal input is OpenAI's GPT-4V model (GPT-4 with vision), released in September 2023, which takes both text and images and comes with better **Optical Character Recognition (OCR)** than previous versions to read text from images. Images can be translated into descriptive words, then existing text filters are applied. This mitigates the risk of generating unconstrained image captions.

As the list shows, text is a common input modality that can be converted into various outputs like image, audio, and video. The outputs can also be converted back into text or within the same modality. LLMs have driven rapid progress for text-focused domains. These models enable a diverse range of capabilities via different modalities and domains. The LLM categories are the main focus of this book; however, we'll also occasionally look at other models, text-to-image in particular. These models typically use a Transformer architecture trained on massive datasets via self-supervised learning.

The rapid progress shows the potential of generative AI across diverse domains. Within the industry, there is a growing sense of excitement around AI's capabilities and its potential impact on business operations. But there are key challenges such as data availability, compute requirements, bias in data, evaluation difficulties, potential misuse, and other societal impacts that need to be addressed going forward, which we'll discuss in *Chapter 10, The Future of Generative Models*.

Let's delve a bit more into this progress and pose the question why now?

Why now?

The success of generative AI coming into the public spotlight in 2022 can be attributed to several interlinked drivers. The development and success of generative models have relied on improved algorithms, considerable advances in compute power and hardware design, the availability of large, labeled datasets, and an active and collaborative research community helping to evolve a set of tools and techniques.

Developing more sophisticated mathematical and computational methods has played a vital role in advancing generative models. The backpropagation algorithm introduced in the 1980s by Geoffrey Hinton, David Rumelhart, and Ronald Williams is one such example. It provided a way to effectively train multi-layer neural networks.

In the 2000s, neural networks began to regain popularity as researchers developed more complex architectures. However, it was the advent of DL, a type of neural network with numerous layers, that marked a significant turning point in the performance and capabilities of these models. Interestingly, although the concept of DL has existed for some time, the development and expansion of generative models correlate with significant advances in hardware, particularly **Graphics Processing Units (GPUs)**, which have been instrumental in propelling the field forward.

As mentioned, the availability of cheaper and more powerful hardware has been a key factor in the development of deeper models. This is because DL models require a lot of computing power to train and run. This concerns all aspects of processing power, memory, and disk space. This graph shows the cost of computer storage over time for different mediums such as disks, solid state, flash, and internal memory in terms of price in dollars per terabyte (adapted from *Our World in Data* by Max Roser, Hannah Ritchie, and Edouard Mathieu; https://ourworldindata. org/grapher/historical-cost-of-computer-memory-and-storage:

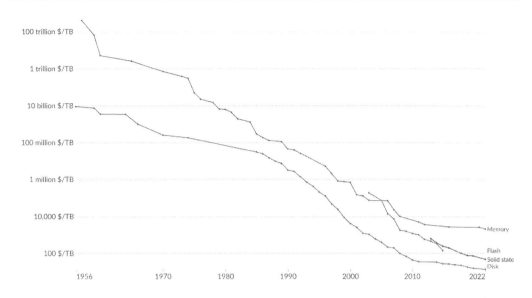

Figure 1.4: Cost of computer storage since the 1950s in dollars (unadjusted) per terabyte

While, in the past, training a DL model was prohibitively expensive, as the cost of hardware has come down, it has become possible to train bigger models on much larger datasets. The model size is one of the factors determining how well a model can approximate (as measured in perplexity) the training dataset.

The importance of the number of parameters in an LLM: The more parameters a model has, the higher its capacity to capture relationships between words and phrases as knowledge. As a simple example of these higher-order correlations, an LLM could learn that the word "cat" is more likely to be followed by the word "dog" if it is preceded by the word "chase," even if there are other words in between. Generally, the lower a model's perplexity, the better it will perform, for example, in terms of answering questions.

Particularly, it seems that in models with between 2 and 7 billion parameters, new capabilities emerge such as the ability to generate different creative text in formats like poems, code, scripts, musical pieces, emails, and letters, and to answer even open-ended and challenging questions in an informative way.

This trend toward larger models started around 2009, when NVIDIA catalyzed what is often called the **Big Bang of DL**. GPUs are particularly well suited for the matrix/vector computations necessary to train deep learning neural networks, therefore significantly increasing the speed and efficiency of these systems by several orders of magnitude and reducing running times from weeks to days. In particular, NVIDIA's CUDA platform, which allows direct programming of GPUs, has made it easier than ever for researchers and developers to experiment with and deploy complex generative models facilitating breakthroughs in vision, speech recognition, and – more recently – LLMs. Many LLM papers describe the use of NVIDIA A100s for training.

In the 2010s, several types of generative models started gaining traction. Autoencoders, a kind of neural network that can learn to compress data from the input layer to a representation, and then reconstruct the input, served as a basis for more advanced models like **Variational Autoencoders (VAEs)**, which were first proposed in 2013. VAEs, unlike traditional autoencoders, use variational inference to learn the distribution of data, also called the latent space of input data. Around the same time, GANs were proposed by Ian Goodfellow and others in 2014.

Over the past decade, significant advancements have been made in the fundamental algorithms used in DL, such as better optimization methods, more sophisticated model architectures, and improved regularization techniques. Transformer models, introduced in 2017, built upon this progress and enabled the creation of large-scale models like GPT-3. Transformers rely on attention mechanisms and resulted in a further leap in the performance of generative models. These models, such as Google's BERT and OpenAI's GPT series, can generate highly coherent and contextually relevant text.

The development of transfer learning techniques, which allow a model pre-trained on one task to be fine-tuned on another, similar task, has also been significant. These techniques have made it more efficient and practical to train large generative models. Moreover, part of the rise of generative models can be attributed to the development of software libraries and tools (TensorFlow, PyTorch, and Keras) specifically designed to work with these artificial neural networks, streamlining the process of building, training, and deploying them.

In addition to the availability of cheaper and more powerful hardware, the availability of large datasets of labeled data has also been a key factor in the development of generative models. This is because DL models, particularly generative ones, require vast amounts of text data for effective training. The explosion of data available from the internet, particularly in the last decade, has created a suitable environment for such models to thrive. As the internet has become more popular, it has become easier to collect large datasets of text, images, and other data.

This has made it possible to train generative models on much larger datasets than would have been possible in the past. To further drive the development of generative models, the research community has been developing benchmarks and other challenges, like the mentioned MMLU and ImageNet for image classification, and has started to do the same for generative models.

In summary, generative modeling is a fascinating and rapidly evolving field. It has the potential to revolutionize the way we interact with computers and create original content. I am excited to see what the future holds for this field.

Understanding LLMs

Text generation models, such as GPT-4 by OpenAI, can generate coherent and grammatically correct text in different languages and formats. These models have practical applications in fields like content creation and NLP, where the ultimate goal is to create algorithms capable of understanding and generating natural language text.

Language modeling aims to predict the next word, character, or even sentence based on the previous ones in a sequence. In this sense, language modeling serves as a way of encoding the rules and structures of a language in a way that can be understood by a machine. LLMs capture the structure of human language in terms of grammar, syntax, and semantics. These models form the backbone of larger NLP tasks, such as content creation, translation, summarization, machine translation, and text-editing tasks such as spelling correction.

At its core, language modeling, and more broadly NLP, relies heavily on the quality of representation learning. A generative language model encodes information about the text that it has been trained on and generates new text based on those learnings, thereby taking on the task of text generation.

Representation learning is about a model learning its internal representations of raw data to perform a machine learning task, rather than relying only on engineered feature extraction. For example, an image classification model based on representation learning might learn to represent images according to visual features like edges, shapes, and textures. The model isn't told explicitly what features to look for – it learns representations of the raw pixel data that help it make predictions.

Recently, LLMs have found applications for tasks like essay generation, code development, translation, and understanding genetic sequences. More broadly, applications of language models involve multiple areas, such as:

- **Question answering**: AI chatbots and virtual assistants can provide personalized and efficient assistance, reducing response times in customer support and thereby enhancing customer experience. These systems can be used in specific contexts like restaurant reservations and ticket booking.

- **Automatic summarization**: Language models can create concise summaries of articles, research papers, and other content, enabling users to consume and understand information rapidly.

- **Sentiment analysis**: By analyzing opinions and emotions in texts, language models can help businesses understand customer feedback and opinions more efficiently.

- **Topic modeling**: LLMs can discover abstract topics and themes across a corpus of documents. It identifies word clusters and latent semantic structures.

- **Semantic search**: LLMs can focus on understanding meaning within individual documents. It uses NLP to interpret words and concepts for improved search relevance.

- **Machine translation**: Language models can translate texts from one language into another, supporting businesses in their global expansion efforts. New generative models can perform on par with commercial products (for example, Google Translate).

Despite the remarkable achievements, language models still face limitations when dealing with complex mathematical or logical reasoning tasks. It remains uncertain whether continually increasing the scale of language models will inevitably lead to new reasoning capabilities. Further, LLMs are known to return the most probable answers within the context, which can sometimes yield fabricated information, termed hallucinations. This is a feature as well as a bug since it highlights their creative potential. We'll talk about hallucinations in *Chapter 5, Building a Chatbot Like ChatGPT*, but for now, let's discuss the technical background of LLMs in some more detail.

What is a GPT?

LLMs are deep neural networks adept at understanding and generating human language. The current generation of LLMs such as ChatGPT are deep neural network architectures that utilize the transformer model and undergo pre-training using unsupervised learning on extensive text data, enabling the model to learn language patterns and structures. Models have evolved rapidly, enabling the creation of versatile foundational AI models suitable for a wide range of downstream tasks and modalities, ultimately driving innovation across various applications and industries.

The notable strength of the latest generation of LLMs as conversational interfaces (chatbots) lies in their ability to generate coherent and contextually appropriate responses, even in open-ended conversations. By generating the next word based on the preceding words repeatedly, the model produces fluent and coherent text often indistinguishable from text produced by humans. However, ChatGPT has been observed to "sometimes write plausible sounding but incorrect or nonsensical answers," as expressed in a disclaimer by OpenAI. This is referred to as a hallucination and is just one of the concerns around LLMs.

A **transformer** is a DL architecture, first introduced in 2017 by researchers at Google and the University of Toronto (in an article called *Attention Is All You Need*; Vaswani and colleagues), that comprises self-attention and feed-forward neural networks, allowing it to effectively capture the word relationships in a sentence. The attention mechanism enables the model to focus on various parts of the input sequence.

Generative Pre-Trained Transformers (GPTs), on the other hand, were introduced by researchers at OpenAI in 2018 together with the first of their eponymous GPT models, GPT-1 (*Improving Language Understanding by Generative Pre-Training*; Radford and others). The pre-training process involves predicting the next word in a text sequence, enhancing the model's grasp of language as measured in the quality of the output. Following pre-training, the model can be fine-tuned for specific language processing tasks like sentiment analysis, language translation, or chat. This combination of unsupervised and supervised learning enables GPT models to perform better across a range of NLP tasks and reduces the challenges associated with training LLMs.

The size of the training corpus for LLMs has been increasing drastically. GPT-1, introduced by OpenAI in 2018, was trained on BookCorpus with 985 million words. BERT, released in the same year, was trained on a combined corpus of BookCorpus and English Wikipedia, totaling 3.3 billion words. Now, training corpora for LLMs reach up to trillions of tokens.

This graph illustrates how LLMs have been growing:

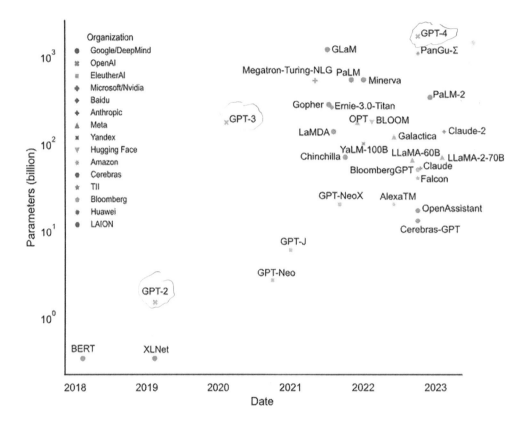

Figure 1.5: LLMs from BERT to GPT-4 – size, training budget, and organizations. For the proprietary models, parameter sizes are often estimates.

The size of the data points indicates training cost in terms of petaFLOPs and petaFLOP/s-days. A petaFLOP/s day is a unit of throughput that consists of performing 10 to the power of 15 operations per day. Training operations in the calculations are estimated as the approximate number of addition and multiplication operations based on the GPU utilization efficiency.

For some models, especially proprietary and closed-source models, this information is not known – in these cases, I've placed a cross. For example, for XLNet, the paper doesn't give information about compute in flops; however, the training was done on 512 TPU v3 chips over 2.5 days.

The development of GPT models has seen considerable progress, with OpenAI's GPT-n series leading the way in creating foundational AI models. GPT models can also work with modalities beyond text for input and output, as seen in GPT-4's ability to process image input alongside text. Additionally, they serve as a foundation for text-to-image technologies like diffusion and parallel decoding, enabling the development of **Visual Foundation Models (VFMs)** for systems that work with images.

A **foundation model** (sometimes known as a **base model**) is a large model that was trained on an immense quantity of data at scale so that it can be adapted to a wide range of downstream tasks. In GPT models, this pre-training is done via self-supervised learning.

Trained on 300 billion tokens, GPT-3 has 175 billion parameters, an unprecedented size for DL models. GPT-4 is the most recent in the series, though its size and training details have not been published due to competitive and safety concerns. However, different estimates suggest it has between 200 and 500 billion parameters. Sam Altman, the CEO of OpenAI, has stated that the cost of training GPT-4 was more than $100 million.

ChatGPT, a conversation model, was released by OpenAI in November 2022. Based on prior GPT models (particularly GPT-3) and optimized for dialogue, it uses a combination of human-generated roleplaying conversations and a dataset of human labeler demonstrations of the desired model behavior. The model exhibits excellent capabilities such as wide-ranging knowledge retention and precise context tracking in multi-turn dialogues.

Another substantial advancement came in March 2023 with GPT-4. GPT-4 provides superior performance on various evaluation tasks coupled with significantly better response avoidance to malicious or provocative queries due to six months of iterative alignment during training.

OpenAI has been coy about the technical details; however, information has been circulating that, with about 1.8 trillion parameters, GPT-4 is more than 10x the size of GPT-3. Further, OpenAI was able to keep costs reasonable by utilizing a **Mixture of Experts (MoE)** model consisting of 16 experts within their model, each having about 111 billion parameters.

Apparently, GPT-4 was trained on about 13 trillion tokens. However, these are not unique tokens since they count repeated presentation of the data in each epoch. Training was conducted for 2 epochs for text-based data and 4 for code-based data. For fine-tuning, the dataset consisted of millions of rows of instruction fine-tuning data. Another rumor, again to be taken with a grain of salt, is that OpenAI might be applying speculative decoding on GPT-4's inference, with the idea that a smaller model (oracle model) could be predicting the large model's responses, and these predicted responses could help speed up decoding by feeding them into the larger model, thereby skipping tokens. This is a risky strategy because – depending on the threshold of the confidence of the oracle's responses – the quality could deteriorate.

There's also a multi-modal version of GPT-4 that incorporates a separate vision encoder, trained on joined image and text data, giving the model the capability to read web pages and transcribe what's in images and video.

As can be seen in *Figure 1.5*, there are quite a few models besides OpenAI's, some of which are suitable as a substitute for the OpenAI closed-source models, which we will have a look at.

Other LLMs

Other notable foundational GPT models besides OpenAI's include Google DeepMind's **PaLM 2**, the model behind Google's chatbot Bard. Although GPT-4 leads most benchmarks in performance, these and other models demonstrate a comparable performance in some tasks and have contributed to advancements in generative transformer-based language models.

PaLM 2, released in May 2023, was trained with the focus of improving multilingual and reasoning capabilities while being more compute efficient. Using evaluations at different compute scales, the authors (Anil and others; *PaLM 2 Technical Report*) estimated an optimal scaling of training data sizes and parameters. PaLM 2 is smaller and exhibits faster and more efficient inference, allowing for broader deployment and faster response times for a more natural pace of interaction.

Extensive benchmarking across different model sizes has shown that PaLM 2 has significantly improved quality on downstream tasks, including multilingual common sense and mathematical reasoning, coding, and natural language generation, compared to its predecessor PaLM.

PaLM 2 was also tested on various professional language-proficiency exams. The exams used were for Chinese (HSK 7-9 Writing and HSK 7-9 Overall), Japanese (J-Test A-C Overall), Italian (PLIDA C2 Writing and PLIDA C2 Overall), French (TCF Overall), and Spanish (DELE C2 Writing and DELE C2 Overall). Across these exams, which were designed to test C2-level proficiency, considered mastery or advanced professional level according to the **CEFR (Common European Framework of Reference for Languages)**, PaLM 2 achieved mostly high-passing grades.

The releases of the **LLaMa** and **LLaMa 2** series of models, with up to 70B parameters, by Meta AI in February and July 2023, respectively, have been highly influential by enabling the community to build on top of them, thereby kicking off a Cambrian explosion of open-source LLMs. LLaMa triggered the creation of models such as Vicuna, Koala, RedPajama, MPT, Alpaca, and Gorilla. LLaMa 2, since its recent release, has already inspired several very competitive coding models, such as WizardCoder.

Optimized for dialogue use cases, at their release, the LLMs outperformed other open-source chat models on most benchmarks and seem on par with some closed-source models based on human evaluations. The LLaMa 2 70B model performs on par or better than PaLM (540B) on almost all benchmarks, but there is still a large performance gap between LLaMa 2 70B and GPT-4 and PaLM-2-L.

LLaMa 2 is an updated version of LLaMa 1 trained on a new mix of publicly available data. The pre-training corpus size has increased by 40% (2 trillion tokens of data), the context length of the model has doubled, and grouped-query attention has been adopted.

Variants of LLaMa 2 with different parameter sizes (7B, 13B, 34B, and 70B) have been released. While LLaMa was released under a non-commercial license, the LLaMa 2 are open to the general public for research and commercial use.

LLaMa 2-Chat has undergone safety evaluation results compared to other open-source and closed-source models. Human raters judged the safety violations of model generations across approximately 2,000 adversarial prompts, including both single and multi-turn prompts.

Claude and **Claude 2** are AI assistants created by Anthropic. Evaluations suggest Claude 2, released in July 2023, is one of the best GPT-4 competitors in the market. It improves on previous versions in helpfulness, honesty, and lack of stereotype bias based on human feedback comparisons. It also performs well on standardized tests like GRE and MBE. Key model improvements include an expanded context size of up to 200K tokens, far larger than most available models, and being commercial or open source. It also performs better on use cases like coding, summarization, and long document understanding.

The model card Anthropic has created is fairly detailed, showing Claude 2 still has limitations in areas like confabulation, bias, factual errors, and potential for misuse, problems it has in common with all LLMs. Anthropic is working to address these through techniques like data filtering, debiasing, and safety interventions.

The development of LLMs has been limited to a few players due to high computational requirements. In the next section, we'll look into who these organizations are.

Major players

Training a large number of parameters on large-scale datasets requires significant compute power and a skilled data science and data engineering team. Meta's LLaMa 2 model, with a size of up to 70 billion parameters, was trained on 1.4 trillion tokens, while PaLM 2, reportedly consisting of 340 billion parameters – smaller than their previous LLMs – appears to have a larger scale of training data in at least 100 languages. Modern LLMs can cost anywhere from 10 million to over 100 million US dollars in computing costs for training.

Only a few companies, such as those shown in *Figure 1.5*, have been able to successfully train and deploy very large models. Major companies like Microsoft and Google have invested in start-ups and collaborations to support the development of these models. Universities, such as KAUST, Carnegie Mellon University, Nanyang Technological University, and Tel Aviv University, have also contributed to the development of these models. Some projects are developed through collaborations between companies and universities, as seen in the cases of Stable Diffusion, Soundify, and DreamFusion.

There are quite a few companies and organizations developing generative AI in general, as well as LLMs, and they are releasing them on different terms – here's just a few:

- **OpenAI** have released GPT-2 as open source; however, subsequent models have been closed source but open for public usage on their website or through an API.

- **Google** (including Google's **DeepMind** division) have developed a number of LLMs, starting from BERT and – more recently – Chinchilla, Gopher, PaLM, and PaLM2. They previously released the code and weights (parameters) of a few of their models under open-source licensing, even though recently they have moved toward more secrecy in their development.

- **Anthropic** have released the Claude and Claude 2 models for public usage on their website. The API is in private beta. The models themselves are closed source.

- **Meta** have released models like RoBERTa, BART, and LLaMa 2, including parameters of the models (although often under a non-commercial license) and the source code for setting up and training the models.

- **Microsoft** have developed models like Turing-NLG and Megatron-Turing NLG but have focused on integrating OpenAI models into products over releasing their own models. The training code and parameters for phi-1 have been released for research use.

- **Stability AI**, the company behind Stable Diffusion, released the model weights under a non-commercial license.

- The French AI startup **Mistral** has unveiled its free-to-use, open-license 7B model, outperforming similar-sized models, generated from private datasets, and developed with the intent to support the open generative AI community, while also offering commercial products.

- **EleutherAI** is a grassroots collection of researchers developing open-access models like GPT-Neo and GPT-J, fully open source and available to the public.

- **Aleph Alpha**, **Alibaba**, and **Baidu** are providing API access or integrating their models into products rather than releasing parameters or training code.

There are a few more notable institutions, such as the **Technology Innovation Institute** (TII), an Abu Dhabi government-funded research institution, which open-sourced Falcon LLM for research and commercial usage.

The complexity of estimating parameters in generative AI models suggests that smaller companies or organizations without sufficient computation power and expertise may struggle to deploy these models successfully; although, recently, after the publication of the LLaMa models, we've seen smaller companies making significant breakthroughs, for example, in terms of coding ability.

In the next section, we'll review the progress that DL and generative models have been making over recent years that has led up to the current explosion of their apparent capabilities and the attention these models have been getting.

Let's get into the nitty-gritty details – how do these LLMs work under the hood? How do GPT models work?

How do GPT models work?

Generative pre-training has been around for a while, employing methods such as Markov models or other techniques. However, language models such as BERT and GPT were made possible by the transformer deep neural network architecture (Vaswani and others, *Attention Is All You Need*, 2017), which has been a game-changer for NLP. Designed to avoid recursion to allow parallel computation, the Transformer architecture, in different variations, continues to push the boundaries of what's possible within the field of NLP and generative AI.

Transformers have pushed the envelope in NLP, especially in translation and language understanding. **Neural Machine Translation (NMT)** is a mainstream approach to machine translation that uses DL to capture long-range dependencies in a sentence. Models based on transformers outperformed previous approaches, such as using recurrent neural networks, particularly Long Short-Term Memory (LSTM) networks.

The transformer model architecture has an encoder-decoder structure, where the encoder maps an input sequence to a sequence of hidden states, and the decoder maps the hidden states to an output sequence. The hidden state representations consider not only the inherent meaning of the words (their semantic value) but also their context in the sequence.

The encoder is made up of identical layers, each with two sub-layers. The input embedding is passed through an attention mechanism, and the second sub-layer is a fully connected feed-forward network. Each sub-layer is followed by a residual connection and layer normalization. The output of each sub-layer is the sum of the input and the output of the sub-layer, which is then normalized.

The decoder uses this encoded information to generate the output sequence one item at a time, using the context of the previously generated items. It also has identical modules, with the same two sub-layers as the encoder.

In addition, the decoder has a third sub-layer that performs **Multi-Head Attention (MHA)** over the output of the encoder stack. The decoder also uses residual connections and layer normalization. The self-attention sub-layer in the decoder is modified to prevent positions from attending to subsequent positions. This masking, combined with the fact that the output embeddings are offset by one position, ensures that the predictions for position i can only depend on the known outputs at positions less than i. These are indicated in the diagram here (source: Yuening Jia, Wikimedia Commons):

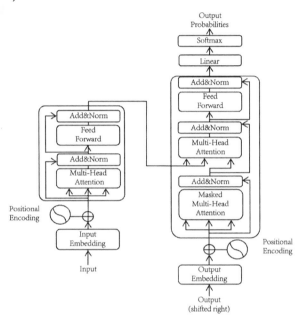

Figure 1.6: The Transformer architecture

The architectural features that have contributed to the success of transformers are:

- **Positional encoding**: Since the transformer doesn't process words sequentially but instead processes all words simultaneously, it lacks any notion of the order of words. To remedy this, information about the position of words in the sequence is injected into the model using positional encodings. These encodings are added to the input embeddings representing each word, thus allowing the model to consider the order of words in a sequence.

- **Layer normalization**: To stabilize the network's learning, the transformer uses a technique called layer normalization. This technique normalizes the model's inputs across the features dimension (instead of the batch dimension as in batch normalization), thus improving the overall speed and stability of learning.

- **Multi-head attention**: Instead of applying attention once, the transformer applies it multiple times in parallel – improving the model's ability to focus on different types of information and thus capturing a richer combination of features.

A key reason for the success of transformers has been their ability to maintain performance across longer sequences better than other models, for example, recurrent neural networks.

The basic idea behind attention mechanisms is to compute a weighted sum of the values (usually referred to as values or content vectors) associated with each position in the input sequence, based on the similarity between the current position and all other positions. This weighted sum, known as the context vector, is then used as an input to the subsequent layers of the model, enabling the model to selectively attend to relevant parts of the input during the decoding process.

To enhance the expressiveness of the attention mechanism, it is often extended to include multiple so-called *heads*, where each head has its own set of query, key, and value vectors, allowing the model to capture various aspects of the input representation. The individual context vectors from each head are then concatenated or combined in some way to form the final output.

Early attention mechanisms scaled quadratically with the length of the sequences (context size), rendering them inapplicable to settings with long sequences. Different mechanisms have been tried out to alleviate this. Many LLMs use some form of **Multi-Query Attention (MQA)**, including OpenAI's GPT-series models, Falcon, SantaCoder, and StarCoder.

MQA is an extension of MHA, where attention computation is replicated multiple times. MQA improves the performance and efficiency of language models for various language tasks. By removing the heads dimension from certain computations and optimizing memory usage, MQA allows for 11 times better throughput and 30% lower latency in inference tasks compared to baseline models without MQA.

LLaMa 2 and a few other models used **Grouped-Query Attention (GQA)**, which is a practice used in autoregressive decoding to cache the key (K) and value (V) pairs for the previous tokens in the sequence, speeding up attention computation. However, as the context window or batch sizes increase, the memory costs associated with the KV cache size in MHA models also increase significantly. To address this, the key and value projections can be shared across multiple heads without much degradation of performance.

There have been many other proposed approaches to obtain efficiency gains, such as sparse, low-rank self-attention, and latent bottlenecks, to name just a few. Other work has tried to extend sequences beyond the fixed input size; architectures such as transformer-XL reintroduce recursion by storing hidden states of already encoded sentences to leverage them in the subsequent encoding of the next sentences.

The combination of these architectural features allows GPT models to successfully tackle tasks that involve understanding and generating text in human language and other domains. The overwhelming majority of LLMs are transformers, as are many other state-of-the-art models we will encounter in the different sections of this chapter, including models for image, sound, and 3D objects.

As the name suggests, a particularity of GPTs lies in pre-training. Let's see how these LLMs are trained!

Pre-training

The transformer is trained in two phases using a combination of unsupervised pre-training and discriminative task-specific fine-tuning. The goal during pre-training is to learn a general-purpose representation that transfers to a wide range of tasks.

The unsupervised pre-training can follow different objectives. In **Masked Language Modeling** (**MLM**), introduced in *BERT: Pre-training of Deep Bidirectional Transformers for Language Understanding* by Devlin and others (2019), the input is masked out, and the model attempts to predict the missing tokens based on the context provided by the non-masked portion. For example, if the input sentence is "The cat [MASK] over the wall," the model would ideally learn to predict "jumped" for the mask.

In this case, the training objective minimizes the differences between predictions and the masked tokens according to a loss function. Parameters in the models are then iteratively updated according to these comparisons.

Negative Log-Likelihood (NLL) and **Perplexity (PPL)** are important metrics used in training and evaluating language models. NLL is a loss function used in ML algorithms, aimed at maximizing the probability of correct predictions. A lower NLL indicates that the network has successfully learned patterns from the training set, so it will accurately predict the labels of the training samples. It's important to mention that NLL is a value constrained within a positive interval.

PPL, on the other hand, is an exponentiation of NLL, providing a more intuitive way to understand the model's performance. Smaller PPL values indicate a well-trained network that can predict accurately while higher values indicate poor learning performance. Intuitively, we could say that a low perplexity means that the model is less surprised by the next word. Therefore, the goal in pre-training is to minimize perplexity, which means the model's predictions align more with the actual outcomes.

In comparing different language models, perplexity is often used as a benchmark metric across various tasks. It gives an idea about how well the language model is performing, where a lower perplexity indicates the model is more certain of its predictions. Hence, a model with lower perplexity would be considered better performing in comparison to others with higher perplexity.

The first step in training an LLM is **tokenization**. This process involves building a vocabulary, which **maps** tokens to unique numerical representations so that they can be processed by the model, given that LLMs are mathematical functions that require numerical inputs and outputs.

Tokenization

Tokenizing a text means splitting it into tokens (words or subwords), which then are converted to IDs through a look-up table mapping words in text to corresponding lists of integers.

Before training the LLM, the tokenizer – more precisely, its dictionary – is typically fitted to the entire training dataset and then frozen. It's important to note that tokenizers do not produce arbitrary integers. Instead, they output integers within a specific range – from 0 to $V\text{-}1$, where V represents the vocabulary size of the tokenizer.

Definitions:

Token: A token is an instance of a sequence of characters, typically forming a word, punctuation mark, or number. Tokens serve as the base elements for constructing sequences of text.

Tokenization: This refers to the process of splitting text into tokens. A tokenizer splits on whitespace and punctuation to break text into individual tokens.

Examples:

Consider the following text:

"The quick brown fox jumps over the lazy dog!"

This would get split into the following tokens:

["The", "quick", "brown", "fox", "jumps", "over", "the", "lazy", "dog", "!"]

Each word is an individual token, as is the punctuation mark.

There are a lot of tokenizers that work according to different principles, but common types of tokenizers employed in models are **Byte-Pair Encoding** (BPE), WordPiece, and SentencePiece. For example, LLaMa 2's BPE tokenizer splits numbers into individual digits and uses bytes to decompose unknown UTF-8 characters. The total vocabulary size is 32K tokens.

It is necessary to point out that LLMs can only generate outputs based on a sequence of tokens that does not exceed its context window. This context window refers to the length of the longest sequence of tokens that an LLM can use. Typical context window sizes for LLMs can range from about 1,000 to 10,000 tokens.

Next, it is worth talking at least briefly about the scale of these architectures, and why these models are as large as they are.

Scaling

As we've seen in *Figure 1.5*, language models have been becoming bigger over time. That corresponds to a long-term trend in machine learning that models get bigger as computing resources get cheaper, enabling higher performance. In a paper from 2020 by researchers from OpenAI, Kaplan and others (*Scaling laws for neural language models*, 2020) discussed scaling laws and the choice of parameters.

Interestingly, they compare lots of different architecture choices and, among other things, show that transformers outperform LSTMs as language models in terms of perplexity in no small part due to the improved use of long contexts. While recurrent networks plateau after less than 100 tokens, transformers improve throughout the whole context. Therefore, transformers not only come with better training and inference speed but also give better performance when looking at relevant contexts.

Further, they found a power-law relationship between performance and each of the following factors: dataset size, model size (number of parameters), and the amount of computational resources required for training. This implies that to improve performance by a certain factor, one of these elements must be scaled up by the power of that factor; however, for optimal performance, all three factors must be scaled in tandem to avoid bottlenecks.

Researchers at DeepMind (*An empirical analysis of compute-optimal large language model training*, Hoffmann and others, 2022) analyzed the training compute and dataset size of LLMs and concluded that LLMs are undertrained in terms of compute budget and dataset size as suggested by scaling laws.

They predicted that large models would perform better if substantially smaller and trained for much longer, and – in fact – validated their prediction by comparing a 70-billion-parameter Chinchilla model on a benchmark to their Gopher model, which consists of 280 billion parameters.

However, more recently, a team at Microsoft Research has challenged these conclusions and surprised everyone (*Textbooks Are All You Need*; Gunaseka and colleagues, June 2023), finding that a small network (350M parameters) trained on high-quality datasets can give very competitive performance. We'll discuss this model again in *Chapter 6, Developing Software with Generative AI,* and we'll discuss the implications of scaling in *Chapter 10, The Future of Generative Models.*

It will be instructive to observe whether model sizes for LLMs keep increasing at the same rate as they have. This is an important question since it determines if the development of LLMs will be firmly in the hands of large organizations. It could be that there's a saturation of performance at a certain size, which only changes in the approach can overcome. However, we could see new scaling laws linking performance with data quality.

After pre-training, a major step is how models are prepared for specific tasks either by fine-tuning or prompting. Let's see what this task conditioning is about!

Conditioning

Conditioning LLMs refers to adapting the model for specific tasks. It includes fine-tuning and prompting:

- **Fine-tuning** involves modifying a pre-trained language model by training it on a specific task using supervised learning. For example, to make a model more amenable to chats with humans, the model is trained on examples of tasks formulated as natural language instructions (instruction tuning). For fine-tuning, pre-trained models are usually trained again using **Reinforcement Learning from Human Feedback (RLHF)** to be helpful and harmless.
- **Prompting techniques** present problems in text form to generative models. There are a lot of different prompting techniques, starting from simple questions to detailed instructions. Prompts can include examples of similar problems and their solutions. Zero-shot prompting involves no examples, while few-shot prompting includes a small number of examples of relevant problem and solution pairs.

These conditioning methods continue to evolve, becoming more effective and useful for a wide range of applications. Prompt engineering and conditioning methods will be explored further in *Chapter 8, Customizing LLMs and Their Output.*

How to try out these models

You can access OpenAI's model through their website or their API. If you want to try other LLMs on your laptop, open-source LLMs are a good place to get started. There is a whole zoo of stuff out there!

You can access these models through Hugging Face or other providers, as we'll see starting in *Chapter 3, Getting Started with LangChain.* You can even download these open-source models, fine-tune them, or fully train them. We'll fine-tune a model in *Chapter 8, Customizing LLMs and Their Output.*

Generative AI is extensively used in generating 3D images, avatars, videos, graphs, and illustrations for virtual or augmented reality, video games graphic design, logo creation, image editing, or enhancement. The most popular model category here is for text-conditioned image synthesis, specifically text-to-image generation. As mentioned, in this book, we'll focus on LLMs, since they have the broadest practical application, but we'll also have a look at image models, which sometimes can be quite useful.

In the next section, we'll be reviewing state-of-the-art methods for text-conditioned image generation. I'll highlight the progress made in the field so far, but also discuss existing challenges and potential future directions.

What are text-to-image models?

Text-to-image models are a powerful type of generative AI that creates realistic images from textual descriptions. They have diverse use cases in creative industries and design for generating advertisements, product prototypes, fashion images, and visual effects. The main applications are:

- **Text-conditioned image generation**: Creating original images from text prompts like "a painting of a cat in a field of flowers." This is used for art, design, prototyping, and visual effects.
- **Image inpainting**: Filling in missing or corrupted parts of an image based on the surrounding context. This can restore damaged images (denoising, dehazing, and deblurring) or edit out unwanted elements.
- **Image-to-image translation**: Converting input images to a different style or domain specified through text, like "make this photo look like a Monet painting."
- **Image recognition**: Large foundation models can be used to recognize images, including classifying scenes, but also object detection, for example, detecting faces.

Models like Midjourney, DALL-E 2, and Stable Diffusion provide creative and realistic images derived from textual input or other images. These models work by training deep neural networks on large datasets of image-text pairs. The key technique used is diffusion models, which start with random noise and gradually refine it into an image through repeated denoising steps.

Popular models like Stable Diffusion and DALL-E 2 use a text encoder to map input text into an embedding space. This text embedding is fed into a series of conditional diffusion models, which denoise and refine a latent image in successive stages. The final model output is a high-resolution image aligned with the textual description.

Two main classes of models are used: **Generative Adversarial Networks** (**GANs**) and diffusion models. GAN models like StyleGAN or GANPaint Studio can produce highly realistic images, but training is unstable and computationally expensive. They consist of two networks that are pitted against each other in a game-like setting – the generator, which generates new images from text embeddings and noise, and the discriminator, which estimates the probability of the new data being real. As these two networks compete, GANs get better at their task, generating realistic images and other types of data.

The setup for training GANs is illustrated in this diagram (taken from *A Survey on Text Generation Using Generative Adversarial Networks*, G de Rosa and J P. Papa, 2022; `https://arxiv.org/pdf/2212.11119.pdf`):

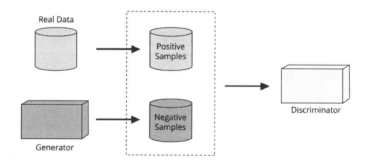

Figure 1.7: GAN training

Diffusion models have become popular and promising for a wide range of generative tasks, including text-to-image synthesis. These models offer advantages over previous approaches, such as GANs, by reducing computation costs and sequential error accumulation. Diffusion models operate through a process like diffusion in physics. They follow a **forward diffusion process** by adding noise to an image until it becomes uncharacteristic and noisy. This process is analogous to an ink drop falling into a glass of water and gradually diffusing.

The unique aspect of generative image models is the **reverse diffusion process**, where the model attempts to recover the original image from a noisy, meaningless image. By iteratively applying noise removal transformations, the model generates images of increasing resolutions that align with the given text input. The final output is an image that has been modified based on the text input. An example of this is the Imagen text-to-image model (*Photorealistic Text-to-Image Diffusion Models with Deep Language Understanding* by Google Research, May 2022), which incorporates frozen text embeddings from LLMs, pre-trained on text-only corpora. A text encoder first maps the input text to a sequence of embeddings. A cascade of conditional diffusion models takes the text embeddings as input and generates images.

The denoising process is demonstrated in this plot (source: user Benlisquare via Wikimedia Commons):

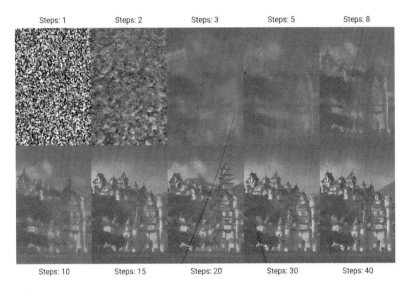

Figure 1.8: European-style castle in Japan, created using the Stable Diffusion V1-5 AI diffusion model

In *Figure 1.8*, only some steps within the 40-step generation process are shown. You can see the image generation step by step, including the U-Net denoising process using the **Denoising Diffusion Implicit Model (DDIM)** sampling method, which repeatedly removes Gaussian noise, and then decodes the denoised output into pixel space.

With diffusion models, you can see a wide variety of outcomes using only minimal changes to the initial setting of the model or – as in this case – numeric solvers and samplers. Although they sometimes produce striking results, the instability and inconsistency are a significant challenge to applying these models more broadly.

Stable Diffusion was developed by the CompVis group at LMU Munich (*High-Resolution Image Synthesis with Latent Diffusion Models* by Blattmann and others, 2022). The Stable Diffusion model significantly cuts training costs and sampling time compared to previous (pixel-based) diffusion models. The model can be run on consumer hardware equipped with a modest GPU (for example, the GeForce 40 series). By creating high-fidelity images from text on consumer GPUs, the Stable Diffusion model democratizes access. Further, the model's source code and even the weights have been released under the CreativeML OpenRAIL-M license, which doesn't impose restrictions on reuse, distribution, commercialization, and adaptation.

Significantly, Stable Diffusion introduced operations in latent (lower-dimensional) space representations, which capture the essential properties of an image, in order to improve computational efficiency. A VAE provides latent space compression (called *perceptual compression* in the paper), while a U-Net performs iterative denoising.

Stable Diffusion generates images from text prompts through several clear steps:

1. It starts by producing a random tensor (random image) in the latent space, which serves as the noise for our initial image.
2. A noise predictor (U-Net) takes in both the latent noisy image and the provided text prompt and predicts the noise.
3. The model then subtracts the latent noise from the latent image.
4. *Steps 2* and *3* are repeated for a set number of sampling steps, for instance, 40 times, as shown in the plot.
5. Finally, the decoder component of the VAE transforms the latent image back into pixel space, providing the final output image.

A **VAE** is a model that encodes data into a learned, smaller representation (encoding). These representations can then be used to generate new data similar to that used for training (decoding). This VAE is trained first.

A **U-Net** is a popular type of **convolutional neural network (CNN)** that has a symmetric encoder-decoder structure. It is commonly used for image segmentation tasks, but in the context of Stable Diffusion, it can help to introduce and remove noise in the image. The U-Net takes a noisy image (seed) as input and processes it through a series of convolutional layers to extract features and learn semantic representations.

These convolutional layers, typically organized in a contracting path, reduce the spatial dimensions while increasing the number of channels. Once the contracting path reaches the bottleneck of the U-Net, it then expands through a symmetric expanding path. In the expanding path, transposed convolutions (also known as upsampling or deconvolutions) are applied to progressively upsample the spatial dimensions while reducing the number of channels.

For training the image generation model in the latent space itself **(latent diffusion model)**, a loss function is used to evaluate the quality of the generated images. One commonly used loss function is the **Mean Squared Error (MSE)** loss, which quantifies the difference between the generated image and the target image. The model is optimized to minimize this loss, encouraging it to generate images that closely resemble the desired output.

This training was performed on the LAION-5B dataset, consisting of billions of image-text pairs, derived from Common Crawl data, comprising billions of image-text pairs from sources such as Pinterest, WordPress, Blogspot, Flickr, and DeviantArt.

The following images illustrate text-to-image generation from a text prompt with diffusion (source: Ramesh and others, *Hierarchical Text-Conditional Image Generation with CLIP Latents*, 2022; https://arxiv.org/abs/2204.06125):

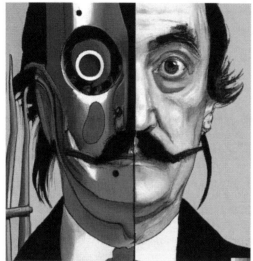 

vibrant portrait painting of Salvador Dali with a robotic half face   a shiba inu wearing a beret and black turtleneck

Figure 1.9: Image generation from text prompts

Overall, image generation models such as Stable Diffusion and Midjourney process textual prompts into generated images, leveraging the concept of forward and reverse diffusion processes and operating in a lower-dimensional latent space for efficiency. But what about the conditioning for the model in the text-to-image use case?

The conditioning process allows these models to be influenced by specific input textual prompts or input types like depth maps or outlines for greater precision to create relevant images. These embeddings are then processed by a text transformer and fed to the noise predictor, steering it to produce an image that aligns with the text prompt.

It's out of the scope of this book to provide a comprehensive survey of generative AI models for all modalities. However, let's get a bit of an overview of what models can do for other domains.

What can AI do in other domains?

Generative AI models have demonstrated impressive capabilities across modalities including sound, music, video, and 3D shapes. In the audio domain, models can synthesize natural speech, generate original music compositions, and even mimic a speaker's voice and the patterns of rhythm and sound (prosody). Speech-to-text systems can convert spoken language into text [**Automatic Speech Recognition (ASR)**]. For video, AI systems can create photorealistic footage from text prompts and perform sophisticated editing like object removal. 3D models learned to reconstruct scenes from images and generate intricate objects from textual descriptions.

The following table summarizes some recent models in these domains:

Model	Organization	Year	Domain	Architecture	Performance
3D-GQN	DeepMind	2018	3D	Deep, iterative, latent variable density models	3D scene generation from 2D images
Jukebox	OpenAI	2020	Music	VQ-VAE + transformer	High-fidelity music generation in different styles
Whisper	OpenAI	2022	Sound/speech	Transformer	Near human-level speech recognition
Imagen Video	Google	2022	Video	Frozen text transformers + video diffusion models	High-definition video generation from text
Phenaki	Google & UCL	2022	Video	Bidirectional masked transformer	Realistic video generation from text
TecoGAN	U. Munich	2022	Video	Temporal coherence module	High-quality, smooth video generation
DreamFusion	Google	2022	3D	NeRF + Diffusion	High-fidelity 3D object generation from text

					High linguistic quality speech generation maintaining speaker's identity
AudioLM	Google	2023	Sound/ speech	Tokenizer + transformer LM + detokenizer	High linguistic quality speech generation maintaining speaker's identity
AudioGen	Meta AI	2023	Sound/ speech	Transformer + text guidance	High-quality conditional and unconditional audio generation
Universal Speech Model (USM)	Google	2023	Sound/ speech	Encoder-decoder transformer	State-of-the-art multilingual speech recognition

Table 1.1: Models for audio, video, and 3D domains

Underlying many of these innovations are advances in deep generative architectures like GANs, diffusion models, and transformers. Leading AI labs at Google, OpenAI, Meta, and DeepMind are pushing the boundaries of what's possible.

Summary

With the rise of computing power, deep neural networks, transformers, generative adversarial networks, and VAEs model the complexity of real-world data much more effectively than previous generations of models, pushing the boundaries of what's possible with AI algorithms. In this chapter, we explored the recent history of DL and AI and generative models such as LLMs and GPTs, together with the theoretical ideas underpinning them, especially the Transformer architecture. We also explained the basic concepts of models for image generation, such as the Stable Diffusion model, and finally discussed applications beyond text and images, such as sound and video.

The next chapter will explore the tooling of generative models, particularly LLMs, with the LangChain framework, focusing on the fundamentals, the implementation, and the use of this particular tool in exploiting and extending the capability of LLMs.

Questions

I think it's a good habit to check that you've digested the material when reading a technical book. For this purpose, I've created a few questions relating to the content of this chapter. Let's see if you can answer them:

1. What is a generative model?
2. Which applications exist for generative models?
3. What is an LLM and what does it do?
4. How can we get better performance from LLMs?
5. What are the conditions that make these models possible?
6. Which companies and organizations are the big players in developing LLMs?
7. What is a transformer and what does it consist of?
8. What does GPT stand for?
9. How does Stable Diffusion work?
10. What is a VAE?

If you struggle to answer these questions, please refer to the corresponding sections in this chapter to ensure that you've understood the material.

Join our community on Discord

Join our community's Discord space for discussions with the authors and other readers:

`https://packt.link/lang`

2

LangChain for LLM Apps

Large Language Models (LLMs) like GPT-4 have demonstrated immense capabilities in generating human-like text. However, simply accessing LLMs via APIs has limitations. Instead, combining them with other data sources and tools can enable more powerful applications. In this chapter, we will introduce LangChain as a way to overcome LLM limitations and build innovative language-based applications. We aim to demonstrate the potential of combining recent AI advancements with a robust framework like LangChain.

We will start by outlining some challenges faced when using LLMs on their own, like the lack of external knowledge, incorrect reasoning, and the inability to take action. LangChain provides solutions to these issues through different integrations and off-the-shelf components for specific tasks. We will walk through examples of how developers can use LangChain's capabilities to create customized natural language processing solutions, outlining the components and concepts involved.

The goal is to illustrate how LangChain enables building dynamic, data-aware applications that go beyond what is possible by simply accessing LLMs via API calls. Lastly, we will talk about important concepts related to LangChain, such as chains, action plan generation, and memory, which are important concepts to understand how LangChain works.

The main sections of this chapter are:

- Going beyond stochastic parrots
- What is LangChain?
- Exploring key components of LangChain
- How does LangChain work?
- Comparing LangChain with other frameworks

Going beyond stochastic parrots

LLMs have gained significant attention and popularity due to their ability to generate human-like text and understand natural language, which makes them useful in scenarios that revolve around content generation, text classification, and summarization. However, their apparent fluency obscures serious deficiencies that constrain real-world utility. The concept of **stochastic parrots** helps to elucidate this fundamental issue.

Stochastic parrots refers to LLMs that can produce convincing language but lack any true comprehension of the meaning behind words. Coined by researchers Emily Bender, Timnit Gebru, Margaret Mitchell, and Angelina McMillan-Major in their influential paper *On the Dangers of Stochastic Parrots* (2021), the term critiques models that mindlessly mimic linguistic patterns. Without being grounded in the real world, models can produce responses that are inaccurate, irrelevant, unethical, or make little logical sense.

Simply scaling up compute and data does not impart reasoning capabilities or common sense. LLMs struggle with challenges like the compositionality gap (*Measuring and Narrowing the Compositionality Gap in Language Models* by Ofir Press and colleagues; 2023). This means LLMs cannot connect inferences or adapt responses to new situations. Overcoming these obstacles requires augmenting LLMs with techniques that add true comprehension. Raw model scale alone cannot transform stochastic parroting into beneficial systems. Innovations like prompting, chain-of-thought reasoning, retrieval grounding, and others are needed to educate models.

Let's look at this argument in a bit more detail. If you wish to skip these details, please move on to the next section. We'll continue here by looking at the limitations of LLMs, ways to overcome those limitations, and how LangChain facilitates applications that systematically mitigate the shortcomings and extend the functionality of LLMs.

What are the limitations of LLMs?

As has been established, LLMs offer impressive capabilities but suffer from limitations that hinder their effectiveness in certain scenarios. Understanding these limitations is crucial when developing applications. Some pain points associated with LLMs include:

- **Outdated knowledge**: LLMs rely solely on their training data. Without external integration, they cannot provide recent real-world information.
- **Inability to take action**: LLMs cannot perform interactive actions like searches, calculations, or lookups. This severely limits functionality.

- **Lack of context**: LLMs struggle to incorporate relevant context like previous conversations and the supplementary details that are needed for coherent and useful responses.

- **Hallucination risks**: Insufficient knowledge on certain topics can lead to the generation of incorrect or nonsensical content by LLMs if not properly grounded.

- **Biases and discrimination**: Depending on the data they were trained on, LLMs can exhibit biases that can be religious, ideological, or political in nature.

- **Lack of transparency**: The behavior of large, complex models can be opaque and difficult to interpret, posing challenges to alignment with human values.

- **Lack of context**: LLMs may struggle to understand and incorporate context from previous prompts or conversations. They may not remember previously mentioned details or may fail to provide additional relevant information beyond the given prompt.

Let's illustrate some of these limitations a bit more since they are very important. As mentioned, LLMs face significant limitations in their lack of real-time knowledge and inability to take actions themselves, which restricts their effectiveness in many real-world contexts. For instance, LLMs have no inherent connection to external information sources. They are confined to the training data used to develop them, which inevitably becomes increasingly outdated over time. An LLM would have zero awareness of current events that occurred after its training data cut-off date. Asking an LLM about breaking news or the latest societal developments would leave it unable to construct responses without external grounding.

Additionally, LLMs cannot interact dynamically with the world around them. They cannot check the weather, look up local data, or access documents. With no ability to perform web searches, interface with APIs, run calculations, or take any practical actions based on new prompts, LLMs operate solely within the confines of pre-existing information. Even when discussing topics contained in its training data, an LLM struggles to incorporate real-time context and specifics without retrieving external knowledge. For example, an LLM could fluently discuss macroeconomic principles used in financial analysis, but it would fail to actually conduct analysis by retrieving current performance data and computing relevant statistics. Without dynamic lookup abilities, its financial discussion remains generic and theoretical. Similarly, an LLM may eloquently describe a past news event but then falter if asked for the latest developments on the same story today.

Architecting solutions that combine LLMs with external data sources, analytical programs, and tool integrations can help overcome these limitations. But in isolation, LLMs lack connection to the real-world context, which is often essential for useful applications. Their impressive natural language abilities need appropriate grounding and actions to produce substantive insights beyond eloquent but hollow text.

Let's look at a few examples of problems with LLMs. The cut-off day issue is illustrated here in the OpenAI ChatGPT interface asking about LangChain:

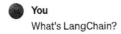

You
What's LangChain?

ChatGPT
As of my last knowledge update in January 2022, I don't have specific information about "LangChain." It's possible that there have been developments or new entities with that name since then.

If LangChain is a term or entity that emerged or gained significance after my last update, I recommend checking the latest online sources, such as news articles, official websites, or other reliable platforms for the most recent information. If it's a relatively new or niche topic, it might be best to look for specialized sources or announcements related to the field or industry associated with LangChain.

Figure 2.1: ChatGPT – a lack of up-to-date information

In this case, the model was able to correctly catch the problem and give the correct feedback – this is not always the case, though. If you access the model through other endpoints or use other models, it might just make up the information (hallucinate). Also, it might not have knowledge about certain entities, or it may refer to different entities entirely. Asking the same question in the OpenAI playground, I got this response:

USER   What is LangChain?

ASSISTANT   LangChain is a decentralized platform that aims to revolutionize the global
                language learning industry. It leverages blockchain technology to provide
                a secure and transparent learning environment, connecting language
                learners directly with native speakers and qualified tutors. The platform
                offers various language learning tools, including interactive lessons,
                practice exercises, and real-time conversations, all facilitated by its
                decentralized network. LangChain also incorporates a reward system using
                its native cryptocurrency, enabling learners to earn tokens by achieving
                language learning milestones and facilitating peer-to-peer transactions
                within the platform. Overall, LangChain aims to provide an efficient,
                affordable, and engaging language learning experience for users
                worldwide.

Figure 2.2: OpenAI playground with GPT 3.5

In this case, we can see that the model talks about a different LangChain, which is a decentralized blockchain-based translation platform. This is a problem of relevance, which can be referred to as a hallucination. It can be remedied by accessing external data, such as weather APIs, user preferences, or relevant information from the web, and this is essential for creating personalized and accurate language-driven applications.

LLMs struggle with certain tasks that involve logical reasoning or math problems. As an example, even advanced LLMs perform poorly at high-school level math and cannot perform simple math operations that they haven't seen before. Again, we can illustrate this with a simple demonstration:

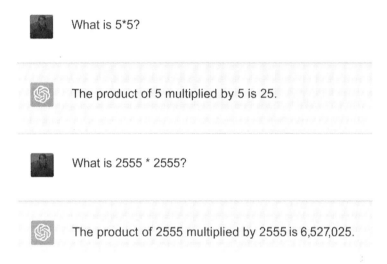

Figure 2.3: ChatGPT math solving

As you can see, the model comes up with the correct response for the first question but fails with the second. Just in case you were wondering what the true result is, if we use a calculator, we get this:

```
(base) ~ % bc -l
bc 1.06
Copyright 1991-1994, 1997, 1998, 2000 Free Software Foundation, Inc.
This is free software with ABSOLUTELY NO WARRANTY.
For details type `warranty'.
2555 * 2555
6528025
```

Figure 2.4: Multiplication with a calculator (BC)

The LLM hasn't stored the result of the calculation or hasn't encountered it often enough in the training data for it to be reliably remembered as encoded in its weights. Therefore, it fails to correctly come up with the solution. An LLM is not a suitable tool for the job in this case.

Deploying chatbots and other applications using LLMs requires thoughtful design and monitoring to address risks like bias and inappropriate content. For instance, Microsoft's Tay chatbot was taken offline shortly after launch in 2016 due to offensive tweets resulting from toxic interactions.

As for reasoning, for example, an LLM may correctly identify a fruit's density and water's density when asked about those topics independently, but it would struggle to synthesize those facts to determine if the fruit will float (this being a multi-hop question). The model fails to bridge its disjointed knowledge.

Let's see how we can address these challenges.

How can we mitigate LLM limitations?

Mitigating these limitations includes techniques like:

- **Retrieval augmentation**: This technique accesses knowledge bases to supplement an LLM's outdated training data, providing external context and reducing hallucination risk.
- **Chaining**: This technique integrates actions like searches and calculations.
- **Prompt engineering**: This involves the careful crafting of prompts by providing critical context that guides appropriate responses.
- **Monitoring, filtering, and reviews**: This involves ongoing and effective oversight of emerging issues regarding the application's input and output to detect issues. Both manual reviews and automated filters then correct potential problems with the output. This includes the following:

    a. **Filters**, like block lists, sensitivity classifiers, and banned word filters, can automatically flag issues.

    b. **Constitutional principles** monitor and filter unethical or inappropriate content.

    c. **Human reviews** provide insight into model behavior and output.

- **Memory**: Retains conversation context by persisting conversation data and context across interactions.
- **Fine-tuning**: Training and tuning the LLM on more appropriate data for the application domain and principles. This adapts the model's behavior for its specific purpose.

To re-emphasize what we previously mentioned, raw model scale alone cannot impart compositional reasoning or other missing capabilities. Explicit techniques like elicit prompting and chain-of-thought reasoning are needed to overcome the compositionality gap. Approaches like self-ask prompting mitigate these flaws by encouraging models to methodically decompose problems.

Integrating such tools into training pipelines provides the otherwise lacking faculties. Prompting supplies context, chaining enables inference steps, and retrieval incorporates facts. Together, these transform stochastic parrots into reasoning engines.

Thoughtful prompt engineering and fine-tuning prepare models for real-world use. Ongoing monitoring then catches any emerging issues, both through automation and human review. Filters act as a first line of defense. Adopting constitutional AI principles also encourages building models capable of behaving ethically. This comprehensive approach combines preparation, vigilance, and inherently beneficial design.

Connecting LLMs to external data further reduces hallucination risks and enhances responses with accurate, up-to-date information. However, securely integrating sources like databases adds complexity. Frameworks like LangChain simplify this while providing structure and oversight for responsible LLM use. They allow composing prompted model queries and data sources to surmount standalone LLM deficits. With diligent augmentation, we can create AI systems previously not viable due to innate model limitations. This brings us to our next topic of discussion.

What is an LLM app?

Combining LLMs with other tools into applications using specialized tooling, LLM-powered applications have the potential to transform our digital world. This is often done via a chain of one or multiple prompted calls to LLMs but can also make use of other external services (such as APIs or data sources) to achieve tasks.

Traditional software applications typically follow a multi-layer architecture:

Figure 2.5: A traditional software application

The client layer handles user interaction. The frontend layer handles presentation and business logic. The backend layer processes logic, APIs, computations, etc. Lastly, the database stores and retrieves data.

In contrast, an **LLM app** is an application that utilizes an LLM to understand natural language prompts and generate responsive text outputs. LLM apps typically have the following components:

- A client layer to collect user input as text queries or decisions.
- A prompt engineering layer to construct prompts that guide the LLM.
- An LLM backend to analyze prompts and produce relevant text responses.
- An output parsing layer to interpret LLM responses for the application interface.
- Optional integration with external services via function APIs, knowledge bases, and reasoning algorithms to augment the LLM's capabilities.

In the simplest possible cases, the frontend, parsing, and knowledge base parts are sometimes not explicitly defined, leaving us with just the client, the prompt, and the LLM:

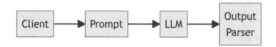

Figure 2.6: A simple LLM application

LLM apps can integrate external services via:

- Function APIs to access web tools and databases.
- Advanced reasoning algorithms for complex logic chains.
- Retrieval augmented generation via knowledge bases.

Retrieval augmented generation (RAG), which we will discuss in *Chapter 5, Building a Chatbot like ChatGPT*, enhances the LLM with external knowledge. These extensions expand the capabilities of LLM apps beyond the LLM's knowledge alone. For instance:

- Function calling allows parameterized API requests.
- SQL functions enable conversational database queries.
- Reasoning algorithms like chain-of-thought facilitate multi-step logic.

This is illustrated here:

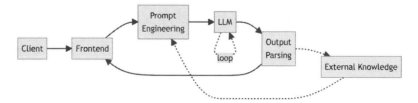

Figure 2.7: An advanced LLM application

As can be seen in the preceding figure, the client layer collects user text queries and decisions. Prompt engineering constructs guide the LLM, considering external knowledge or capability (or earlier interactions) without changes to the model itself. The LLM backend dynamically understands and responds to the prompts based on its training. Output parsing interprets the LLM text for the frontend. A knowledge base can enhance the LLM's information, and optionally, like a database backend in a traditional app, information can be written to it.

LLM applications are important for several reasons:

- The LLM backend handles language in a nuanced, human-like way without hardcoded rules.
- Responses can be personalized and contextualized based on past interactions.
- Advanced reasoning algorithms enable complex, multi-step inference chains.
- Dynamic responses based on the LLM or on up-to-date information retrieved in real time.

The key capability LLM apps use is the ability to understand nuanced language in prompts and generate coherent, human-like text responses. This facilitates more natural interactions and workflows compared to traditional code.

The LLM provides human-like language capabilities without manual coding. Therefore, there is no need to manually anticipate and code every language scenario in advance. The integration of LLMs with external services, knowledge, and reasoning algorithms eases the development of innovative applications.

But responsible data practices are critical – PII should be kept off public platforms and models should be fine-tuned in-house when needed. Both the frontend and the output parser could include moderation and enforcing rules about behavior, privacy, and security. Future research must address concerns around potential misuse, biases, and limitations.

We will see a lot of examples of LLM apps throughout this book; here are a few that we'll encounter:

- **Chatbots and virtual assistants**: These apps use LLMs like ChatGPT to have natural conversations with users and assist with tasks like scheduling, customer service, and information lookup.
- **Intelligent search engines**: LLM apps can parse search queries written in natural language and generate relevant results.
- **Automated content creation**: Apps can leverage LLMs to generate content like articles, emails, code, and more based on a text prompt.

- **Question answering**: Users can ask an LLM app questions in plain language and receive informative answers that are quickly sourced from the model's knowledge.

- **Sentiment analysis**: You can analyze customer feedback, reviews, and social posts using an LLM app to summarize sentiment and extract key themes.

- **Text summarization**: You can automatically generate concise summaries of longer text documents and articles using an LLM backend.

- **Data analysis**: You can use LLMs for automated data analysis and visualization to extract insights.

- **Code generation**: You can set up software pair-programming assistants that can help solve business problems.

The true power of LLMs lies not in LLMs being used in isolation but in LLMs being combined with other sources of knowledge and computation. The LangChain framework aims to enable precisely this kind of integration, facilitating the development of context-aware, reasoning-based applications. LangChain addresses pain points associated with LLMs and provides an intuitive framework for creating customized NLP solutions.

What is LangChain?

Created in 2022 by Harrison Chase, LangChain is an open-source Python framework for building LLM-powered applications. It provides developers with modular, easy-to-use components for connecting language models with external data sources and services. The project has attracted millions in venture capital funding from the likes of Sequoia Capital and Benchmark, who supplied funding to Apple, Cisco, Google, WeWork, Dropbox, and many other successful companies.

LangChain simplifies the development of sophisticated LLM applications by providing reusable components and pre-assembled chains. Its modular architecture abstracts access to LLMs and external services into a unified interface. Developers can combine these building blocks to carry out complex workflows.

Building impactful LLM apps involves challenges like prompt engineering, bias mitigation, productionizing, and integrating external data. LangChain reduces this learning curve through its abstractions and composable structure.

Beyond basic LLM API usage, LangChain facilitates advanced interactions like conversational context and persistence through agents and memory. This allows for chatbots, gathering external data, and more.

In particular, LangChain's support for chains, agents, tools, and memory allows developers to build applications that can interact with their environment in a more sophisticated way and store and reuse information over time. Its modular design makes it easy to build complex applications that can be adapted to a variety of domains. Support for action plans and strategies improves the performance and robustness of applications. The support for memory and access to external information reduces hallucinations, thus enhancing reliability.

The key benefits LangChain offers developers are:

- **Modular architecture** for flexible and adaptable LLM integrations.
- **Chaining together** multiple services beyond just LLMs.
- Goal-driven agent interactions instead of isolated calls.
- **Memory and persistence** for statefulness across executions.
- **Open-source access** and community support.

As mentioned, LangChain is open source and written in Python, although companion projects exist that are implemented in JavaScript or – more precisely – TypeScript (LangChain.js), and the fledgling Langchain.rb project for Ruby, which comes with a Ruby interpreter for code execution. In this book, we focus on the Python flavor of the framework.

While resources like documentation, courses, and communities help accelerate the learning process, developing expertise in applying LLMs takes dedicated time and effort. For many developers, the learning curve can be a blocking factor to impactfully leveraging LLMs.

There are active discussions on a Discord chat server, multiple blogs, and regular meetups taking place in various cities, including San Francisco and London. There's even a chatbot, ChatLangChain, that can answer questions about the LangChain documentation. It's built using LangChain and FastAPI and is available online through the documentation website!

LangChain comes with many extensions and a larger ecosystem that is developing around it. As mentioned, it has an immense number of integrations already, with many new ones being added every week. This screenshot highlights a few of the integrations (source: `integrations.langchain.com`):

Figure 2.8: LangChain integrations as of September 2023

As for the broader ecosystem, LangSmith is a platform that complements LangChain by providing robust debugging, testing, and monitoring capabilities for LLM applications. For example, developers can quickly debug new chains by viewing detailed execution traces. Alternative prompts and LLMs can be evaluated against datasets to ensure quality and consistency. Usage analytics empower data-driven decisions around optimizations.

LlamaHub and LangChainHub provide open libraries of reusable elements to build sophisticated LLM systems in a simplified manner. **LlamaHub** is a library of data loaders, readers, and tools created by the LlamaIndex community. It provides utilities to easily connect LLMs to diverse knowledge sources. The loaders ingest data for retrieval, while tools enable models to read/write to external data services. LlamaHub simplifies the creation of customized data agents to unlock LLM capabilities.

LangChainHub is a central repository for sharing artifacts like prompts, chains, and agents used in LangChain. Inspired by the Hugging Face Hub, it aims to be a one-stop resource for discovering high-quality building blocks to compose complex LLM apps. The initial launch focuses on a collection of reusable prompts. Future plans involve adding support for chains, agents, and other key LangChain components.

LangFlow and **Flowise** are UIs that allow chaining LangChain components in an executable flowchart by dragging sidebar components onto the canvas and connecting them together to create your pipeline. This is a quick way to experiment and prototype pipelines and is illustrated in the following screenshot of Flowise (source: `https://github.com/FlowiseAI/Flowise`):

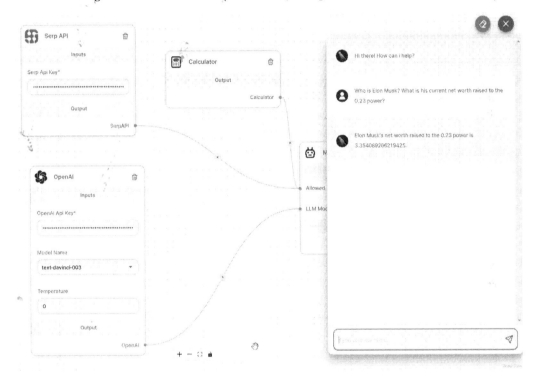

Figure 2.9: Flowise UI with an agent that uses an LLM, a calculator, and a search tool

You can see an agent (discussed later in this chapter) that is connected to a search interface (**Serp API**), an LLM, and a calculator. LangChain and LangFlow can be deployed locally, for example, using the Chainlit library, or on different platforms, including Google Cloud. The `langchain-serve` library helps to deploy both LangChain and LangFlow on the Jina AI cloud as LLM-apps-as-a-service with a single command.

While still relatively new, LangChain unlocks more advanced LLM applications via its combination of components like memory, chaining, and agents. It aims to simplify what can otherwise be complex LLM application development. Hence, it is crucial at this point in the chapter that we shift focus to the workings of LangChain and its components.

Exploring key components of LangChain

Chains, agents, memory, and tools enable the creation of sophisticated LLM applications that go beyond basic API calls to a single LLM. In the following dedicated subsections on these key concepts, we'll consider how they enable the development of capable systems by combining language models with external data and services.

We won't dive into implementation patterns in this chapter; however, we will discuss in more detail what some of these components are good for. By the end, you should have the level of understanding that's required to architect systems with LangChain. Let's start with chains!

What are chains?

Chains are a critical concept in LangChain for composing modular components into reusable pipelines. For example, developers can put together multiple LLM calls and other components in a sequence to create complex applications for things like chatbot-like social interactions, data extraction, and data analysis. In the most generic terms, a chain is a sequence of calls to components, which can include other chains. The most innocuous example of a chain is probably the `PromptTemplate`, which passes a formatted response to a language model.

Prompt chaining is a technique that can be used to improve the performance of LangChain applications, which involves chaining together multiple prompts to autocomplete a more complex response. More complex chains integrate models with tools like `LLMMath`, for math-related queries, or `SQLDatabaseChain`, for querying databases. These are called **utility chains**, because they combine language models with specific tools.

Chains can even enforce policies, like moderating toxic outputs or aligning with ethical principles. LangChain implements chains to make sure the content of the output is not toxic, does not otherwise violate OpenAI's moderation rules (`OpenAIModerationChain`), or that it conforms to ethical, legal, or custom principles (`ConstitutionalChain`).

An LLMCheckerChain verifies statements to reduce inaccurate responses using a technique called self-reflection. The LLMCheckerChain can prevent hallucinations and reduce inaccurate responses by verifying the assumptions underlying the provided statements and questions. In a paper by researchers at Carnegie Mellon, Allen Institute, University of Washington, NVIDIA, UC San Diego, and Google Research in May 2023 (*SELF-REFINE: Iterative Refinement with Self-Feedback*), this strategy has been found to improve task performance by about 20% on average across a benchmark including dialogue responses, math reasoning, and code reasoning.

A few chains can make autonomous decisions. Like agents, router chains can decide which tool to use based on their descriptions. A RouterChain can dynamically select which retrieval system, such as prompts or indexes, to use.

Chains deliver several key benefits:

- **Modularity**: Logic is divided into reusable components.
- **Composability**: Components can be sequenced flexibly.
- **Readability**: Each step in a pipeline is clear.
- **Maintainability**: Steps can be added, removed, and swapped.
- **Reusability**: Common pipelines become configurable chains.
- **Tool integration**: Easily incorporate LLMs, databases, APIs, etc.
- **Productivity**: Quickly build prototypes of configurable chains.

Together, these benefits enable the encapsulation of complex workflows into easy-to-understand and adaptable chained pipelines.

Typically, developing a LangChain chain involves breaking down a workflow into logical steps, like data loading, processing, model querying, and so on. Well-designed chains embrace single-responsibility components being pipelined together. Steps should be stateless functions to maximize reusability. Configurations should be made customizable. Robust error handling with exceptions and errors is critical for reliability. Monitoring and logging can be enabled with different mechanisms, including callbacks.

Let's discuss agents next and how they make their decisions!

What are agents?

Agents are a key concept in LangChain for creating systems that interact dynamically with users and environments over time. An agent is an autonomous software entity that is capable of taking actions to accomplish goals and tasks.

Chains and agents are similar concepts and it's worth unpicking their differences. The core idea in LangChain is the compositionality of LLMs and other components to work together. Both chains and agents do that, but in different ways. Both extend LLMs, but agents do so by orchestrating chains while chains compose lower-level modules. While chains define reusable logic by sequencing components, agents leverage chains to take goal-driven actions. Agents combine and orchestrate chains. The agent observes the environment, decides which chain to execute based on that observation, takes the chain's specified action, and repeats.

Agents decide which actions to take using LLMs as reasoning engines. The LLM is prompted with available tools, user input, and previous steps. It then selects the next action or final response.

Tools (discussed later in this chapter) are functions the agent calls to take real-world actions. Providing the right tools and effectively describing them is critical for agents to accomplish goals.

The agent executor runtime orchestrates the loop of querying the agent, executing tool actions, and feeding observations back. This handles lower-level complexities like error handling, logging, and parsing.

Agents provide several key benefits:

- **Goal-oriented execution**: Agents can plan chains of logic targeting specific goals.
- **Dynamic responses**: Observing environment changes lets agents react and adapt.
- **Statefulness**: Agents can maintain memory and context across interactions.
- **Robustness**: Errors can be handled by catching exceptions and trying alternate chains.
- **Composition**: Agent logic combines reusable component chains.

Together, this enables agents to handle complex, multi-step workflows and continuously interactive applications like chatbots.

In the section about the limitations of LLMs, we've seen that for calculations, a simple calculator outperforms a model consisting of billions of parameters. In this case, an agent can decide to pass the calculation to a calculator or to a Python interpreter. We can see a simple app here, where an agent is connected to both an OpenAI model and a Python function:

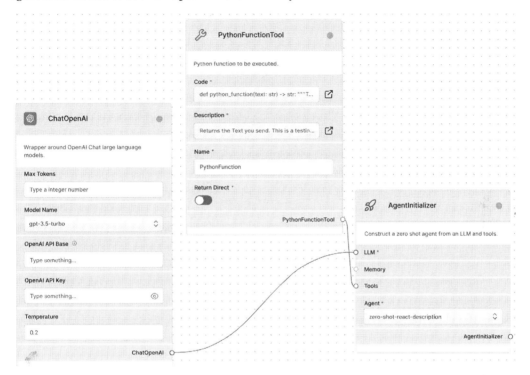

Figure 2.10: A simple LLM app with a Python function visualized in LangFlow

Based on the input, the agent can decide to run a Python function. Each agent also decides which tool to use and when. We'll look more at the mechanics of how this works in *Chapter 4, Building Capable Assistants.*

A key limitation of agents and chains is their statelessness – each execution occurs in isolation without retaining prior context. This is where the concept of memory becomes critical. Memory in LangChain refers to persisting information across chain executions to enable statefulness.

What is memory?

In LangChain, memory refers to the persisting state between executions of a chain or agent. Robust memory approaches unlock key benefits for developers building conversational and interactive applications. For example, storing chat history context in memory improves the coherence and relevance of LLM responses over time.

Rather than treating each user input as an isolated prompt, chains can pass conversational memory to models on each call to provide consistency. Agents can also persist facts, relationships, and deductions about the world in memory. This knowledge remains available even as real-world conditions change, keeping the agent contextually informed. Memory of objectives and completed tasks allows agents to track progress on multi-step goals across conversations. In addition, retaining information in memory reduces the number of calls to LLMs for repetitive information. This lowers API usage and costs, while still providing the agent or chain with the needed context.

LangChain provides a standard interface for memory, integrations with storage options like databases, and design patterns for effectively incorporating memory into chains and agents.

Several memory options exist – for example:

- `ConversationBufferMemory` stores all messages in model history. This increases latency and costs.
- `ConversationBufferWindowMemory` retains only recent messages.
- `ConversationKGMemory` summarizes exchanges as a knowledge graph for integration into prompts.
- `EntityMemory` backed by a database persists agent state and facts.

Moreover, LangChain integrates many database options for durable storage:

- SQL options like Postgres and SQLite enable relational data modeling.
- NoSQL choices like MongoDB and Cassandra facilitate scalable unstructured data.
- Redis provides an in-memory database for high-performance caching.
- Managed cloud services like AWS DynamoDB remove infrastructure burdens.

Beyond databases, purpose-built memory servers like Remembrall and Motörhead offer optimized conversational context. The right memory approach depends on factors like persistence needs, data relationships, scale, and resources, but robustly retaining state is key for conversational and interactive applications.

LangChain's memory integrations, from short-term caching to long-term databases, enable the building of stateful, context-aware agents. Architecting effective memory patterns unlocks the next generation of capable and reliable AI systems. LangChain comes with a long list of tools that we can use in applications. A short section will not be able to do this justice; however, I'll attempt to give a brief overview.

What are tools?

Tools provide modular interfaces for agents to integrate external services like databases and APIs. Toolkits group tools that share resources. Tools can be combined with models to extend their capability. LangChain offers tools like document loaders, indexes, and vector stores, which facilitate the retrieval and storage of data for augmenting data retrieval in LLMs.

There are many tools available, and here are just a few examples:

- **Machine translator**: A language model can use a machine translator to better comprehend and process text in multiple languages. This tool enables non-translation-dedicated language models to understand and answer questions in different languages.

- **Calculator**: Language models can utilize a simple calculator tool to solve math problems. The calculator supports basic arithmetic operations, allowing the model to accurately solve mathematical queries in datasets specifically designed for math problem-solving.

- **Maps**: By connecting with the Bing Map API or similar services, language models can retrieve location information, assist with route planning, provide driving distance calculations, and offer details about nearby points of interest.

- **Weather**: Weather APIs provide language models with real-time weather information for cities worldwide. Models can answer queries about current weather conditions or forecast the weather for specific locations within varying time periods.

- **Stocks**: Connecting with stock market APIs like Alpha Vantage allows language models to query specific stock market information such as opening and closing prices, highest and lowest prices, and more.

- **Slides**: Language models equipped with slide-making tools can create slides using high-level semantics provided by APIs such as the python-pptx library or image retrieval from the internet based on given topics. These tools facilitate tasks related to slide creation that are required in various professional fields.

- **Table processing**: APIs built with pandas DataFrames enable language models to perform data analysis and visualization tasks on tables. By connecting to these tools, models can provide users with a more streamlined and natural experience for handling tabular data.

- **Knowledge graphs**: Language models can query knowledge graphs using APIs that mimic human querying processes, such as finding candidate entities or relations, sending SPARQL queries, and retrieving results. These tools assist in answering questions based on factual knowledge stored in knowledge graphs.

- **Search engine**: By utilizing search engine APIs like Bing Search, language models can interact with search engines to extract information and provide answers to real-time queries. These tools enhance the model's ability to gather information from the web and deliver accurate responses.

- **Wikipedia**: Language models equipped with Wikipedia search tools can search for specific entities on Wikipedia pages, look up keywords within a page, or disambiguate entities with similar names. These tools facilitate question-answering tasks using content retrieved from Wikipedia.

- **Online shopping**: Connecting language models with online shopping tools allows them to perform actions like searching for items, loading detailed information about products, selecting item features, going through shopping pages, and making purchase decisions based on specific user instructions.

Additional tools include AI Painting, which allows language models to generate images using AI image generation models; 3D Model Construction, enabling language models to create 3D models using a sophisticated 3D rendering engine; Chemical Properties, assisting in resolving scientific inquiries about chemical properties using APIs like PubChem; and database tools that facilitate natural language access to database data for executing SQL queries and retrieving results.

These various tools provide language models with additional functionalities and capabilities to perform tasks beyond text processing. By connecting with these tools via APIs, language models can enhance their abilities in areas such as translation, math problem-solving, location-based queries, weather forecasting, stock market analysis, slide creation, table processing and analysis, image generation, text-to-speech conversion, and many more specialized tasks.

All these tools can give us advanced AI functionality, and there's virtually no limit to the tools available. We can easily build custom tools to extend the capability of LLMs, as we'll see in the next chapter. The use of different tools expands the scope of applications for language models and enables them to handle various real-world tasks more efficiently and effectively.

After discussing chains, agents, memory, and tools, let's put this all together to get a picture of how LangChain fits all of them together as moving parts.

How does LangChain work?

The LangChain framework simplifies building sophisticated LLM applications by providing modular components that facilitate connecting language models with other data and services. The framework organizes capabilities into modules spanning from basic LLM interaction to complex reasoning and persistence.

These components can be combined into pipelines also called chains that sequence the following actions:

- Loading documents
- Embedding for retrieval
- Querying LLMs
- Parsing outputs
- Writing memory

Chains match modules to application goals, while agents leverage chains for goal-directed interactions with users. They repeatedly execute actions based on observations, plan optimal logic chains, and persist memory across conversations.

The modules, ranging from simple to advanced, are:

- **LLMs and chat models**: Provide interfaces to connect and query language models like GPT-3. Support async, streaming, and batch requests.
- **Document loaders**: Ingest data from sources into documents with text and metadata. Enable loading files, webpages, videos, etc.
- **Document transformers**: Manipulate documents via splitting, combining, filtering, translating, etc. Help adapt data for models.
- **Text embeddings**: Create vector representations of text for semantic search. Different methods for embedding documents vs. queries.
- **Vector stores**: Store embedded document vectors for efficient similarity search and retrieval.
- **Retrievers**: General interface to return documents based on a query. Can leverage vector stores.
- **Tools**: Interfaces that agents use to interact with external systems.

- **Agents**: Goal-driven systems that use LLMs to plan actions based on environment observations.

- **Toolkits**: Initialize groups of tools that share resources like databases.

- **Memory**: Persist information across conversations and workflows by reading/writing session data.

- **Callbacks**: Hook into pipeline stages for logging, monitoring, streaming, and others. Callbacks enable monitoring chains.

Together, the preceding capabilities facilitate the building of robust, efficient, and capable LLM applications with LangChain. Each of them has its own complexity and importance, so it's important to explain a bit more.

LangChain offers interfaces to connect with and query LLMs like GPT-3 and chat models. These interfaces support asynchronous requests, streaming responses, and batch queries. This provides a flexible API for integrating different language models.

Although LangChain doesn't supply models itself, it supports integration through LLM wrappers with various language model providers, enabling the app to interact with chat models as well as text embedding model providers. Supported providers include OpenAI, HuggingFace, Azure, and Anthropic. Providing a standardized interface means being able to effortlessly swap out models to save money and energy or get better performance. We'll go into some of these options in *Chapter 3, Getting Started with LangChain*.

A core building block of LangChain is the prompt class, which allows users to interact with LLMs by providing concise instructions or examples. Prompt engineering helps optimize prompts for optimal model performance. Templates give flexibility in terms of input and the available collection of prompts is battle-tested in a range of applications. We'll discuss prompts starting in *Chapter 3, Getting Started with LangChain*, and prompt engineering is the topic of *Chapter 8, Customizing LLMs and Their Output*.

Document loaders allow ingesting data from various sources into documents containing text and metadata. This data can then be manipulated via document transformers – splitting, combining, filtering, translating, etc. These tools adapt external data for use in LLMs.

Data loaders include modules for storing data and utilities for interacting with external systems, like web searches or databases, and most importantly data retrieval. Examples are Microsoft Word documents (.docx), **HyperText Markup Language (HTML)**, and other common formats such as PDF, text files, JSON, and CSV. Other tools will send emails to prospective customers, post funny puns for your followers, or send Slack messages to your coworkers. We'll look at these in *Chapter 5, Building a Chatbot like ChatGPT*.

Text embedding models create vector representations of text that capture semantic meaning. This enables semantic search by finding text with the most similar vector representations. Vector stores build on this by indexing embedded document vectors for efficient similarity-based retrieval.

Vector stores come in when working with large documents, where the document needs to be chunked up in order to be passed to the LLM. These parts of the document would be stored as embeddings, which means that they are vector representations of the information. All these tools enhance the LLMs' knowledge and improve their performance in applications like question answering and summarization.

There are numerous integrations for vector storage. These include Alibaba Cloud OpenSearch, AnalyticDB for PostgreSQL, Meta AI's Annoy library for **Approximate Nearest Neighbor (ANN)** search, Cassandra, Chroma, Elasticsearch, **Facebook AI Similarity Search (Faiss)**, MongoDB Atlas Vector Search, PGVector as a vector similarity search for Postgres, Pinecone, scikit-learn (SKLearnVectorStore for k-nearest neighbor search), and many more. We'll explore these in *Chapter 5, Building a Chatbot like ChatGPT*.

While the next chapters will dig into the details of some usage patterns and use cases of LangChain components, the following resources provide invaluable information on LangChain's components and how they can be assembled into pipelines.

For full details on the dozens of available modules, refer to the comprehensive LangChain API reference: https://api.python.langchain.com/. There are also hundreds of code examples demonstrating real-world use cases: https://python.langchain.com/docs/use_cases/.

There are a few other frameworks besides LangChain; however, we'll see that LangChain is one of the most prominent and feature rich of them.

Comparing LangChain with other frameworks

LLM application frameworks have been developed to provide specialized tooling that can harness the power of LLMs effectively to solve complex problems. A few libraries have emerged that meet the requirements of effectively combining generative AI models with other tools to build LLM applications.

There are several open-source frameworks for building dynamic LLM applications. They all offer value in developing cutting-edge LLM applications. This graph shows their popularity over time (data source: GitHub star history, `https://star-history.com/`):

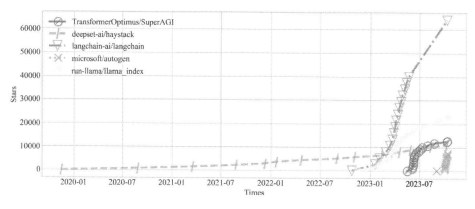

Figure 2.11: Comparison of popularity between different frameworks in Python

We can see the number of stars on GitHub over time for each project. Haystack is the oldest of the compared frameworks, having started in early 2020 (as per the earliest GitHub commits). It is also the least popular in terms of stars on GitHub. LangChain, LlamaIndex (previously called GPTIndex), and SuperAGI were started in late 2022 or early 2023, and they have all fallen short in popularity in a noticeably brief time compared to LangChain, which has been growing impressively. AutoGen is a project recently released by Microsoft that has already garnered some interest. In this book, we'll see a lot of the functionality of LangChain and explore its features, which are the reason its popularity is exploding right now.

LlamaIndex focuses on advanced retrieval rather than on the broader aspects of LLM apps. Similarly, Haystack focuses on creating large-scale search systems with components designed specifically for scalable information retrieval using retrievers, readers, and other data handlers combined with semantic indexing via pre-trained models.

LangChain excels at chaining LLMs together using agents to delegate actions to models. Its use cases emphasize prompt optimization and context-aware information retrieval/generation; however, with its Pythonic highly modular interface and its huge collection of tools, it is the number-one tool to implement complex business logic.

SuperAGI has similar features to LangChain. It even comes with a marketplace, a repository for tools and agents. However, it's not as extensive and well supported as LangChain.

AutoGen simplifies the building, orchestrating, and optimizing of complex workflows powered by LLMs. Its key innovation is enabling customizable conversational agents that automate coordination between different LLMs, humans, and tools via automated chat. AutoGen streamlines agent definition and interaction to automatically compose optimal LLM-based workflows.

I haven't included AutoGPT (and similar tools like AutoLlama), a recursive application that breaks down tasks, because its reasoning capability, based on human and LLM feedback, is very limited compared to LangChain. As a consequence, it's often caught in logic loops and regularly repeats steps. I've also omitted a few libraries that concentrate on prompt engineering, for example, Promptify.

There are other LLM app frameworks in languages such as Rust, JavaScript, Ruby, and Java. For example, Dust, written in Rust, focuses on the design of LLM apps and their deployment.

Frameworks like LangChain aim to lower barriers by providing guardrails, conventions, and pre-built modules, but foundational knowledge remains important for avoiding pitfalls and maximizing value from LLMs. Investing in education pays dividends when delivering capable, responsible applications.

Summary

LLMs produce convincing language but have significant limitations in terms of reasoning, knowledge, and access to tools. The LangChain framework simplifies the building of sophisticated applications powered by LLMs that can mitigate these shortcomings. It provides developers with modular, reusable building blocks like chains for composing pipelines and agents for goal-oriented interactions. These building blocks fit together as LLM apps that come with extended capabilities.

As we saw in this chapter, chains allow sequencing calls to LLMs, databases, APIs, and more to accomplish multi-step workflows. Agents leverage chains to take actions based on observations for managing dynamic applications. Memory persists information across executions to maintain state. Together, these concepts enable developers to overcome the limitations of individual LLMs by integrating external data, actions, and context. In other words, LangChain reduces complex orchestration into customizable building blocks.

In the next chapters, we'll build on these LangChain fundamentals to create capable, real-world applications. We'll implement conversational agents combining LLMs with knowledge bases and advanced reasoning algorithms. By leveraging LangChain's capabilities, developers can unlock the full potential of LLMs to power the next generation of AI software. In the next chapter, we'll implement our first apps with Langchain!

Questions

Please see if you can come up with answers to these questions. I'd recommend you go back to the corresponding sections of this chapter if you are unsure about any of them:

1. What are the limitations of LLMs?
2. What are stochastic parrots?
3. What are LLM applications?
4. What is LangChain and why should you use it?
5. What are LangChain's key features?
6. What is a chain in LangChain?
7. What is an agent?
8. What is memory and why do we need it?
9. What kind of tools are available in LangChain?
10. How does LangChain work?

Join our community on Discord

Join our community's Discord space for discussions with the authors and other readers:

`https://packt.link/lang`

3

Getting Started with LangChain

In this book, we'll write a lot of code and test many different integrations and tools. Therefore, in this chapter, we'll give basic setup instructions for all the libraries needed with the most common dependency management tools such as Docker, Conda, pip, and Poetry. This will ensure that you can run all the practical examples in this book.

Next, we'll go through model integrations that we can use such as OpenAI's ChatGPT, models on Hugging Face, Jina AI, and others. Further, we'll introduce, set up, and work with a few providers in turn. For each of them, we will show how to get an API key token.

In the end, as a practical example, we'll go through an example of a real-world application, an LLM app that could help customer service agents, one of the main areas where LLMs could prove to be game-changing. This will give us a bit more context around using LangChain, and we can introduce tips and tricks for using it effectively.

The main sections are as follows:

- How to set up the dependencies for this book
- Model integrations
- Building an application for customer service

We'll start the chapter by setting up the environment for the book on our computer.

How to set up the dependencies for this book

We'll assume at least a basic familiarity with Python, Jupyter, and environments in this book, but let's quickly walk through this together. You can safely skip this section if you are confident about your setup or if you plan to install libraries separately for each chapter or application.

Please make sure you have Python version 3.10 or higher installed. You can install it from python. org or your platform's package manager. If you use Docker, Conda, or Poetry, an appropriate Python version should be installed automatically as part of the instructions. You should also install Jupyter Notebook or JupyterLab to run the example notebooks interactively.

Environment management tools like Docker, Conda, Pip, and Poetry help create reproducible Python environments for projects. They install dependencies and isolate projects. This table gives an overview of these options for managing dependencies:

Tool	Pros	Cons
pip	Default Python package manager Simple commands to install packages `requirements.txt` for tracking dependencies	Can't install non-Python system dependencies No built-in virtual environment management (see venv or other tools) Limited dependency resolution
Poetry	Intuitive interface Robust dependency resolution Built-in virtual environment management Lock files and version control	Less common than Pip or Conda Limited non-Python dependency management
Conda	Manages Python and non-Python dependencies Handles complex dependency trees Supports multiple Python versions Built-in virtual environment management	Slower than native package managers Large disk usage
Docker	Provides fully isolated and reproducible environments Easily shared and distributed Guaranteed consistency across systems	Additional platform knowledge required Larger disk usage Slower startup times

Table 3.1: Comparison of tools for managing dependencies

For developers, Docker, which provides isolation via containers, is a good option. The downside is that it uses a lot of disk space and is more complex than the other options. For data scientists, I'd recommend Conda or Poetry.

Conda handles intricate dependencies efficiently, although it can be excruciatingly slow in large environments. Poetry resolves dependencies well and managed environments; however, it doesn't capture system dependencies.

All tools allow sharing and replicating dependencies from configuration files. You can find a set of instructions and the corresponding configuration files in the book's repository at https:// github.com/benman1/generative_ai_with_langchain.

This includes these files:

- `requirements.txt` for pip
- `pyproject.toml` for Poetry
- `langchain_ai.yaml` for Conda
- `Dockerfile` for Docker

Depending on whether system dependencies are managed, they can require additional tweaks with more setup, as in the case with pip and poetry. My preference is Conda because it strikes the right balance for me of complexity versus isolation.

As mentioned, we won't spend much time on installation but rather breeze through each of the different tools in turn. For all instructions, please make sure you have the book's repository downloaded (using the GitHub user interface) or cloned on your computer, and you've changed into the project's root directory.

If you encounter issues during the installation process, consult the respective documentation or raise an issue on the GitHub repository of this book. The different installations have been tested at the time of the release of this book; however, things can change, and we will update the GitHub README online to include workarounds for potential problems that could arise.

For each tool, the key steps are installing the tool, using the configuration file from the repository, and activating the environment. This sets up a reproducible environment to run all the examples in the book (with very few exceptions, which will be noted).

Let's go from the simplest to the most complex. We'll start with pip!

pip

pip is the default Python package manager. To use Pip:

1. If it's not already included in your Python distribution, install pip following the instructions here: https://pip.pypa.io/.

2. Use a virtual environment for isolation (for example, venv).

3. Install the dependencies from `requirements.txt`:

```
pip install -r requirements.txt
```

Poetry

Poetry is relatively new, but is popular with Python developers and data scientists because of its convenience. It manages dependencies and virtual environments. To use Poetry:

1. Install poetry by following the instructions at `https://python-poetry.org/`.

2. Run `poetry install` to install the dependencies.

Conda

Conda manages Python environments and dependencies. To use Conda:

1. Install Miniconda or Anaconda following the instructions from this link: `https://docs.continuum.io/anaconda/install/`.

2. Create the environment from `langchain_ai.yml`:

```
conda env create --file langchain_ai.yaml
```

3. Activate the environment:

```
conda activate langchain_ai
```

Docker

Docker provides isolated, reproducible environments using containers. To use Docker:

1. Install Docker Engine; follow the installation instructions here: `https://docs.docker.com/get-docker/`.

2. Build the Docker image from the Dockerfile in this repository:

```
docker build -t langchain_ai
```

3. Run the Docker container interactively:

```
docker run -it langchain_ai
```

Let's move on and see some of the models that you can use with LangChain!

There are many cloud providers of models, where you can use the model through an interface; other sources allow you to download a model to your computer.

With the help of LangChain, we can interact with all of these – for example, through **Application Programming Interface (APIs)**, or we can call models that we have downloaded on our computer. Let's start with models accessed through APIs with cloud providers.

Exploring API model integrations

Before properly starting with generative AI, we need to set up access to models such as LLMs or text-to-image models so we can integrate them into our applications. As discussed in *Chapter 1, What Is Generative AI?*, there are various LLMs by tech giants, like GPT-4 by OpenAI, BERT and PaLM-2 by Google, LLaMA by Meta, and many more.

For LLMs, OpenAI, Hugging Face, Cohere, Anthropic, Azure, Google Cloud Platform's Vertex AI (PaLM-2), and Jina AI are among the many providers supported in LangChain; however, this list is growing all the time. You can check out the full list of supported integrations for LLMs at `https://integrations.langchain.com/llms`.

Here's a screenshot of this page as of the time of writing (October 2023), which includes both cloud providers and interfaces for local models:

Figure 3.1: LLM integrations in LangChain

LangChain implements three different interfaces – we can use chat models, LLMs, and embedding models. Chat models and LLMs are similar in that they both process text input and produce text output. However, there are some differences in the types of input and output they handle. Chat models are specifically designed to handle a list of chat messages as input and generate a chat message as output. They are commonly used in chatbot applications where conversations are exchanged. You can find chat models at https://python.langchain.com/docs/integrations/chat.

Finally, text embedding models are used to convert text inputs into numerical representations called embeddings. We'll focus on text generation in this chapter, and discuss embeddings, vector databases, and neural search in *Chapter 5, Building a Chatbot Like ChatGPT*. Suffice it to say here that these embeddings are a way to capture and extract information from the input text. They are widely used in natural language processing tasks like sentiment analysis, text classification, and information retrieval. Embedding models are listed at https://python.langchain.com/docs/integrations/text_embedding.

As for image models, the big developers include OpenAI (DALL-E), Midjourney, Inc. (Midjourney), and Stability AI (Stable Diffusion). LangChain currently doesn't have out-of-the-box handling of models that are not for text; however, its documentation describe how to work with Replicate, which also provides an interface to Stable Diffusion models.

For each of these providers, to make calls against their API, you'll first need to create an account and obtain an API key. This is free of charge for all providers and, with some of them, you don't even have to give them your credit card details.

To set an API key in an environment, in Python, we can execute the following lines:

```python
import os
os.environ["OPENAI_API_KEY"] = "<your token>"
```

Here, OPENAI_API_KEY is the environment key that is appropriate for OpenAI. Setting the keys in your environment has the advantage of not needing to include them as parameters in your code every time you use a model or service integration.

You can also expose these variables in your system environment from your terminal. In Linux and macOS, you can set a system environment variable from the terminal using the export command:

```
export OPENAI_API_KEY=<your token>
```

To permanently set the environment variable in Linux or macOS, you would need to add the preceding line to the ~/.bashrc or ~/.bash_profile file, respectively, and then reload the shell using the command source ~/.bashrc or source ~/.bash_profile.

In Windows, you can set a system environment variable from the command prompt using the set command:

```
set OPENAI_API_KEY=<your token>
```

To permanently set the environment variable in Windows, you can add the preceding line to a batch script.

My personal choice is to create a config.py file, where all the keys are stored. I then import a function from this module that will load all these keys into the environment. If you look for this file in the Github repository, you'll notice that it is missing. This is on purpose (in fact, I've disabled the tracking of this file in Git) since I don't want to share my keys with other people for security reasons (and because I don't want to pay for anyone else's usage).

My config.py looks like this:

```
import os

OPENAI_API_KEY = "... "
# I'm omitting all other keys

def set_environment():
    variable_dict = globals().items()
    for key, value in variable_dict:
        if "API" in key or "ID" in key:
            os.environ[key] = value
```

You can set all your keys in the config.py file. This function, set_environment(), loads all the keys into the environment as mentioned. Anytime you want to run an application, you import the function and run it like so:

```
from config import set_environment
set_environment()
```

Now, let's go through a few prominent model providers in turn. We'll give an example of usage for each of them. Let's start with a fake LLM that we can use for testing purposes. This will help to illustrate the general idea of calling language models in LangChain.

Fake LLM

The fake LLM allows you to simulate LLM responses during testing without needing actual API calls. This is useful for rapid prototyping and unit testing agents. Using the FakeLLM avoids hitting rate limits during testing. It also allows you to mock various responses to validate that your agent handles them properly. Overall, it enables fast agent iteration without needing a real LLM.

For example, you could initialize a FakeLLM that returns "Hello" as follows:

```
from langchain.llms import FakeLLM


fake_llm = FakeLLM(responses=["Hello"])
```

You can execute this example in either Python directly or in a notebook.

The fake LLM is only for testing purposes. The LangChain documentation has an example of tool use with LLMs. This is a bit more complex than the previous example but gives a hint of the capabilities we have at our fingertips:

```
from langchain.llms.fake import FakeListLLM
from langchain.agents import load_tools
from langchain.agents import initialize_agent
from langchain.agents import AgentType


tools = load_tools(["python_repl"])
responses = ["Action: Python_REPL\nAction Input: print(2 + 2)", "Final
Answer: 4"]
llm = FakeListLLM(responses=responses)


agent = initialize_agent(
    tools, llm, agent=AgentType.ZERO_SHOT_REACT_DESCRIPTION, verbose=True
)
agent.run("whats 2 + 2")
```

We set up an agent that makes decisions based on the React strategy that we explained in *Chapter 2, LangChain for LLM Apps* (ZERO_SHOT_REACT_DESCRIPTION). We run the agent with a text: the question what's 2 + 2.

As you can see, we connect a tool, a Python **Read-Eval-Print Loop (REPL)**, that will be called depending on the output of the LLM. `FakeListLLM` will give two responses (`"Action: Python_REPL\nAction Input: print(2 + 2)"` and `"Final Answer: 4"`) that won't change based on the input.

We can also observe how the fake LLM output leads to a call to the Python interpreter, which returns 4. Please note that the action must match the name attribute of the tool, `PythonREPLTool`, which starts like this:

```python
class PythonREPLTool(BaseTool):
    """A tool for running python code in a REPL."""

    name = "Python_REPL"
    description = (
        "A Python shell. Use this to execute python commands. "
        "Input should be a valid python command. "
        "If you want to see the output of a value, you should print it out
"
        "with `print(...)`."
    )
```

As you can see in the preceding code block, the names and descriptions of the tools are passed to the LLM, which then decides an action based on the information provided. The action can be executing a tool or planning.

The output of the Python interpreter is passed to the fake LLM, which ignores the observation and returns 4. Obviously, if we change the second response to `"Final Answer: 5"`, the output of the agent wouldn't correspond to the question.

In the next sections, we'll make our example more meaningful by using an actual LLM rather than a fake one. One of the first providers anyone will think of is OpenAI.

OpenAI

As explained in *Chapter 1, What Is Generative AI?*, OpenAI is an American AI research laboratory that is the current market leader in generative AI models, especially LLMs. They offer a range of models with various levels of power suitable for different tasks. We'll see, in this chapter, how to interact with OpenAI models with the LangChain and the OpenAI Python client libraries. OpenAI also offers an **Embedding** class for text embedding models.

We will use OpenAI for our applications but will also try LLMs from other organizations. When you send a prompt to an LLM API, it processes the prompt word by word, breaking down (tokenizing) the text into individual tokens. The number of tokens directly correlates with the amount of text.

When using commercial LLMs like GPT-3 and GPT-4 via APIs, each token has an associated cost based on factors like the LLM model and API pricing tiers. Token usage refers to how many tokens from the model's quota have been consumed to generate a response. Strategies like using smaller models, summarizing outputs, and preprocessing inputs help reduce the tokens required to get useful results. Being aware of token usage is key for optimizing productivity within budget constraints when leveraging commercial LLMs.

We need to obtain an OpenAI API key first. To create an API key, follow these steps:

1. You need to create a login at `https://platform.openai.com/`.
2. Set up your billing information.
3. You can see the API keys under **Personal | View API Keys**.
4. Click on **Create new secret key** and give it a name.

Here's how this should look on the OpenAI platform:

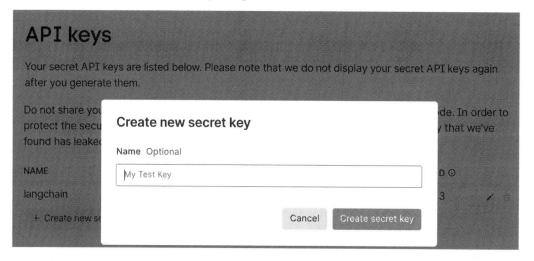

Figure 3.2: OpenAI API platform – Create new secret key

After clicking **Create secret key**, you should see the message **API key generated**. You need to copy the key to your clipboard and keep it. We can set the key as an environment variable (OPENAI_API_KEY) or pass it as a parameter every time you construct a class for OpenAI calls.

We can use the OpenAI language model class to set up an LLM to interact with. Let's create an agent that calculates using this model – I am omitting the imports from the previous example:

```
from langchain.llms import OpenAI
llm = OpenAI(temperature=0., model="text-davinci-003")


agent = initialize_agent(
    tools, llm, agent=AgentType.ZERO_SHOT_REACT_DESCRIPTION, verbose=True
)
agent.run("whats 4 + 4")
```

We should be seeing this output:

```
> Entering new chain...
 I need to add two numbers
Action: Python_REPL
Action Input: print(4 + 4)
Observation: 8

Thought: I now know the final answer
Final Answer: 4 + 4 = 8

> Finished chain.
'4 + 4 = 8'
```

The agent comes up with the right solution. It's a simple problem, but I still find it fascinating to be able to put my question in natural language. During the course of this book, we'll try to come up with solutions to more complex problems. But for now, let's move on to the next provider and more examples!

Hugging Face

Hugging Face is a very prominent player in the NLP space and has considerable traction in open-source and hosting solutions. The company is an American company that develops tools for building machine learning applications. Its employees develop and maintain the Transformers Python library, which is used for NLP tasks, includes implementations of state-of-the-art and popular models like Mistral 7B, BERT, and GPT-2, and is compatible with PyTorch, TensorFlow, and JAX.

Hugging Face also provides the Hugging Face Hub, a platform for hosting Git-based code repositories, machine learning models, datasets, and web applications, which provides over 120k models, 20k datasets, and 50k demo apps (spaces) for machine learning. It is an online platform where people can collaborate and facilitate machine learning development.

These tools allow users to load and use models, embeddings, and datasets from Hugging Face. The HuggingFaceHub integration, for example, provides access to different models for tasks like text generation and text classification. The HuggingFaceEmbeddings integration allows users to work with sentence-transformer models.

Hugging Face offer various other libraries within their ecosystem, including Datasets for dataset processing, Evaluate for model evaluation, Simulate for simulation, and Gradio for machine learning demos.

In addition to their products, Hugging Face has been involved in initiatives such as the BigScience Research Workshop, where they released an open LLM called BLOOM with 176 billion parameters. They have received significant funding, including a $40 million Series B round and a recent Series C funding round led by Coatue and Sequoia at a $2 billion valuation. Hugging Face has also formed partnerships with companies like Graphcore and Amazon Web Services to optimize their offerings and make them available to a broader customer base.

To use Hugging Face as a provider for your models, you can create an account and API keys at https://huggingface.co/settings/profile. Additionally, you can make the token available in your environment as HUGGINGFACEHUB_API_TOKEN.

Let's see an example, where we use an open-source model developed by Google, the Flan-T5-XXL model:

```
from langchain.llms import HuggingFaceHub
llm = HuggingFaceHub(
    model_kwargs={"temperature": 0.5, "max_length": 64},
    repo_id="google/flan-t5-xxl"
)
prompt = "In which country is Tokyo?"
completion = llm(prompt)
print(completion)
```

We get the response "japan".

The LLM takes a text input, a question in this case, and returns a completion. The model has a lot of knowledge and can come up with answers to knowledge questions.

Google Cloud Platform

There are many models and functions available through **Google Cloud Platform (GCP)** and Vertex AI, GCP's machine learning platform. GCP provides access to LLMs like LaMDA, T5, and PaLM. Google has also updated the Google Cloud **Natural Language (NL)** API with a new LLM-based model for **Content Classification**. This updated version offers an expansive pre-trained classification taxonomy to help with ad targeting and content-based filtering. The NL API's improved v2 classification model is enhanced with over 1,000 labels and supports 11 languages with improved accuracy (it is unclear, however, which model is used under the hood).

For models with GCP, you need to have the gcloud **command-line interface (CLI)** installed. You can find the instructions here: `https://cloud.google.com/sdk/docs/install`.

You can then authenticate and print a key token with this command from the terminal:

```
gcloud auth application-default login
```

You also need to enable Vertex AI for your project. To enable Vertex AI, install the Google Vertex AI SDK with the `pip install google-cloud-aiplatform` command. If you've followed the instructions on GitHub as indicated in the previous section, you should already have this installed.

Then we have to set up the Google Cloud project ID. You have different options for this:

- Using `gcloud config set project my-project`
- Passing a constructor argument when initializing the LLM
- Using `aiplatform.init()`
- Setting a GCP environment variable

I found all these options work fine. You can find more details about these options in the Vertex documentation. The GCP environment variable works well with the `config.py` file that I mentioned earlier. I found the `gcloud` command very convenient though, so I went with this. Please make sure you set the project ID before you move on.

If you haven't enabled it, you should get a helpful error message pointing you to the right website, where you click **Enable**.

Let's run a model!

```
from langchain.llms import VertexAI
from langchain import PromptTemplate, LLMChain
template = """Question: {question}
Answer: Let's think step by step."""
prompt = PromptTemplate(template=template, input_variables=["question"])
llm = VertexAI()
llm_chain = LLMChain(prompt=prompt, llm=llm, verbose=True)
question = "What NFL team won the Super Bowl in the year Justin Beiber was
born?"
llm_chain.run(question)
```

We should see this response:

```
[1m> Entering new chain...[0m
Prompt after formatting:
[[Question: What NFL team won the Super Bowl in the year Justin Beiber was
born?
Answer: Let's think step by step.[0m
[1m> Finished chain.[0m
Justin Beiber was born on March 1, 1994. The Super Bowl in 1994 was won by
the San Francisco 49ers.
```

I've set verbose to True to see the model's reasoning process. It's quite impressive that it produces the right response even given a misspelling of the name. The step-by-step prompt instruction is key to the correct answer.

Vertex AI offers a range of models tailored for tasks like following instructions, conversation, and code generation/assistance:

- **text-bison** is fine-tuned to follow natural language instructions, with a max input of 8,192 tokens and an output of 1,024.

- **chat-bison** is optimized for multi-turn conversation with a max input of 4,096 tokens, an output of 1,024 tokens, and up to 2,500 turns.

- **code-bison** generates code from natural language descriptions, with a max input of 4,096 tokens and an output of 2,048 tokens.

- **codechat-bison** is a chatbot that is fine-tuned to help with code-related questions. It has an input limit of 4,096 tokens and an output limit of 2,048 tokens.

- **code-gecko** suggests code completions. It has a max input length of 2,048 tokens and an output of 64 tokens.

These models also have different input/output limits and training data and are often updated. For more detailed and up-to-date information about models, including when models have been updated, you can check out the documentation at https://cloud.google.com/vertex-ai/docs/generative-ai/learn/overview.

We can also generate code. Let's see if the code-bison model can solve **FizzBuzz**, a common interview question for entry-level software developer positions:

```
question = """
Given an integer n, return a string array answer (1-indexed) where:

answer[i] == "FizzBuzz" if i is divisible by 3 and 5.
answer[i] == "Fizz" if i is divisible by 3.
answer[i] == "Buzz" if i is divisible by 5.
answer[i] == i (as a string) if none of the above conditions are true.
"""

llm = VertexAI(model_name="code-bison")
llm_chain = LLMChain(prompt=prompt, llm=llm)
print(llm_chain.run(question))
```

We are getting this response:

```python
answer = []
for i in range(1, n + 1):
    if i % 3 == 0 and i % 5 == 0:
        answer.append("FizzBuzz")
    elif i % 3 == 0:
        answer.append("Fizz")
    elif i % 5 == 0:
        answer.append("Buzz")
    else:
        answer.append(str(i))

return answer
```

Would you hire code-bison for your team?

Jina AI

Jina AI, founded in February 2020 by Han Xiao and Xuanbin He, is a German AI company based in Berlin that specializes in providing cloud-native neural search solutions with models for text, image, audio, and video. Their open-source neural search ecosystem enables businesses and developers to easily build scalable and highly available neural search solutions, allowing for efficient information retrieval. Recently, Jina AI launched **Finetuner**, a tool that enables the fine-tuning of any deep neural network to specific use cases and requirements.

The company raised $37.5 million in funding through three rounds, with their most recent funding coming from a Series A round in November 2021. Notable investors in Jina AI include GGV Capital and Canaan Partners.

You can set up a login at `https://chat.jina.ai/api`.

On the platform, we can set up APIs for different use cases such as image caption, text embedding, image embedding, visual question answering, visual reasoning, image upscale, or Chinese text embedding.

Here, we are setting up a Visual Question Answering API with the recommended model:

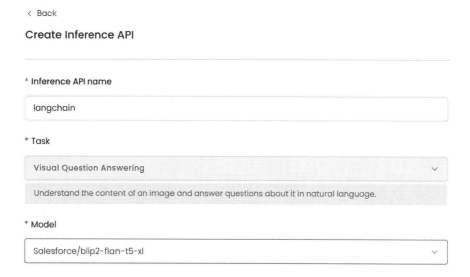

Figure 3.3: Visual Question Answering API in Jina AI

We get examples for client calls in Python and cURL, and a demo, where we can ask a question. This is cool, but unfortunately, these APIs are not available yet through LangChain. We can implement such calls ourselves by subclassing the LLM class in LangChain as a custom LLM interface.

Let's set up another chatbot, this time powered by Jina AI. We can generate the API token, which we can set as `JINACHAT_API_KEY`, at `https://chat.jina.ai/api`.

Let's translate from English to French here:

```
from langchain.chat_models import JinaChat
from langchain.schema import HumanMessage
chat = JinaChat(temperature=0.)


messages = [
    HumanMessage(
        content="Translate this sentence from English to French: I love
generative AI!"
    )
]
chat(messages)
```

We should be seeing :

```
AIMessage(content="J'adore l'IA générative !", additional_kwargs={},
example=False).
```

We can set different temperatures, where a low temperature makes the responses more predictable. In this case, it makes only a minor difference. We are starting the conversation with a system message clarifying the purpose of the chatbot.

Let's ask for some food recommendations:

```
from langchain.schema import SystemMessage
chat = JinaChat(temperature=0.)


chat(
    [
        SystemMessage(
            content="You help a user find a nutritious and tasty food to
eat in one word."
        ),
```

```
        HumanMessage(
            content="I like pasta with cheese, but I need to eat more
    vegetables, what should I eat?"
        )
    ]
)
```

I get this response in Jupyter – your answer could vary:

```
AIMessage(content='A tasty and nutritious option could be a vegetable
pasta dish. Depending on your taste, you can choose a sauce that
complements the vegetables. Try adding broccoli, spinach, bell peppers,
and zucchini to your pasta with some grated parmesan cheese on top. This
way, you get to enjoy your pasta with cheese while incorporating some
veggies into your meal.', additional_kwargs={}, example=False)
```

It ignored the one-word instruction, but I liked reading the ideas. I think I should try this for my son. With other chatbots, I got `Ratatouille` as a suggestion.

It's important to understand the difference in LangChain between LLMs and chat models. LLMs are text completion models that take a string prompt as input and output a string completion. As mentioned, chat models are like LLMs but are specifically designed for conversations. They take a list of chat messages as input, labeled with the speaker, and return a chat message as output.

Both LLMs and chat models implement the base language model interface, which includes methods such as `predict()` and `predict_messages()`. This shared interface allows for interchangeability between diverse types of models in applications and between chat and LLM models.

Replicate

Established in 2019, Replicate Inc. is a San Francisco-based start-up that presents a streamlined process to AI developers, where they can implement and publish AI models with minimal code input through the utilization of cloud technology. The platform works with private as well as public models and enables model inference and fine-tuning. The firm, deriving its most recent funding from a Series A funding round of which the invested total was $12.5 million, was spearheaded by Andreessen Horowitz, and involved the participation of Y Combinator, Sequoia, and various independent investors.

Ben Firshman, who drove open-source product efforts at Docker, and Andreas Jansson, a former machine learning engineer at Spotify, co-founded Replicate Inc. with the mutual aspiration to eliminate the technical barriers that were hindering the mass acceptance of AI. Consequently, they created Cog, an open-source tool that packs machine learning models into a standard production-ready container that can run on any current operating system and automatically generate an API. These containers can also be deployed on clusters of GPUs through the Replicate platform. As a result, developers can concentrate on other essential tasks, thereby enhancing their productivity.

Replicate has lots of models available on their platform: `https://replicate.com/explore`.

You can authenticate with your GitHub credentials at `https://replicate.com/`. If you then click on your user icon at the top left, you'll find the API tokens – just copy the API key and make it available in your environment as `REPLICATE_API_TOKEN`. To run bigger jobs, you need to set up your credit card (under **billing**).

Here is a simple example for creating an image:

```
from langchain.llms import Replicate

text2image = Replicate(
    model="stability-ai/stable-diffusion:db21e45d3f7023abc2a46ee38a23973f6
dce16bb082a930b0c49861f96d1e5bf",
    input={"image_dimensions": "512x512"},
)
image_url = text2image("a book cover for a book about creating generative
ai applications in Python")
```

I got this image:

Figure 3.4: A book cover for a book about generative AI with Python – Stable Diffusion

I think it's a nice image – is that an AI chip that creates art?

Others

There are a lot more providers, and we'll encounter quite a few throughout the book. Sadly, as you'll see, I faced issues with Azure and Anthropic, two major providers. Let's still have a quick look at them!

Azure

Azure, the cloud computing platform run by Microsoft, integrates with OpenAI to provide powerful language models like GPT-3, Codex, and Embeddings. It offers access, management, and development of applications and services through its global data centers for use cases such as writing assistance, summarization, code generation, and semantic search. It provides capabilities like **software as a service (SaaS)**, **platform as a service (PaaS)**, and **infrastructure as a service (IaaS)**.

By authenticating either through GitHub or Microsoft credentials, we can create an account on Azure at https://azure.microsoft.com/.

We can then create new API keys under **Cognitive Services | Azure OpenAI**. There are a few more steps involved, and personally, I found this process frustrating. After going through account validation a few times, getting denied, and trying to contact Microsoft customer service, I gave up. For this reason, I don't have a practical example with Azure. Your mileage might vary – if you are already using Microsoft services, this process could be pain-free for you.

After setting up, the models should be accessible through the `AzureOpenAI()` class interface in LangChain.

Anthropic

Anthropic is an AI start-up and public-benefit corporation based in the United States. It was founded in 2021 by former members of OpenAI, including siblings Daniela Amodei and Dario Amodei. The company specializes in developing general AI systems and language models with a focus on responsible AI usage. As of July 2023, Anthropic has raised $1.5 billion in funding. They have also worked on projects like Claude, an AI chatbot like OpenAI's ChatGPT, and have researched the interpretability of machine learning systems, specifically the Transformer architecture.

Unfortunately, Claude is not available to the general public (yet). You need to apply for access to use Claude and set the `ANTHROPIC_API_KEY` environment variable.

Next, let's see how to run models locally.

Exploring local models

We can also run local models from LangChain. The advantages of running models locally are complete control over the model and not sharing any data over the internet.

 Please note that we don't need an API token for local models!

Let's preface this with a note of caution: an LLM is big, which means that it'll take up a lot of disk space or system memory. The use cases presented in this section should run even on old hardware, like an old MacBook; however, if you choose a big model, it can take an exceptionally long time to run or may crash the Jupyter notebook. One of the main bottlenecks is memory requirement. In rough terms, if quantized (roughly, compressed; we'll discuss quantization in *Chapter 8, Customizing LLMs and Their Output*), 1 billion parameters correspond to 1 GB of RAM (please note that not all models will come quantized).

You can also run these models on hosted resources or services such as Kubernetes or Google Colab. These will let you run on machines with a lot of memory and different hardware including **Tensor Processing Units (TPUs)** or **GPUs**.

We'll have a look here at Hugging Face's `transformers`, `llama.cpp`, and GPT4All. These tools provide huge power and are full of great functionality too broad to cover in this chapter. Let's start by showing how we can run a model with the transformers library by Hugging Face.

Hugging Face Transformers

I'll quickly show the general recipe for setting up and running a pipeline:

```python
from transformers import pipeline
import torch

generate_text = pipeline(
    model="aisquared/dlite-v1-355m",
    torch_dtype=torch.bfloat16,
    trust_remote_code=True,
    device_map="auto",
    framework="pt"
)
generate_text("In this chapter, we'll discuss first steps with generative
AI in Python.")
```

Running the preceding code will download everything that's needed for the model such as the tokenizer and model weights from Hugging Face. This model is quite small (355 million parameters) but relatively performant and instruction-tuned for conversations. We can then run a text completion to give us some inspiration for this chapter.

I haven't included `accelerate` in the main requirements, but I've included the transformers library. If you don't have all libraries installed, make sure you execute this command:

```
pip install transformers accelerate torch
```

To plug this pipeline into a LangChain agent or chain, we can use it the same way that we've seen in the other examples in this chapter:

```python
from langchain import PromptTemplate, LLMChain

template = """Question: {question}
Answer: Let's think step by step."""
prompt = PromptTemplate(template=template, input_variables=["question"])
llm_chain = LLMChain(prompt=prompt, llm=generate_text)
```

```
question = "What is electroencephalography?"

print(llm_chain.run(question))
```

In this example, we also see the use of a `PromptTemplate` that gives specific instructions for the task.

`llama.cpp` is a C++ port of Facebook's LLaMA, LLaMA 2, and other derivative models with a similar architecture. Let's have a look at this next.

llama.cpp

Written and maintained by Georgi Gerganov, `llama.cpp` is a C++ toolkit that executes models based on architectures based on or like LLaMA, one of the first large open-source models, which was released by Meta, and which spawned the development of many other models in turn. One of the main use cases of `llama.cpp` is to run models efficiently on the CPU; however, there are also some options for GPU.

Please note that you need to have an **md5 checksum** tool installed. This is included by default in several Linux distributions such as Ubuntu. On macOS, you can install it with brew like this:

```
brew install md5sha1sum
```

We need to download the llama.cpp repository from GitHub. You can do this online by choosing one of the download options on GitHub, or you can use a `git` command from the terminal like this:

```
git clone https://github.com/ggerganov/llama.cpp.git
```

Then we need to install the Python requirements, which we can do with the pip package installer — let's also switch to the `llama.cpp` project root directory for convenience:

```
cd llama.cpp
pip install -r requirements.txt
```

You might want to create a Python environment before you install the requirements, but this is up to you. In my case, I received an error message at the end that a few libraries were missing, so I had to execute this command:

```
pip install 'blosc2==2.0.0' cython FuzzyTM
```

Now we need to compile `llama.cpp`. We can parallelize the build with 4 processes:

```
make -C . -j4 # runs make in subdir with 4 processes
```

To get the Llama model weights, you need to sign up with the T&Cs and wait for a registration email from Meta. There are tools such as the `llama` model downloader in the `pyllama` project, but please be advised that they might not conform to the license stipulations by Meta.

There are also many other models with more permissive licensing such as Falcon or Mistral, Vicuna, OpenLLaMA, or Alpaca. Let's assume you download the model weights and the tokenizer model for the OpenLLaMA 3B model using the link on the ***llama.cpp*** GitHub page. The model file should be about 6.8 Gigabyes big, the tokenizer is much smaller. You can move the two files into the `models/3B` directory.

You can download models in much bigger sizes such as 13B, 30B, and 65B; however, a note of caution is in order here: these models are big both in terms of memory and disk space. We have to convert the model to llama.cpp format, which is called ggml, using the convert script:

```
python3 convert.py models/3B/ --ctx 2048.
```

Then we can optionally quantize the models to save memory when doing inference. Quantization refers to reducing the number of bits that are used to store weight:

```
./quantize ./models/3B/ggml-model-f16.gguf ./models/3B/ggml-model-q4_0.bin
q4_0
```

This last file is much smaller than the previous files and will take up much less space in memory as well, which means that you can run it on smaller machines. Once we have chosen a model that we want to run, we can integrate it into an agent or a chain, for example, as follows:

```
llm = LlamaCpp(
    model_path="./ggml-model-q4_0.bin",
    verbose=True
)
```

GPT4All Is a fantastic tool that not only includes running but also serving and customizing models.

GPT4All

This tool is closely related to llama.cpp, and it's based on an interface with llama.cpp. Compared to llama.cpp, however, it's much more convenient to use and much easier to install. The setup instructions for this book already include the gpt4all library, which is needed.

As for model support, GPT4All supports a large array of Transformer architectures:

- GPT-J
- LLaMA (via llama.cpp)
- Mosaic ML's MPT architecture
- Replit
- Falcon
- BigCode's StarCoder

You can find a list of all available models on the project website, where you can also see their results in important benchmarks: `https://gpt4all.io/`.

Here's a quick example of text generation with GPT4All:

```
from langchain.llms import GPT4All
model = GPT4All(model="mistral-7b-openorca.Q4_0.gguf", n_ctx=512, n_
threads=8)
response = model(
    "We can run large language models locally for all kinds of
applications, "
)
```

Executing this should first download (if not downloaded yet) the model, which is one of the best chat model available through GPT4All, pre-trained by the French startup Mistral AI, and fine-tuned by the OpenOrca AI initiative. This model requires 3.83 GB of harddisk to store and 8 GB of RAM to run. Then we should hopefully see some convincing arguments for running LLMs locally.

This should serve as a first introduction to integrations with local models. In the next section, we'll discuss building a text classification application in LangChain to assist customer service agents. The goal is to categorize customer emails based on intent, extract sentiment, and generate summaries to help agents understand and respond faster.

Building an application for customer service

Customer service agents are responsible for answering customer inquiries, resolving issues, and addressing complaints. Their work is crucial for maintaining customer satisfaction and loyalty, which directly affects a company's reputation and financial success.

Generative AI can assist customer service agents in several ways:

- **Sentiment classification**: This helps identify customer emotions and allows agents to personalize their responses.
- **Summarization**: This enables agents to understand the key points of lengthy customer messages and save time.
- **Intent classification**: Similar to summarization, this helps predict the customer's purpose and allows for faster problem-solving.
- **Answer suggestions**: This provides agents with suggested responses to common inquiries, ensuring that accurate and consistent messaging is provided.

These approaches combined can help customer service agents respond more accurately and in a timely manner, improving customer satisfaction. Customer service is crucial for maintaining customer satisfaction and loyalty. Generative AI can help agents in several ways – sentiment analysis to gauge emotion, summarization to identify key points, and intent classification to determine purpose. Combined, these can enable more accurate, timely responses.

LangChain provides the flexibility to leverage different models. LangChain comes with many integrations that can enable us to tackle a wide range of text problems. We have a choice between many different integrations to perform these tasks.

We can access all kinds of models for open-domain classification and sentiment and smaller transformer models through Hugging Face for focused tasks. We'll build a prototype that uses sentiment analysis to classify email sentiment, summarization to condense lengthy text, and intent classification to categorize the issue.

Given a document such as an email, we want to classify it into different categories related to intent, extract the sentiment, and provide a summary. We will work on other projects for question-answering in *Chapter 5, Building a Chatbot Like ChatGPT*.

We could ask any LLM to give us an open-domain (any category) classification or choose between multiple categories. In particular, because of their large training size, LLMs are enormously powerful models, especially when given few-shot prompts, for sentiment analysis that don't need any additional training. This was analyzed by Zengzhi Wang and others in their April 2023 study, *Is ChatGPT a Good Sentiment Analyzer? A Preliminary Study*.

A prompt for an LLM for sentiment analysis could be something like this:

```
Given this text, what is the sentiment conveyed? Is it positive, neutral,
or negative?
```

```
Text: {sentence}
Sentiment:
```

LLMs can also be highly effective at summarization, much better than any previous models. The downside can be that these model calls are slower than more traditional machine learning models and more expensive.

If we want to try out more traditional or smaller models, we can rely on libraries such as spaCy or access them through specialized providers. Cohere and other providers have text classification and sentiment analysis as part of their capabilities. For example, NLP Cloud's model list includes spaCy and many others: `https://docs.nlpcloud.com/#models-list`.

Many Hugging Face models are supported for these tasks, including:

- Document question-answering
- Summarization
- Text classification
- Text question-answering
- Translation

We can execute these models either locally by running a `pipeline` in transformer, remotely on the Hugging Face Hub server (`HuggingFaceHub`), or as a tool through the `load_huggingface_tool()` loader.

Hugging Face contains thousands of models, many fine-tuned for particular domains. For example, **ProsusAI/finbert** is a BERT model that was trained on a dataset called **Financial PhraseBank** and can analyze the sentiment of financial text. We could also use any local model. For text classification, the models tend to be much smaller, so this would be less of a drag on resources. Finally, text classification could also be a case for embeddings, which we'll discuss in *Chapter 5*, *Building a Chatbot Like ChatGPT*.

I've decided to try and manage as much as I can with smaller models that I can find on Hugging Face for this exercise.

We can list the 5 most downloaded models on Hugging Face Hub for text classification through the Hugging Face API:

```
from huggingface_hub import list_models

def list_most_popular(task: str):
```

```
    for rank, model in enumerate(
        list_models(filter=task, sort="downloads", direction=-1)
):

        if rank == 5:
            break
        print(f"{model.id}, {model.downloads}\n")


list_most_popular("text-classification")
```

Let's see the list:

Model	Downloads
distilbert-base-uncased-finetuned-sst-2-english	40,672,289
cardiffnlp/twitter-roberta-base-sentiment	9,292,338
MoritzLaurer/DeBERTa-v3-base-mnli-fever-anli	7,907,049
cardiffnlp/twitter-roberta-base-irony	7,023,579
SamLowe/roberta-base-go_emotions	6,706,653

Table 3.2: The most popular text classification models on Hugging Face Hub

Generally, we should see that these models are about small ranges of categories such as sentiment, emotions, irony, or well-formedness. Let's use a sentiment model with a customer email, which should be a common use case in customer service.

I've asked GPT-3.5 to put together a rambling customer email complaining about a coffee machine – I've shortened it a bit here. You can find the full email on GitHub. Let's see what our sentiment model has to say:

```
from transformers import pipeline


customer_email = """
I am writing to pour my heart out about the recent unfortunate experience
I had with one of your coffee machines that arrived broken. I anxiously
unwrapped the box containing my highly anticipated coffee machine.
However, what I discovered within broke not only my spirit but also any
semblance of confidence I had placed in your brand.
```

```
Its once elegant exterior was marred by the scars of travel, resembling a
war-torn soldier who had fought valiantly on the fields of some espresso
battlefield. This heartbreaking display of negligence shattered my dreams
of indulging in daily coffee perfection, leaving me emotionally distraught
and inconsolable
"""

sentiment_model = pipeline(
    task="sentiment-analysis",
    model="cardiffnlp/twitter-roberta-base-sentiment"
)
print(sentiment_model(customer_email))
```

The sentiment model we are using here, Twitter-roBERTa-base, was trained on tweets, so it might not be the most adequate use case. Apart from emotion sentiment analysis, this model can also perform other tasks such as emotion recognition (anger, joy, sadness, or optimism), emoji prediction, irony detection, hate speech detection, offensive language identification, and stance detection (favor, neutral, or against).

For the sentiment analysis, we'll get a rating and a numeric score that expresses confidence in the label. These are the labels:

- 0 – negative
- 1 – neutral
- 2 – positive

Please make sure you have all the dependencies installed according to instructions in order to execute this. I am getting this result:

```
[{'label': 'LABEL_0', 'score': 0.5822020173072815}]
```

Not a happy camper.

For comparison, if the email says "I am so angry and sad, I want to kill myself," we should get a score of close to 0.98 for the same label. We could try out other models or train better models once we have established metrics to work against.

Let's move on!

Here are the 5 most popular models for summarization as well (downloads at the time of writing, October 2023):

Model	Downloads
facebook/bart-large-cnn	4,637,417
t5-small	2,492,451
t5-base	1,887,661
sshleifer/distilbart-cnn-12-6	715,809
t5-large	332,854

Table 3.3: The most popular summarization models on Hugging Face Hub

All these models have a small footprint, which is nice, but to apply them in earnest, we should make sure they are reliable enough.

Let's execute the summarization model remotely on a server. Please note that you need to have your HUGGINGFACEHUB_API_TOKEN set for this to work:

```python
from langchain import HuggingFaceHub

summarizer = HuggingFaceHub(
    repo_id="facebook/bart-large-cnn",
    model_kwargs={"temperature":0, "max_length":180}
)
def summarize(llm, text) -> str:
    return llm(f"Summarize this: {text}!")

summarize(summarizer, customer_email)
```

After executing this, I see this summary:

```
A customer's coffee machine arrived ominously broken, evoking a profound
sense of disbelief and despair. "This heartbreaking display of negligence
shattered my dreams of indulging in daily coffee perfection, leaving me
emotionally distraught and inconsolable," the customer writes. "I hope
this email finds you amidst an aura of understanding, despite the tangled
mess of emotions swirling within me as I write to you," he adds.
```

This summary is just passable, but not very convincing. There is still a lot of rambling in the summary. We could try other models or just go for an LLM with a prompt asking to summarize. We'll look at summarization in much more detail in *Chapter 4, Building Capable Assistants*. Let's move on.

It could be quite useful to know what kind of issue the customer is writing about. Let's ask Vertex AI:

 Before you execute the following code, make sure you have authenticated with GCP and you've set your GCP project according to the instructions mentioned in the section about Vertex AI.

```
from langchain.llms import VertexAI
from langchain import PromptTemplate, LLMChain

template = """Given this text, decide what is the issue the customer is
concerned about. Valid categories are these:
* product issues
* delivery problems
* missing or late orders
* wrong product
* cancellation request
* refund or exchange
* bad support experience
* no clear reason to be upset

Text: {email}
Category:
"""
prompt = PromptTemplate(template=template, input_variables=["email"])
llm = VertexAI()
llm_chain = LLMChain(prompt=prompt, llm=llm, verbose=True)
print(llm_chain.run(customer_email))
```

We get product issues back, which is correct for the long email example that I am using here.

I hope it was exciting to see how quickly we can throw a few models and tools together in Lang-Chain to get something that looks actually useful. With thoughtful implementation, such AI automation can complement human agents – handling frequent questions to allow focusing on complex problems. Overall, this demonstrates generative AI's potential to enhance customer service workflows.

We could easily expose this in a graphical interface for customer service agents to see and interact with. This is something we will do in the next chapter.

Let's wrap up!

Summary

In this chapter, we walked through four distinct ways of installing LangChain and other libraries needed in this book as an environment. Then, we introduced several providers of models for text and images. For each of them, we explained where to get the API token, and demonstrated how to call a model.

Finally, we developed an LLM app for text categorization (intent classification) and sentiment analysis in a use case for customer service. This showcases LangChain's ease in orchestrating multiple models to create useful applications. By chaining together various functionalities in LangChain, we can help reduce response times in customer service and make sure answers are accurate and to the point.

In *Chapter 4*, *Building Capable Assistants* and *Chapter 5*, *Building a Chatbot Like ChatGPT*, we'll dive more into use cases such as question answering in chatbots through augmentation with tools and retrieval.

Questions

Please look to see whether you can provide answers to these questions. I'd recommend you go back to the corresponding sections of this chapter if you are unsure about any of them:

1. How do you install LangChain?
2. List at least 4 cloud providers of LLMs apart from OpenAI!
3. What are Jina AI and Hugging Face?
4. How do you generate images with LangChain?
5. How do you run a model locally on your own machine rather than through a service?
6. How do you perform text classification in LangChain?
7. How can we help customer service agents in their work through generative AI?

Join our community on Discord

Join our community's Discord space for discussions with the authors and other readers:

`https://packt.link/lang`

4

Building Capable Assistants

As LLMs continue to advance, a key challenge is transforming their impressive fluency into reliably capable assistants. This chapter explores methods for instilling greater intelligence, productivity, and trustworthiness in LLMs. The unifying theme across these approaches is enhancing LLMs through prompts, tools, and structured reasoning techniques. We'll have sample applications that demonstrate these techniques in this chapter.

We will begin by addressing the critical weakness of hallucinated content through automatic fact-checking. By verifying claims against the available evidence, we can reduce the spread of misinformation. We will continue by discussing a key strength of LLMs with important applications – summarization, which we'll go into with the integration of prompts at different levels of sophistication, and the map reduce approach for very long documents. We will then move on to information extraction from documents with function calls, which leads to the topic of tool integrations. We'll implement an application that showcases how connecting external data and services can augment LLMs' limited world knowledge. Finally, we will further extend this application through the application of reasoning strategies.

In short, this chapter covers:

- Mitigating hallucinations through fact-checking
- Summarizing information
- Extracting information from documents
- Answering questions with tools
- Exploring reasoning strategies

Let's get started with addressing hallucinations through automatic fact-checking!

Mitigating hallucinations through fact-checking

As discussed in previous chapters, hallucination in LLMs refers to the generated text being unfaithful or nonsensical compared to the input. It contrasts with faithfulness, where outputs stay consistent with the source. Hallucinations can spread misinformation like disinformation, rumors, and deceptive content. This poses threats to society, including distrust in science, polarization, and democratic processes.

Journalism and archival studies have researched misinformation extensively. Fact-checking initiatives provide training and resources to journalists and independent checkers, allowing expert verification at scale. Addressing false claims is crucial to preserving information integrity and combatting detrimental societal impacts.

One technique to address hallucinations is automatic fact-checking – verifying claims made by LLMs against evidence from external sources. This allows for catching incorrect or unverified statements.

Fact-checking involves three main stages:

1. **Claim detection**: Identify parts needing verification
2. **Evidence retrieval**: Find sources supporting or refuting the claim
3. **Verdict prediction**: Assess claim veracity based on evidence

Alternative terms for the last two stages are justification production and verdict prediction.

We can see the general idea of these three stages illustrated in the following diagram (source – `https://github.com/Cartus/Automated-Fact-Checking-Resources` by Zhijiang Guo):

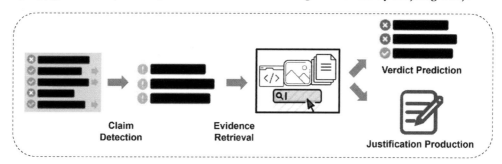

Figure 4.1: Automatic fact-checking pipeline in three stages

Pre-trained LLMs contain extensive world knowledge that can be prompted for facts. Additionally, external tools can search knowledge bases, Wikipedia, textbooks, and corpora for evidence. By grounding claims in data, fact-checking makes LLMs more reliable.

Pre-trained LLMs contain extensive world knowledge from their training data. Starting with the 24-layer BERT-Large in 2018, language models have been pre-trained on large knowledge bases such as Wikipedia; therefore, they would be able to answer knowledge questions from Wikipedia or – since their training set increasingly includes other sources – the internet, textbooks, arXiv, and GitHub.

We can prompt them with masking and other techniques to retrieve facts for evidence. For example, to answer the question "Where is Microsoft's headquarters located?", the question would be rewritten as "Microsoft's headquarters is in [MASK]" and fed into a language model for the answer.

Alternatively, we can integrate external tools to search knowledge bases, Wikipedia, textbooks, and other corpora. The key idea is verifying hallucinated claims by grounding them in factual data sources.

Automatic fact-checking provides a way to make LLMs more reliable by checking that their responses align with real-world evidence. In the next sections, we'll demonstrate this approach.

In LangChain, we have a chain available for fact-checking with prompt chaining, where a model actively questions the assumptions that went into a statement. In this self-checking chain, LLMCheckerChain, the model is prompted sequentially – first, to make the assumptions explicit, which looks like this:

```
Here's a statement: {statement}\nMake a bullet point list of the
assumptions you made when producing the above statement.\n
```

Please note that this is a string template, where the elements in curly brackets will be replaced by variables. Next, these assumptions are fed back to the model in order to check them one by one with a prompt like this:

```
Here is a bullet point list of assertions:
    {assertions}
    For each assertion, determine whether it is true or false. If it is
false, explain why.\n\n
```

Finally, the model is tasked to make a final judgment:

```
In light of the above facts, how would you answer the question
'{question}'
```

LLMCheckerChain does this all by itself, as this example shows:

```
from langchain.chains import LLMCheckerChain
from langchain.llms import OpenAI

llm = OpenAI(temperature=0.7)

text = "What type of mammal lays the biggest eggs?"

checker_chain = LLMCheckerChain.from_llm(llm, verbose=True)

checker_chain.run(text)
```

The model can return different results to this question, some of which are wrong, and some of which it would correctly identify as false. When I was trying this out, I got results such as the blue whale, the North American beaver, and the extinct Giant Moa in response to my question "What type of mammal lays the biggest eggs?". The following is the right answer:

```
Monotremes, a type of mammal found in Australia and parts of New Guinea,
lay the largest eggs in the mammalian world. The eggs of the American
echidna (spiny anteater) can grow as large as 10 cm in length, and
dunnarts (mouse-sized marsupials found in Australia) can have eggs that
exceed 5 cm in length.
• Monotremes can be found in Australia and New Guinea
• The largest eggs in the mammalian world are laid by monotremes
• The American echidna lays eggs that can grow to 10 cm in length
• Dunnarts lay eggs that can exceed 5 cm in length
• Monotremes can be found in Australia and New Guinea - True
• The largest eggs in the mammalian world are laid by monotremes - True
• The American echidna lays eggs that can grow to 10 cm in length - False,
the American echidna lays eggs that are usually between 1 to 4 cm in
length.
• Dunnarts lay eggs that can exceed 5 cm in length - False, dunnarts lay
eggs that are typically between 2 to 3 cm in length.

The largest eggs in the mammalian world are laid by monotremes, which can
be found in Australia and New Guinea. Monotreme eggs can grow to 10 cm in
length.

> Finished chain.
```

So, while this technique does not guarantee correct answers, it can put a stop to some incorrect results. Fact-checking approaches involve decomposing claims into smaller checkable queries, which can be formulated as question-answering tasks. Tools designed for searching domain datasets can assist fact-checkers in finding evidence effectively. Off-the-shelf search engines like Google and Bing can also retrieve both topically and evidentially relevant content to capture the veracity of a statement accurately. We'll apply this approach to return results based on web searches and other applications of this chapter.

In the next section, we'll discuss automating the process of summarizing texts and longer documents such as research papers.

Summarizing information

In today's fast-paced business and research landscape, keeping up with the ever-increasing volume of information can be a daunting task. For engineers and researchers in fields like computer science and artificial intelligence, staying updated with the latest developments is crucial. However, reading and comprehending numerous papers can be time-consuming and labor-intensive. This is where automation comes into play. As engineers, we are driven by the desire to build and innovate and avoid repetitive tasks by automating them through the creation of pipelines and processes. This approach, often mistaken for laziness, allows engineers to focus on more complex challenges and utilize their skills more efficiently.

LLMs excel at condensing text through their strong language understanding abilities. We will explore techniques for summarization using LangChain at increasing levels of sophistication.

Basic prompting

For summarizing a couple of sentences, basic prompting works well. Simply instruct the LLM on the desired length and provide a text:

```
from langchain import OpenAI


prompt = """
Summarize this text in one sentence:

{text}
"""


llm = OpenAI()
summary = llm(prompt.format(text=text))
```

This is similar to what we saw in *Chapter 3*, *Getting Started with LangChain*. text is a string variable that can be any text that we want to summarize.

We can also use the LangChain decorator syntax, which is implemented in the LangChain decorators library, which you should have installed together with all the other dependencies if you followed the instructions in *Chapter 3*, *Getting Started with LangChain*.

LangChain Decorators provides a more Pythonic interface for defining and executing prompts compared to base LangChain, making it easier to leverage the power of LLMs. Function decorators translate prompt documentation into executable code, enabling multiline definitions and natural code flow.

Here's a decorator example for summarization:

```python
from langchain_decorators import llm_prompt
@llm_prompt
def summarize(text:str, length="short") -> str:
    """

    Summarize this text in {length} length:


    {text}
    """

    return


summary = summarize(text="let me tell you a boring story from when I was
young...")
```

The output, the value of the summary variable, I am getting is The speaker is about to share a story from their youth. You can try more meaningful and longer examples for summarization yourself.

The @llm_prompt decorator translates the docstring into a prompt and handles executing it. Parameters are cleanly passed in and outputs are parsed. This abstraction enables prompting in a natural Python style while handling the complexity behind the scenes, making it easy to focus on creating effective prompts. By providing this intuitive interface, LangChain Decorators unlock the power of LLMs for developers.

Prompt templates

For dynamic inputs, prompt templates enable inserting text into predefined prompts. Prompt templates allow variable length limits and modular prompt design.

We can implement this in **LangChain Expression Language (LCEL)**:

```
from langchain import PromptTemplate, OpenAI
from langchain.schema import StrOutputParser
llm = OpenAI()
prompt = PromptTemplate.from_template(
    "Summarize this text: {text}?"
)
runnable = prompt | llm | StrOutputParser()
summary = runnable.invoke({"text": text})
```

LCEL provides a declarative way to compose chains that is more intuitive and productive than directly writing code. Key benefits of LCEL include built-in support for asynchronous processing, batching, streaming, fallbacks, parallelism, and seamless integration with LangSmith tracing.

In this case, runnable is a chain, where the prompt template, the LLM, and the output parser are piped into one another.

Chain of density

Researchers at Salesforce (Adams and colleagues, 2023; *From Sparse to Dense: GPT-4 Summarization with Chain of Density Prompting*) have developed a prompt-guided technique called **Chain of Density (CoD)** to incrementally increase the information density of GPT-4 generated summaries while controlling length.

This is the prompt to use with CoD:

```
template = """Article: { text }
You will generate increasingly concise, entity-dense summaries of the
above article.
Repeat the following 2 steps 5 times.
Step 1. Identify 1-3 informative entities (";" delimited) from the article
which are missing from the previously generated summary.
Step 2. Write a new, denser summary of identical length which covers every
entity and detail from the previous summary plus the missing entities.
A missing entity is:
- relevant to the main story,
- specific yet concise (5 words or fewer),
- novel (not in the previous summary),
- faithful (present in the article),
- anywhere (can be located anywhere in the article).
```

```
Guidelines:
- The first summary should be long (4-5 sentences, ~80 words) yet highly
non-specific, containing little information beyond the entities marked
as missing. Use overly verbose language and fillers (e.g., "this article
discusses") to reach ~80 words.
- Make every word count: rewrite the previous summary to improve flow and
make space for additional entities.
- Make space with fusion, compression, and removal of uninformative
phrases like "the article discusses".
- The summaries should become highly dense and concise yet self-contained,
i.e., easily understood without the article.
- Missing entities can appear anywhere in the new summary.
- Never drop entities from the previous summary. If space cannot be made,
add fewer new entities.
Remember, use the exact same number of words for each summary.
Answer in JSON. The JSON should be a list (length 5) of dictionaries whose
keys are "Missing_Entities" and "Denser_Summary".
"""
```

Please note that you can easily adapt this to any kind of content and provide a different set of guidelines to suit other applications.

The CoD prompt instructs highly powered LLMs such as GPT-4 to produce an initial sparse, verbose summary of an article containing only a few entities. It then iteratively identifies 1–3 missing entities and fuses them into a rewrite of the previous summary in the same number of words.

This repeated rewriting under length constraint forces increasing abstraction, fusion of details, and compression to make room for additional entities in each step. The authors measure statistics like entity density and source sentence alignment to characterize the densification effects.

Through five iterative steps, summaries become highly condensed with more entities per token packed in through creative rewriting. The authors conduct both human preference studies and GPT-4 scoring to evaluate the impact on overall quality across the density spectrum.

The results reveal a trade-off between informativeness gained through density and declining coherence from excessive compression. Optimal density balances concision and clarity, with too many entities overwhelming expression. This method and analysis sheds light on controlling information density in AI text generation.

Please try this out for yourself!

Map-Reduce pipelines

LangChain supports a **map reduce approach** for processing documents using LLMs, which allows for efficient processing and analysis of documents. A chain can be applied to each document individually and then we combine the outputs into a single document.

To summarize long documents, we can first split the document into smaller parts (chunks) that are suitable for the token context length of the LLM, and then a map-reduce chain can summarize these chunks independently before recombining. This scales summarization to any length of text while controlling chunk size.

The key steps are:

1. **Map**: Each document is passed through a summarization chain (LLM chain).
2. **Collapse** (optional): The summarized documents are combined into a single document.
3. **Reduce**: The collapsed document goes through a final LLM chain to produce the output.

So, the map step applies a chain to each document in parallel. The reduce step aggregates the mapped outputs and generates the final result.

Optional collapsing, which may also involve utilizing LLMs, makes sure the data fits within sequence length limits. This compression step can be performed recursively if needed.

This is illustrated in the figure here:

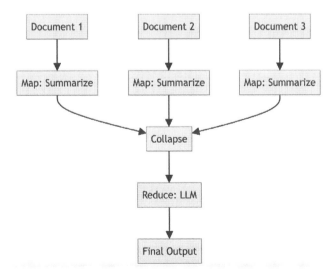

Figure 4.2: Map reduce chain in LangChain

This approach's implications are that it allows the parallel processing of documents and enables the use of LLMs for reasoning, generating, or analyzing individual documents and combining their outputs.

Here's a simple example of loading a PDF document and summarizing it:

```
from langchain.chains.summarize import load_summarize_chain
from langchain import OpenAI
from langchain.document_loaders import PyPDFLoader
pdf_file_path = "<pdf_file_path>"
pdf_loader = PyPDFLoader(pdf_file_path)
docs = pdf_loader.load_and_split()
llm = OpenAI()
chain = load_summarize_chain(llm, chain_type="map_reduce")
chain.run(docs)
```

The variable `pdf_file_path` is a string with the path of a PDF file. Please replace the file path with the path to a PDF document.

The default prompt for both the map and reduce steps is this:

```
Write a concise summary of the following:


{text}


CONCISE SUMMARY:
```

We can specify any prompt for each step. In the text summarization application developed for this chapter on GitHub, we can see how to pass other prompts. On LangChainHub, we can see the question-answering-with-sources prompt, which takes a reduce/combine prompt like this:

```
Given the following extracted parts of a long document and a question,
create a final answer with references (\"SOURCES\"). \nIf you don't know
the answer, just say that you don't know. Don't try to make up an answer.\
nALWAYS return a \"SOURCES\" part in your answer.\n\nQUESTION: {question}\
n=========\nContent: {text}
```

In the preceding prompt, we could formulate a concrete question, but equally, we could give the LLM a more abstract instruction to extract assumptions and implications.

The text would be the summaries from the map steps. An instruction like that would help against hallucinations. Other examples of instructions could be translating the document into a different language or rephrasing in a certain style.

By changing the prompt, we can ask any question to be answered from these documents. This can be built out into an automation tool that can quickly summarize the content of long texts in a more digestible format, as you should be able to tell from the **summarize** package in the book's GitHub repository, which shows how to focus on different perspectives and structures of the response (adapted from David Shapiro).

The tool on GitHub will summarize the core assertions, implications, and mechanics of a paper in a more concise and simplified manner. It can also answer specific questions about the paper, making it a valuable resource for literature reviews and accelerating scientific research. Overall, the approach aims to benefit researchers by providing a more efficient and accessible way to stay updated on the latest research.

> Thoughtful prompt engineering with LangChain provides powerful summarization capabilities using LLMs. A few practical tips are:
>
> - Start with simpler approaches and move to map-reduce if needed
> - Tune chunk size to balance context limits and parallelism
> - Customize map and reduce prompts for the best results
> - Compress or recursively reduce chunks to fit context limits

Once we start making a lot of calls, especially in the *map* step, if we use a cloud provider, we'll see tokens and, therefore, costs increase. It's time to give this some visibility!

Monitoring token usage

When using LLMs, especially in long loops such as with map operations, it's important to track the token usage and understand how much money you are spending.

For any serious usage of generative AI, we need to understand the capabilities, pricing options, and use cases for different language models. All cloud providers provide different models that cater to various NLP needs. For example, OpenAI exposes powerful language models suitable for solving complex problems with NLP and offers flexible pricing options based on the size and number of tokens used.

For example, ChatGPT models, like GPT-3.5-Turbo, specialize in dialogue applications such as chatbots and virtual assistants. They excel at generating responses with accuracy and fluency. Different models within the InstructGPT family, designed for single-turn instruction following, such as Ada and Davinci, offer varying levels of speed and power. Ada is the fastest model, suitable for applications where speed is crucial, while Davinci is the most powerful model, capable of handling complex instructions. The pricing of models depends on the model's capabilities and ranges from low-cost options like Ada to more expensive options like Davinci.

OpenAI provides DALL·E, Whisper, and API services for various applications, such as image generation, speech transcription, translation, and access to language models. DALL·E is an AI-powered image generation model that can be seamlessly integrated into apps for generating and editing novel images and art. OpenAI offers three tiers of resolution, allowing users to choose the level of detail they need. Higher resolutions offer more complexity and detail, while lower resolutions provide a more abstract representation. The price per image varies based on the resolution.

Whisper is an AI tool that can transcribe speech into text and translate multiple languages into English. It helps capture conversations, facilitates communication, and improves understanding across languages. The cost of using Whisper is based on a per-minute rate.

We can track the token usage in OpenAI models by hooking into the OpenAI callback:

```python
from langchain import OpenAI, PromptTemplate
from langchain.callbacks import get_openai_callback


llm_chain = PromptTemplate.from_template("Tell me a joke about {topic}!")
| OpenAI()
with get_openai_callback() as cb:
    response = llm_chain.invoke(dict(topic="light bulbs"))
    print(response)
    print(f"Total Tokens: {cb.total_tokens}")
    print(f"Prompt Tokens: {cb.prompt_tokens}")
    print(f"Completion Tokens: {cb.completion_tokens}")
    print(f"Total Cost (USD): ${cb.total_cost}")
```

We should see an output with the costs and tokens. I am getting this output when I run this:

```
Q: How many light bulbs does it take to change people's minds?
A: Depends on how stubborn they are!
Total Tokens: 36
Prompt Tokens: 8
```

```
Completion Tokens: 28
Total Cost (USD): $0.00072
```

You can change the parameters of the model and the prompt, and you should see costs and tokens changing as a consequence.

There are two other ways of getting the token usage. As an alternative to the OpenAI callback, the generate() method of the llm class returns a response of type LLMResult instead of a string. This includes token usages and finish reason, for example (from the LangChain docs):

```
input_list = [
    {"product": "socks"},
    {"product": "computer"},
    {"product": "shoes"}
]
llm_chain.generate(input_list)
```

The result looks like this:

```
    LLMResult(generations=[[Generation(text='\n\nSocktastic!', generation_
info={'finish_reason': 'stop', 'logprobs': None})], [Generation(text='\n\
nTechCore Solutions.', generation_info={'finish_reason': 'stop',
'logprobs': None})], [Generation(text='\n\nFootwear Factory.', generation_
info={'finish_reason': 'stop', 'logprobs': None})]], llm_output={'token_
usage': {'prompt_tokens': 36, 'total_tokens': 55, 'completion_tokens':
19}, 'model_name': 'text-davinci-003'})
```

Finally, the chat completions response format in the OpenAI API includes a usage object with token information; for example, it could look like this (excerpt):

```
{
"model": "gpt-3.5-turbo-0613",
"object": "chat.completion",
"usage": {
  "completion_tokens": 17,
  "prompt_tokens": 57,
  "total_tokens": 74
}
}
```

This can be extremely helpful for understanding how much money you are spending on distinct parts of your application. In *Chapter 9, Generative AI in Production.* we'll look at LangSmith and similar tools that provide additional observability of LLMs in action, including their token usage.

Next, we'll look at how to extract certain pieces of information from documents using OpenAI functions with LangChain.

Extracting information from documents

In June 2023, OpenAI announced updates to OpenAI's API, including new capabilities for **function calling**, which enhanced functionality. OpenAI's addition of function calling builds on instruction tuning. By describing functions in a schema, developers can tune LLMs to return structured outputs adhering to that schema – for example, extracting entities from text by outputting them in a predefined JSON format.

Function calling enables developers to create chatbots that can answer questions using external tools or OpenAI plugins. It also allows for converting natural language queries into API calls or database queries and extracting structured data from text.

Developers can now describe functions to the gpt-4-0613 and gpt-3.5-turbo-0613 models and have the models intelligently generate a JSON object containing arguments to call those functions. This feature aims to enhance the connection between GPT models and external tools and APIs, providing a reliable way to retrieve structured data from the models.

The mechanics of the update involve using new API parameters, namely functions, in the /v1/chat/completions endpoint. The functions parameter is defined through a name, description, parameters, and the function to call itself. Developers can describe functions to the model using JSON schema and specify the desired function to be called.

In LangChain, we can use these function calls in OpenAI for information extraction or for calling plugins. For information extraction, we can obtain specific entities and their properties from a text and their properties from a document in an extraction chain with OpenAI chat models. For example, this can help identify the people mentioned in the text. By using the OpenAI functions parameter and specifying a schema, it ensures that the model outputs the desired entities and properties with their appropriate types.

The implications of this approach are that it allows for precise extraction of entities by defining a schema with the desired properties and their types. It also enables specifying which properties are required and which are optional.

The default format for the schema is a dictionary, but we can also define properties and their types in Pydantic, a popular parsing library, providing control and flexibility in the extraction process.

Here's an example of a desired schema for information in a **Curriculum Vitae (CV)**:

```python
from typing import Optional
from pydantic import BaseModel

class Experience(BaseModel):
    start_date: Optional[str]
    end_date: Optional[str]
    description: Optional[str]


class Study(Experience):
    degree: Optional[str]
    university: Optional[str]
    country: Optional[str]
    grade: Optional[str]


class WorkExperience(Experience):
    company: str
    job_title: str


class Resume(BaseModel):
    first_name: str
    last_name: str
    linkedin_url: Optional[str]
    email_address: Optional[str]
    nationality: Optional[str]
    skill: Optional[str]
    study: Optional[Study]
    work_experience: Optional[WorkExperience]
    hobby: Optional[str]
```

We can use this for information extraction from a CV.

Please note that you should set up your environment according to the instructions in *Chapter 3, Getting Started with LangChain*. I've found it most convenient to import my config module here and execute setup_environment(). This adds two extra lines to the beginning of the code:

```
from config import setup_environment
setup_environment()
```

This is my advice – you can take it or leave it.

Here's an example CV from https://github.com/xitanggg/open-resume:

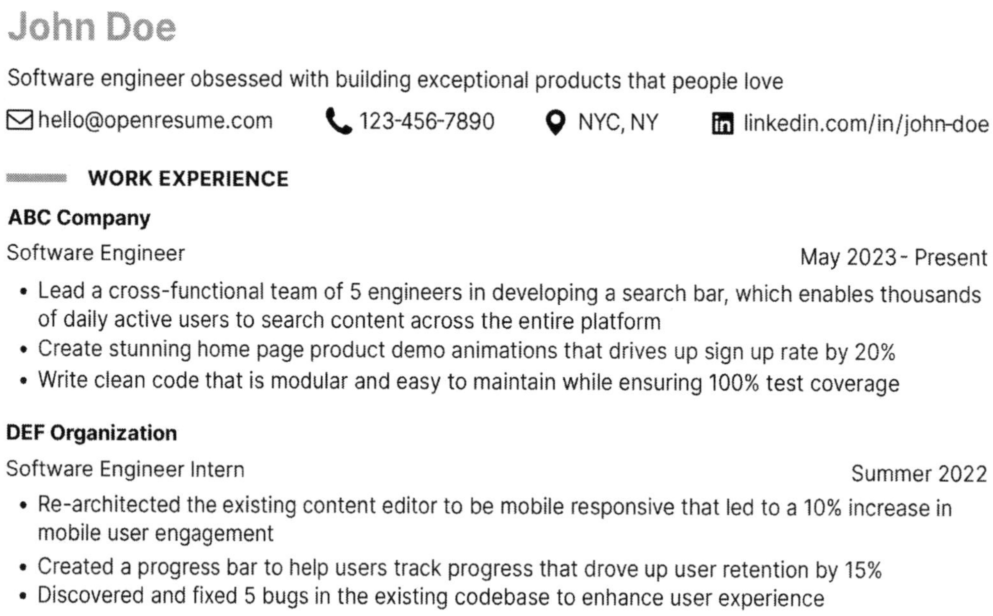

John Doe

Software engineer obsessed with building exceptional products that people love

✉ hello@openresume.com   📞 123-456-7890   📍 NYC, NY   in linkedin.com/in/john-doe

▬▬▬ WORK EXPERIENCE

ABC Company

Software Engineer   May 2023 - Present

- Lead a cross-functional team of 5 engineers in developing a search bar, which enables thousands of daily active users to search content across the entire platform
- Create stunning home page product demo animations that drives up sign up rate by 20%
- Write clean code that is modular and easy to maintain while ensuring 100% test coverage

DEF Organization

Software Engineer Intern   Summer 2022

- Re-architected the existing content editor to be mobile responsive that led to a 10% increase in mobile user engagement
- Created a progress bar to help users track progress that drove up user retention by 15%
- Discovered and fixed 5 bugs in the existing codebase to enhance user experience

Figure 4.3: Extract of an example CV

We are going to try to parse the information from this resume.

Utilizing the create_extraction_chain_pydantic() function in LangChain, we can provide our schema as input, and an output will be an instantiated object that adheres to it. In its most simple terms, we can try this code snippet:

```
from langchain.chains import create_extraction_chain_pydantic
from langchain.chat_models import ChatOpenAI
from langchain.document_loaders import PyPDFLoader
```

```
pdf_file_path = "<pdf_file_path>"
pdf_loader = PyPDFLoader(pdf_file_path)
docs = pdf_loader.load_and_split()
# please note that function calling is not enabled for all models!
llm = ChatOpenAI(model_name="gpt-3.5-turbo-0613")
chain = create_extraction_chain_pydantic(pydantic_schema=Resume, llm=llm)
chain.run(docs)
```

Please note that the pdf_file_path variable should be the relative or absolute path to a pdf file. We should get an output like this:

```
[Resume(first_name='John', last_name='Doe', linkedin_url='linkedin.com/
in/john-doe', email_address='hello@openresume.com', nationality=None,
skill='React', study=None, work_experience=WorkExperience(start_date='May
2023', end_date='Present', description='Lead a cross-functional team of
5 engineers in developing a search bar, which enables thousands of daily
active users to search content across the entire platform. Create stunning
home page product demo animations that drives up sign up rate by 20%.
Write clean code that is modular and easy to maintain while ensuring 100%
test coverage.', company='ABC Company', job_title='Software Engineer'),
hobby=None)]
```

This result is far from perfect – only one work experience gets parsed out. But it's a good start given the little effort we've put in so far. For a complete example, please refer to the GitHub repository. We could add more functionality, for example, to guess personality or leadership capability.

OpenAI injects these function calls into the system message in a certain syntax, which their models have been optimized for. This implies that functions count against the context limit and are correspondingly billed as input tokens.

LangChain natively has the functionality to inject function calls as prompts. This means we can use models from providers other than OpenAI for function calls within LLM apps. We'll look at this now, and we'll build this into an interactive web app with Streamlit.

Instruction tuning and function calling allow models to produce callable code. This leads to tool integrations, where LLM agents can execute these function calls to connect LLMs with live data, services, and runtime environments. In the next section, we'll discuss how tools can augment context by retrieving external knowledge sources to enhance understanding.

Answering questions with tools

LLMs are trained on general corpus data and may not be as effective for tasks that require domain-specific knowledge. On their own, LLMs can't interact with the environment and access external data sources; however, LangChain provides a platform for creating tools that access real-time information and perform tasks such as weather forecasting, making reservations, suggesting recipes, and managing tasks. Tools within the framework of agents and chains allow for the development of applications powered by LLMs that are data-aware and agentic and open up a wide range of approaches to solving problems with LLMs, expanding their use cases, and making them more versatile and powerful.

One important aspect of tools is their capability to work within specific domains or process specific inputs. For example, an LLM lacks inherent mathematical capabilities. However, a mathematical tool like a calculator can accept mathematical expressions or equations as an input and calculate the outcome. The LLM combined with such a mathematical tool performs calculations and provides accurate answers.

Tools leverage contextual dialogue representation to search pertinent data sources related to the user's query. For example, for a question about a historical event, tools could retrieve Wikipedia articles to augment context.

By grounding responses in real-time data, tools reduce hallucinated or incorrect replies. Contextual tool use complements chatbots' core language capabilities to make responses more useful, correct, and aligned with real-world knowledge. Tools provide creative solutions to problems and open up new possibilities for LLMs in various domains. For example, a tool could be developed to enable an LLM to perform advanced retrieval searches, query a database for specific information, automate email writing, or even handle phone calls.

Let's see this in action!

Information retrieval with tools

We have quite a few tools available in LangChain, and – if that's not enough – it's not hard to roll out our own tools. Let's set up an agent with a few tools:

```
from langchain.agents import (
    AgentExecutor, AgentType, initialize_agent, load_tools
)
```

```
from langchain.chat_models import ChatOpenAI


def load_agent() -> AgentExecutor:
    llm = ChatOpenAI(temperature=0, streaming=True)
    # DuckDuckGoSearchRun, wolfram alpha, arxiv search, wikipedia
    # TODO: try wolfram-alpha!
    tools = load_tools(
        tool_names=["ddg-search", "wolfram-alpha", "arxiv", "wikipedia"],
        llm=llm
    )
    return initialize_agent(
        tools=tools, llm=llm, agent=AgentType.ZERO_SHOT_REACT_DESCRIPTION,
verbose=True
    )
```

This function returns AgentExecutor, which is a chain; therefore, if we wanted, we could integrate it into a larger chain. The Zero-Shot agent is a general-purpose action agent, which we'll discuss in the next section.

Please notice the streaming parameter in the ChatOpenAI constructor, which is set to True. This makes for a better user experience since it means that the text response will be updated as it comes in, rather than once all the text has been completed. Currently, only the OpenAI, ChatOpenAI, and ChatAnthropic implementations support streaming.

All the tools mentioned have their specific purpose that's part of the description, which is passed to the language model. These tools here are plugged into the agent:

- **DuckDuckGo**: A search engine that focuses on privacy; an added advantage is that it doesn't require developer signup
- **Wolfram Alpha**: An integration that combines natural language understanding with math capabilities, for questions like "What is 2x+5 = -3x + 7?"
- **arXiv**: Search in academic pre-print publications; this is useful for research-oriented questions
- **Wikipedia**: For any question about entities of significant notoriety

Please note that to use Wolfram Alpha, you have to set up an account and set the `WOLFRAM_ALPHA_APPID` environment variable with the developer token you create at `https://products.wolframalpha.com/api`. Please note that the website can sometimes be a bit slow, and it might take patience to register.

There are a lot of other search tools integrated into LangChain apart from DuckDuckGo that let you utilize Google or Bing search engines or work with meta-search engines. There's an Open-Meteo integration for weather information; however, this information is also available through search.

Building a visual interface

After developing an intelligent agent with LangChain, the natural next step is deploying it in an easy-to-use application. Streamlit provides an ideal framework for this goal. As an open-source platform optimized for ML workflows, Streamlit makes it simple to wrap our agent in an interactive web application. So let's make our agent available as a Streamlit app!

For this application, we'll need the Streamlit, unstructured, and docx libraries, among others. These are in the environment that we set up in *Chapter 3, Getting Started with LangChain*.

Let's write the code for this using the `load_agent()` function we've just defined:

```python
import streamlit as st
from langchain.callbacks import StreamlitCallbackHandler


chain = load_agent()
st_callback = StreamlitCallbackHandler(st.container())


if prompt := st.chat_input():
    st.chat_message("user").write(prompt)
    with st.chat_message("assistant"):
        st_callback = StreamlitCallbackHandler(st.container())
        response = chain.run(prompt, callbacks=[st_callback])
        st.write(response)
```

Please notice that we are using the callback handler in the call to the chain, which means that we'll see responses as they come back from the model. We can start the app locally from the terminal like this:

```
PYTHONPATH=. streamlit run question_answering/app.py
```

We can open our app in the browser. Here's a screenshot that illustrates what the app looks like:

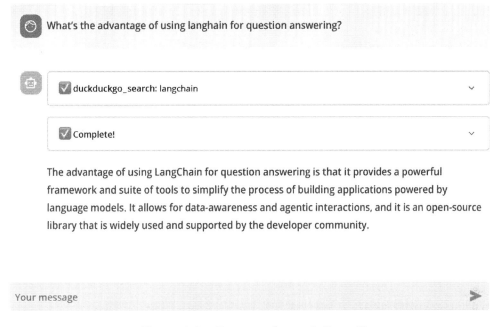

What's the advantage of using langhain for question answering?

duckduckgo_search: langchain   ⌄

Complete!   ⌄

The advantage of using LangChain for question answering is that it provides a powerful framework and suite of tools to simplify the process of building applications powered by language models. It allows for data-awareness and agentic interactions, and it is an open-source library that is widely used and supported by the developer community.

Your message   ➤

Figure 4.4: Question-answering app in Streamlit

Deployment of Streamlit applications can be local or on a server. Alternatively, you can deploy this on Streamlit Community Cloud or on Hugging Face Spaces.

For **Streamlit Community Cloud**, do this:

1. Create a GitHub repository.
2. Go to Streamlit Community Cloud, click on **New app**, and select the new repo.
3. Click **Deploy!**.

As for **Hugging Face Spaces**, it works like this:

1. Create a GitHub repo.
2. Create a Hugging Face account at `https://huggingface.co/`.
3. Go to **Spaces** and click **Create new Space**. In the form, set the fill in a name, type of space as **Streamlit**, and choose the new repo.

The search works quite well although, depending on the tools used, it might still come up with the wrong results. For the question about the mammal with the largest egg, using DuckDuckGo, it comes back with a result that discusses eggs in birds and mammals and sometimes concludes that the ostrich is the mammal with the largest egg, although platypus also comes back sometimes.

Here's the log output (shortened) for the correct reasoning:

```
> Entering new AgentExecutor chain...
I'm not sure, but I think I can find the answer by searching online.
Action: duckduckgo_search
Action Input: "mammal that lays the biggest eggs"
Observation: Posnov / Getty Images. The western long-beaked echidna ...

Final Answer: The platypus is the mammal that lays the biggest eggs.

> Finished chain.
```

You can see that with a powerful framework for automation and problem-solving at your behest, you can compress work that can take hundreds of hours into minutes. You can play around with different research questions to see how the tools are used. The actual implementation in the repository for the book allows you to try out different tools and has an option for self-verification.

Building a Streamlit app offers several key advantages:

- Quickly create an intuitive graphical interface around our chatbot without having to build a complex frontend. Streamlit automatically handles elements like input fields, buttons, and interactive widgets.

- Seamlessly integrate the agent's capabilities into an app tailored for a specific use case, such as customer support or research assistance. The interface can be customized to match the domain.

- Streamlit apps run Python code in real time, enabling seamless connection to the agent's backend API with no added latency. Our LangChain workflows integrate fluidly.

- Easy sharing and deployment options including open-source GitHub repos, personal Streamlit sharing links, and Streamlit Community Cloud. This allows instantly publishing and distributing the app.

- Streamlit's optimized performance for running models and data workflows ensures responsiveness even with large models. Our chatbot can scale gracefully.

- The result is an elegant web interface that lets users interact naturally with our LLM-powered agent. Streamlit handles the complexity behind the scenes.

While our LLM app can provide answers to simple questions, its reasoning abilities are still limited. In the following section, we'll implement more advanced types of agents.

Exploring reasoning strategies

LLMs excel at pattern recognition in data but struggle with the symbolic reasoning required for complex multi-step problems.

Implementing more advanced reasoning strategies would make our research assistant far more capable. Hybrid systems that combine neural pattern completion with deliberate symbolic manipulation can master skills including these:

- Multi-step deductive reasoning to draw conclusions from a chain of facts
- Mathematical reasoning like solving equations through a series of transformations
- Planning tactics to break down a problem into an optimized sequence of actions

By integrating tools together with explicit reasoning steps instead of pure pattern completion, our agent can tackle problems requiring abstraction and imagination, and can arrive at a complex understanding of the world enabling them to hold more meaningful conversations about complex concepts.

An illustration of augmenting LLMs through tools and reasoning is shown here (source – `https://github.com/billxbf/ReWOO`, implementation for the paper *Decoupling Reasoning from Observations for Efficient Augmented Language Models Resources*, by Binfeng Xu and others, May 2023):

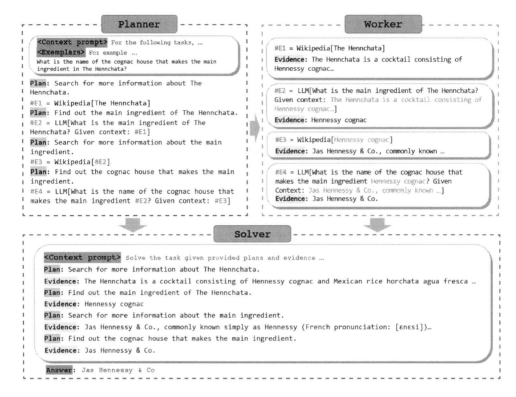

Figure 4.5: Tool-augmented LLM paradigm

The tools are the available resources that the agent can use, such as search engines or databases. The LLMChain is responsible for generating text prompts and parsing the output to determine the next action. The agent class uses the output of the LLMChain to decide which action to take.

While tool-augmented language models combine LLMs with external resources like search engines and databases to enhance reasoning capabilities, this can be further enhanced with agents.

In LangChain, this consists of three parts:

- Tools
- An LLMChain
- The agent itself

There are two key agent architectures:

- Action agents reason iteratively based on observations after each action.

- Plan-and-execute agents plan completely upfront before taking any action.

In **observation-dependent reasoning**, the agent iteratively provides context and examples to an LLM to generate thoughts and actions. Observations from tools are incorporated to inform the next reasoning step. This approach is used in action agents.

An alternative is **plan-and-execute** agents that first create a complete plan and then gather evidence to execute it. The Planner LLM produces a list of plans (**P**). The agent gathers evidence (**E**) using tools. **P** and **E** are combined and fed to the Solver LLM to generate the final output

Plan-and-execute separates planning from execution. Smaller specialized models can be used for the Planner and Solver roles. The trade-off is that plan-and-execute requires more upfront planning.

We can see the reasoning with the observation pattern in the following diagram (source – https://arxiv.org/abs/2305.18323; Binfeng Xu and others, May 2023):

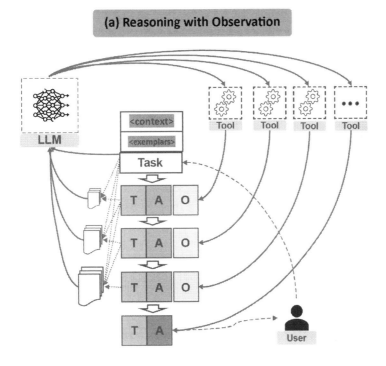

Figure 4.6: Reasoning with observation

Observation-dependent reasoning involves making judgments, predictions, or choices based on the current state of knowledge or the evidence fetched through observation. In each iteration, the agent provides context and examples to the LLM. A user's task is first combined with the context and examples and given to the LLM to initiate reasoning. The LLM generates a thought and an action and then waits for an observation from tools. The observation is added to the prompt to initiate the next call to the LLM. In LangChain, this is an **action agent** (also, **Zero-Shot agent**, `ZERO_SHOT_REACT_DESCRIPTION`), which is the default setting when you create an agent.

As mentioned, plans can also be made ahead of any actions. This strategy (in LangChain, called the **plan-and-execute agent**) is illustrated in the diagram here (source – `https://arxiv.org/abs/2305.18323`; Binfeng Xu and others, May 2023):

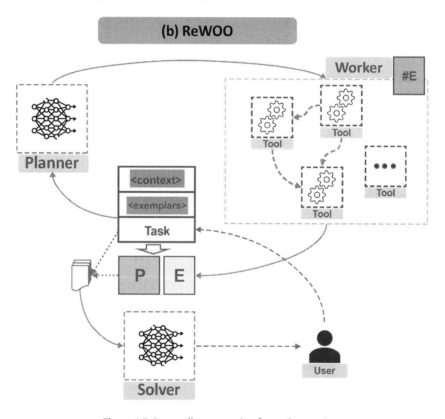

Figure 4.7: Decoupling reasoning from observations

The **Planner** (an LLM), which can be fine-tuned for planning and tool usage, produces a list of plans (**P**) and calls a worker (in LangChain, the agent) to gather evidence (**E**) by using tools. **P** and **E** are combined with the task and then fed into the **Solver** (an LLM) for the final answer. We can write a pseudo algorithm like this:

1. Plan out all the steps (Planner).

2. For each step, determine the proper tools to accomplish the step and execute.

The **Planner** and the **Solver** can be distinct language models. This opens the possibility of using smaller, specialized models for **Planner** and **Solver**, and using fewer tokens for each of the calls.

We can implement plan-and-solve in our research app; let's do it!

First, let's add a strategy variable to the load_agent() function. It can take two values, either plan-and-solve or zero-shot-react. For zero-shot-react, the logic stays the same. For plan-and-solve, we'll define a planner and an executor, which we'll use to create a PlanAndExecute agent executor:

```python
from typing import Literal
from langchain.agents import initialize_agent, load_tools, AgentType
from langchain.chains.base import Chain
from langchain.chat_models import ChatOpenAI
from langchain_experimental.plan_and_execute import (
    load_chat_planner, load_agent_executor, PlanAndExecute
)

ReasoningStrategies = Literal["zero-shot-react", "plan-and-solve"]

def load_agent(
        tool_names: list[str],
        strategy: ReasoningStrategies = "zero-shot-react"
) -> Chain:
    llm = ChatOpenAI(temperature=0, streaming=True)
    tools = load_tools(
        tool_names=tool_names,
        llm=llm
    )
```

```
    if strategy == "plan-and-solve":
        planner = load_chat_planner(llm)
        executor = load_agent_executor(llm, tools, verbose=True)
        return PlanAndExecute(planner=planner, executor=executor,
verbose=True)


    return initialize_agent(
        tools=tools, llm=llm, agent=AgentType.ZERO_SHOT_REACT_DESCRIPTION,
verbose=True
    )
```

Please refer to the version on GitHub (within the question_answering package) for the full version. For example, we might come across output parsing errors. We can handle these by setting handle_parsing_errors in the initialize_agent() method.

Let's define a new variable that's set through a radio button in Streamlit. We'll pass this variable over to the load_agent() function:

```
strategy = st.radio(
    "Reasoning strategy",
    ("plan-and-solve", "zero-shot-react")
)
```

You might have noticed that the load_agent() method takes a list of strings, tool_names. This can be chosen in the **user interface (UI)** as well:

```
tool_names = st.multiselect(
    'Which tools do you want to use?',
    [
        "google-search", "ddg-search", "wolfram-alpha", "arxiv",
        "wikipedia", "python_repl", "pal-math", "llm-math"
    ],
    ["ddg-search", "wolfram-alpha", "wikipedia"])
```

Finally, still in the app, the agent is loaded like this:

```
agent_chain = load_agent(tool_names=tool_names, strategy=strategy)
```

We can execute this agent with Streamlit. We should run the following command in our terminal:

```
PYTHONPATH=. streamlit run question_answering/app.py
```

We should see how Streamlit starts up our application. If we open our browser on the indicated URL (by default, `http://localhost:8501/`), we should see the UI here:

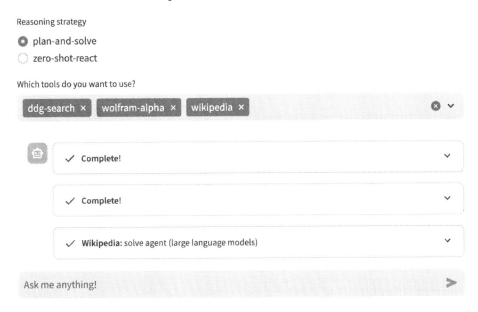

Figure 4.8: Implementing plan-and-execute in our research app

Please have a look at the app in your browser and see the different steps for the question "What is a plan-and-solve agent in the context of LLM?".

The steps look as follows – please note that the result might not be 100% accurate but this is what the agent comes up with:

1. **Define LLMs:** LLMs are AI models that are trained on vast amounts of text data and can generate human-like text based on the input they receive.

2. **Understand the concept of a plan in the context of LLMs:** In the context of large language models, a plan refers to a structured outline or set of steps that the model generates to solve a problem or answer a question.

3. **Understand the concept of a solve agent in the context of LLMs:** A solve agent is an LLM that works as an agent. It is responsible for generating plans to solve problems or answer questions.

4. **Recognize the importance of plans and solve agents in LLMs:** Plans and solve agents help organize the model's thinking process and provide a structured approach to problem-solving or question-answering tasks.

5. **Given the above steps, respond to the user's original question:** In the context of large language models, a plan is a structured outline or set of steps generated by a solve agent to solve a problem or answer a question. A solve agent is a component of a large language model that is responsible for generating these plans.

Accordingly, the first step is to perform a look-up of LLMs:

```
Action:
{
"action": "Wikipedia",
"action_input": "large language models"
}
```

We didn't discuss another aspect of question answering, which is the prompting strategy used in these steps. We'll go into detail about prompting in *Chapter 8, Customizing LLMs and Their Output*, where we talk about prompting techniques, but very quickly, here's an overview:

- Few-shot **chain-of-thought (CoT)** prompting demonstrates step-by-step reasoning to guide the LLM through a thought process.

- Zero-shot CoT prompting elicits reasoning steps without examples by simply instructing the LLM to "think step by step."

- CoT prompting aims to aid understanding of reasoning processes through examples.

Additionally, while in plan-and-solve, complex tasks are broken down into subtask plans that are executed sequentially, this can be extended with more detailed instructions to improve reasoning quality, like emphasizing key variables and common sense.

You can find a very advanced example of augmented information retrieval with LangChain in the BlockAGI project, which is inspired by BabyAGI and AutoGPT, at https://github.com/blockpipe/BlockAGI.

This concludes our introduction to reasoning strategies. All strategies have their problems, which can manifest as calculation errors, missing-step errors, and semantic misunderstandings. However, they help improve the quality of generated reasoning steps, increase accuracy in problem-solving tasks, and enhance LLMs' ability to handle various types of reasoning problems.

Summary

In this chapter, we first talked about the problem of hallucinations and automatic fact-checking, and how to make LLMs more reliable. We implemented a few simple approaches that help to make LLM outputs more accurate. We then looked at and implemented prompting strategies to break down and summarize documents. This can be immensely helpful for digesting large research articles or analyses. Once we get into making a lot of chained calls to LLMs, this can mean we incur a lot of costs. Therefore, I dedicated a subsection to token usage.

The OpenAI API implements functions, which we can use, among other things, for information extraction in documents. We've implemented a remarkably simple version of a CV parser as an example of this functionality that indicates how this could be applied. Tools and function calling are not unique to OpenAI, however. The evolution of instruction tuning, function calling, and tool usage enables models to move beyond freeform text generation into robustly automating tasks by interacting with real systems. The approaches unlock more capable, reliable AI assistants. With LangChain, we can implement different agents that call tools. We've implemented an app with Streamlit that can help answer research questions by relying on external tools such as search engines or Wikipedia. Unlike **Retrieval augmented generation (RAG)**, which we'll discuss in the next chapter and which uses vector search for semantic similarity, tools provide contextual augmentation by directly querying databases, APIs, and other structured external sources. The factual information retrieved by tools supplements the chatbot's internal context.

Finally, we looked at different strategies employed by the agents to make decisions. The main distinction is the point of decision-making. We implemented a plan-and-solve and a zero-shot agent in a Streamlit app.

While this chapter introduced many promising directions for developing capable and trustworthy LLMs, subsequent chapters will expand on the techniques developed here. For example, we'll discuss reasoning with agents in much more detail in *Chapter 6*, *Developing Software with Generative AI,* and *Chapter 7*, *LLMs for Data Science*, and provide an overview of prompting techniques in *Chapter 8*, *Customizing LLMs and Their Output.*

Questions

Please have a look to see if you can come up with the answers to these questions from memory. I'd recommend you go back to the corresponding sections of this chapter if you are unsure about any of them:

1. How can we summarize documents with LLMs?

2. What is the chain of density?

3. What are LangChain decorators and what's the LangChain Expression Language?

4. What is map-reduce in LangChain?

5. How can we count the tokens we are using (and why should we)?

6. How is instruction tuning related to function calling and tool usage?

7. Give some examples of tools that are available in LangChain.

8. Please define two agent paradigms.

9. What is Streamlit and why do we want to use it?

10. How does automated fact-checking work?

Join our community on Discord

Join our community's Discord space for discussions with the authors and other readers:

`https://packt.link/lang`

5

Building a Chatbot like ChatGPT

Chatbots powered by LLMs have demonstrated impressive fluency in conversational tasks like customer service. However, their lack of world knowledge limits their usefulness for domain-specific question answering. In this chapter, we explore how to overcome these limitations through **Retrieval-Augmented Generation (RAG)**. RAG enhances chatbots by grounding their responses in external evidence sources, leading to more accurate and informative answers. This is achieved by retrieving relevant passages from corpora to condition the language model's generation process. The key steps involve encoding corpora into vector embeddings to enable rapid semantic search and integrating retrieval results into the chatbot's prompt.

We will also provide foundations for representing documents as vectors, indexing methods for efficient similarity lookups, and vector databases for managing embeddings. Building on these core techniques, we will demonstrate practical RAG implementations using popular libraries like Milvus and Pinecone. By walking through end-to-end examples, we will showcase how RAG can significantly improve chatbots' reasoning and factual correctness. Finally, we discuss another important topic from the reputational and legal perspective: moderation. LangChain allows you to pass any text through a moderation chain to check whether it contains harmful content.

Throughout the chapter, we'll work on a chatbot implementation with an interface in Streamlit that you can find in the `chat_with_retrieval` directory in the GitHub repository for the book (`https://github.com/benman1/generative_ai_with_langchain`).

In a nutshell, the main topics are:

- What is a chatbot?
- Understanding retrieval and vectors

- Loading and retrieving in LangChain
- Implementing a chatbot
- Moderating responses

We'll begin the chapter by introducing chatbots and the state-of-the-art technology behind them.

What is a chatbot?

Chatbots are AI programs that simulate conversational interactions with users via text or voice. Early chatbots, like **ELIZA** (1966) and **PARRY** (1972), used pattern matching. Recent advances, like LLMs, allow more natural conversations, as seen in systems like **ChatGPT** (2022). However, challenges remain in achieving human-level discourse.

The Turing test, proposed in 1950, established a landmark for assessing intelligence by a computer's ability to impersonate human conversation. Despite limitations, it established a philosophical foundation for AI. However, early systems like ELIZA passed the test using scripted responses without true understanding, calling into question the test's validity as an evaluation of AI. The test also faced criticism for relying on deceit and for limitations in its format that constrained the complexity of questioning. Philosophers like John Searle argued symbolic manipulation alone did not equate to human-level intelligence. Still, the Turing test influenced the conversation on AI capabilities.

Recent chatbots with more advanced natural language processing can better simulate conversational depth. IBM Watson (2011) answered complex questions to beat Jeopardy! champions. Siri (2011), as a voice-based assistant, pioneered integrating chatbots into everyday devices. Systems like Google Duplex (2018) book appointments via phone conversations.

The advent of LLMs like GPT-3 enabled more human-like chatbot systems such as ChatGPT (2022). Yet their abilities remain tightly constrained. True human discourse requires complex reasoning, pragmatics, common sense, and broad contextual knowledge.

Today's benchmarks thus focus more on testing specific task performance to probe the limits of LLMs like GPT-4. While ChatGPT displays remarkable coherence, its lack of grounding can result in plausible but incorrect responses. Understanding these boundaries is crucial for safe, beneficial applications. The goal is no longer merely imitation but developing useful AI alongside a deeper comprehension of the inner workings of adaptive learning systems.

Chatbots analyze user input, understand the intent behind it, and generate appropriate responses. They can be designed to work with text-based messaging platforms or voice-based applications.

Some use cases for chatbots in customer service include providing 24/7 support, handling frequently asked questions, assisting with product recommendations, processing orders and payments, and resolving simple customer issues.

Some more use cases of chatbots include:

- **Appointment scheduling**: Chatbots can help users schedule appointments, book reservations, and manage their calendars.

- **Information retrieval**: Chatbots can provide users with specific information, such as weather updates, news articles, or stock prices.

- **Virtual assistants**: Chatbots can act as personal assistants, helping users with tasks like setting reminders, sending messages, or making phone calls.

- **Language learning**: Chatbots can assist in language learning by providing interactive conversations and language practice.

- **Mental health support**: Chatbots can offer emotional support, provide resources, and engage in therapeutic conversations for mental health purposes.

- **Education**: In educational settings, virtual assistants are being explored as virtual tutors, helping students learn and assess their knowledge, answer questions, and deliver personalized learning experiences.

- **HR and recruitment**: Chatbots can assist in the recruitment process by screening candidates, scheduling interviews, and providing information about job openings.

- **Entertainment**: Chatbots can engage users in interactive games, quizzes, and storytelling experiences.

- **Law**: Chatbots can be used to provide basic legal information, answer common legal questions, assist with legal research, and help users navigate legal processes. They can also help with document preparation, such as drafting contracts or creating legal forms.

- **Medicine**: Chatbots can assist with symptom checking, provide basic medical advice, and offer mental health support. They can improve clinical decision-making by providing relevant information and recommendations to healthcare professionals.

These are just a few examples, and the use cases of chatbots continue to expand across various industries and domains. Chat technology in any field can make information more accessible and provide initial support to individuals seeking assistance. But their inability to reason or analyze limits roles requiring true intelligence. With responsible development, chatbots hold promise for intuitive interfaces in customer service and other domains, even if human-level language mastery remains elusive. Ongoing research aims to develop safe, useful chatbot capabilities.

There is an important distinction between chatbots that merely respond to explicit user prompts versus those with the more advanced ability to proactively initiate conversation and provide information without direct prompting. Intentional chatbots are designed to directly understand and fulfill specific user requests and intentions. However, proactive chatbots aim to anticipate needs and preferences based on prior interactions and contextual cues, taking the conversational initiative to address potential user questions preemptively.

While responsive intentional chatbots can effectively fulfill precise user directions, proactive abilities hold the promise of more natural, efficient human-AI interaction by building loyalty and trust through anticipatory service. However, mastering context and reasoning remains an AI challenge to create proactive yet controllable assistants. Current research is advancing chatbot abilities on both fronts, with the goal of balancing proactive dialog with responsiveness to user intent in fluid, purposeful conversation.

Understanding retrieval and vectors

Retrieval-augmented generation (**RAG**) is a technique that enhances text generation by retrieving and incorporating external knowledge. This grounds the output in factual information rather than relying solely on the knowledge that is encoded in the language model's parameters. **Retrieval-Augmented Language Models** (**RALMs**) specifically refer to retrieval-augmented language models that integrate retrieval into the training and inference process.

Traditional language models generate text autoregressively based only on the prompt. RALMs augment this by first retrieving relevant context from external corpora using semantic search algorithms. Semantic search typically involves indexing documents into vector embeddings, allowing fast similarity lookups via approximate nearest neighbor search.

The retrieved evidence then conditions the language model to produce more accurate, contextually relevant text. This cycle repeats, with RALMs formulating queries dynamically, retrieving information on demand during generation. Active RALMs interleave retrieval and text creation, regenerating uncertain parts by fetching clarifying knowledge.

Overall, RAG and RALMs overcome the limits of language models' memory by grounding responses in external information. As we'll explore more later, efficient storage and indexing of vector embeddings is crucial for enabling real-time semantic search over large document collections.

By incorporating outside knowledge, RALMs generate text that is more useful, nuanced, and factually correct. Their capabilities continue advancing through optimizations in indexing methods, reasoning about retrieval timing, and fusing internal and external contexts.

By grounding LLMs with use-case-specific information through RAG, the quality and accuracy of responses are improved. Through retrieval of relevant data, RAG helps in reducing hallucination responses from LLMs. For example, an LLM used in a healthcare application could retrieve relevant medical information from external sources such as medical literature or databases during inference. This retrieved data can then be incorporated into the context to enhance the generated responses and ensure they are accurate and aligned with domain-specific knowledge.

Since we are talking about vector storage, we need to discuss vector search, which is a technique used to search and retrieve vectors (or embeddings) based on their similarity to a query vector. It is commonly used in applications such as recommendation systems, image and text search, and anomaly detection. We'll start with the fundamentals of embeddings now. Once you understand embeddings, you'll be able to build everything from search engines to chatbots.

Embeddings

An embedding is a numerical representation of content in a way that machines can process and understand. The essence of the process is to convert an object such as an image or some text into a vector that encapsulates its semantic content while discarding irrelevant details as much as possible. An embedding takes a piece of content, such as a word, sentence, or image, and maps it into a multi-dimensional vector space. The distance between two embeddings indicates the semantic similarity between the corresponding concepts (the original content).

Embeddings are representations of data objects generated by machine learning models to represent. They can represent words or sentences as numerical vectors (lists of float numbers). As for the OpenAI language embedding models, the embedding is a vector of 1,536 floating point numbers that represent the text. These numbers are derived from a sophisticated language model that captures semantic content.

As an example, let's say we have the words cat and dog – these could be represented numerically in a space together with all other words in the vocabulary. If the space is 3-dimensional, these could be vectors such as [0.5, 0.2, -0.1] for cat and [0.8, -0.3, 0.6] for dog. These vectors encode information about the relationships of these concepts with other words. Roughly speaking, we would expect the concepts of cat and dog to be closer (more similar) to the concept of animal than to the concept of computer or embedding.

Embeddings can be created using different methods. For texts, one simple method is the **bag-of-words** approach, where each word is represented by a count of how many times it appears in a text. This approach, which in the scikit-learn library is implemented as `CountVectorizer`, was popular until **word2vec** came about. **Word2vec**, which – roughly speaking – learns embeddings by predicting the words in a sentence based on other surrounding words ignoring the word order in a linear model.

We can perform simple vector arithmetic with these vectors, for example, the vector for king minus man plus the vector for woman gives us a vector that comes close to queen. The general idea of embeddings is illustrated in the following figure (source: "Analogies Explained: Towards Understanding Word Embeddings" by Carl Allen and Timothy Hospedales, 2019; `https://arxiv.org/abs/1901.09813`):

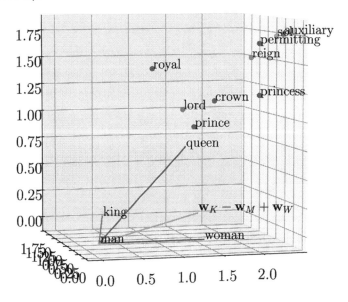

Figure 5.1: Word2vec word embeddings in a 3D space

As for images, embeddings could come from feature extraction stages such as edge detection, texture analysis, and color composition. These features can be extracted over different window sizes to make the representations both scale-invariant and shift-invariant (**scale-space representations**). Nowadays, often, **convolutional neural networks (CNNs)** are pre-trained on large datasets (like ImageNet) to learn a good representation of the image's properties. Since convolutional layers apply a series of filters (or kernels) on the input image to produce a feature map, conceptually this is like scale-space. When a pre-trained CNN then runs over a new image, it can output an embedding vector.

Today, for most domains including texts and images, embeddings usually come from **trans-former-based models**, which consider the context and order of the words in a sentence and the paragraph. Based on the model architecture, most importantly the number of parameters, these models can capture extraordinarily complex relationships. All these models are trained on large datasets to establish the concepts and their relationships.

These embeddings can be used in various tasks. By representing data objects as numerical vectors, we can perform mathematical operations on them and measure their similarity or use them as input for other machine learning models. By calculating distances between embeddings, we can perform tasks like search and similarity scoring, or classify objects, for example by topic or category. For example, we could be performing a simple sentiment classifier by checking if embeddings of product reviews are closer to the concept of positive or negative.

In LangChain, you can obtain an embedding by using the embed_query() method from any embedding class, for example, from the the OpenAIEmbeddings class. Here is an example code snippet:

```
from langchain.embeddings.openai import OpenAIEmbeddings


embeddings = OpenAIEmbeddings()
text = "This is a sample query."
query_result = embeddings.embed_query(text)
print(query_result)
print(len(query_result))
```

This code passes a single string input to the embed_query method and retrieves the corresponding text embedding. The result is stored in the query_result variable. The length of the embedding (the number of dimensions) can be obtained using the len() function. I am assuming you have set the API key as an environment variable, as recommended in *Chapter 3, Getting Started with LangChain*.

You can also obtain embeddings for multiple document inputs using the embed_documents() method. Here is an example:

```
from langchain.embeddings.openai import OpenAIEmbeddings


words = ["cat", "dog", "computer", "animal"]
embeddings = OpenAIEmbeddings()
doc_vectors = embeddings.embed_documents(words)
```

In this case, the `embed_documents()` method is used to retrieve embeddings for multiple text inputs. The result is stored in the `doc_vectors` variable. We could have retrieved embeddings for long documents – instead, we've retrieved the vectors only for each single word.

We can also do arithmetic between these embeddings; for example, we can calculate distances between them:

```
from scipy.spatial.distance import pdist, squareform
import numpy as np
import pandas as pd
X = np.array(doc_vectors)
dists = squareform(pdist(X))
```

This gives us the Euclidean distances between our words as a square matrix. Let's plot them:

```
import pandas as pd

df = pd.DataFrame(
    data=dists,
    index=words,
    columns=words
)
df.style.background_gradient(cmap='coolwarm')
```

The distance plot should look like this:

	cat	dog	computer	animal
cat	0.000000	0.522352	0.575285	0.521214
dog	0.522352	0.000000	0.581203	0.478794
computer	0.575285	0.581203	0.000000	0.591435
animal	0.521214	0.478794	0.591435	0.000000

Figure 5.2: Euclidean distances between embeddings of the words cat, dog, computer, and animal

We can confirm: a cat and a dog are indeed closer to an animal than to a computer. There could be many questions here, for example, if a dog is more an animal than a cat, or why a dog and a cat are only a little more distant from a computer than from an animal. Although these questions can be important in certain applications, let's bear in mind that this is a simple example.

In these examples, we've used OpenAI embeddings – in the examples further on, we'll use embeddings from models served by Hugging Face. There are a few integrations and tools in LangChain that can help with this process, some of which we'll encounter later on in this chapter.

Additionally, LangChain provides a FakeEmbeddings class that can be used to test your pipeline without making actual calls to the embedding providers.

In the context of this chapter, we'll use them for retrieval of related information (semantic search). However, we still need to talk about the integration of these embeddings into apps and broader systems, and this is where vector storage comes in.

Vector storage

As mentioned, in vector search, each data point is represented as a vector in a high-dimensional space. The vectors capture the features or characteristics of the data points. The goal is to find the most similar vectors to a given query vector.

In vector search, every data object in a dataset is assigned a vector embedding. These embeddings are arrays of numbers that can be used as coordinates in a high-dimensional space. The distance between vectors can be computed using distance metrics like cosine similarity or Euclidean distance. To perform a vector search, the query vector (representing the search query) is compared to every vector in the collection. The distance between the query vector and each vector in the collection is calculated, and objects with smaller distances are considered more similar.

To perform vector search efficiently, vector storage mechanisms are used such as vector databases.

 Vector search refers to the process of searching for similar vectors among other stored vectors, for example, in a vector database, based on their similarity to a given query vector. Vector search is commonly used in various applications such as recommendation systems, image and text search, and similarity-based retrieval. The goal of vector search is to efficiently and accurately retrieve vectors that are most similar to the query vector, typically using similarity measures such as the dot product or cosine similarity.

Vector storage refers to the mechanism used to store vector embeddings and is also relevant to how those vector embeddings can be retrieved. Vector storage can be a standalone solution that is specifically designed to store and retrieve vector embeddings efficiently. On the other hand, vector databases are purpose-built to manage vector embeddings and provide several advantages over using standalone vector indices like Faiss.

Let's dive into a few of these concepts a bit more. There are three levels to this:

1. **Indexing** organizes vectors to optimize retrieval, structuring them so that vectors can be retrieved quickly. There are different algorithms like k-d trees or Annoy for this.

2. **Vector libraries** provide functions for vector operations like dot product and vector indexing.

3. **Vector databases** like Milvus or Pinecone are designed to store, manage, and retrieve large sets of vectors. They use indexing mechanisms to facilitate efficient similarity searches on these vectors.

These components work together for the creation, manipulation, storage, and efficient retrieval of vector embeddings. Let's look at these in turn to understand the fundamentals of working with embeddings. Understanding these fundamentals should make it intuitive to work with RAG.

Vector indexing

Indexing in the context of vector embeddings is a method of organizing data to optimize its retrieval and/or storage. It's similar to the concept in traditional database systems, where indexing allows quicker access to data records. For vector embeddings, indexing aims to structure the vectors – roughly speaking – so that similar vectors are stored next to each other, enabling fast proximity or similarity searches.

A typical algorithm applied in this context is **k-dimensional trees (k-d trees)**, but many others, like ball trees, Annoy, and Faiss, are often implemented, especially for high-dimensional vectors, which traditional methods can struggle with.

There are several other types of algorithms commonly used for similarity search indexing. Some of them include:

- **Product quantization (PQ)**: PQ is a technique that divides the vector space into smaller subspaces and quantizes each subspace separately. This reduces the dimensionality of the vectors and allows for efficient storage and search. PQ is known for its fast search speed but may sacrifice some accuracy. Examples of PQ are k-d trees and ball trees. In k-d trees, a binary tree structure is built up that partitions the data points based on their feature values. It is efficient for low-dimensional data but becomes less effective as the dimensionality increases. In ball trees, a tree structure that partitions the data points into nested hyperspheres. It is suitable for high-dimensional data but can be slower than k-d trees for low-dimensional data.

- **Locality sensitive hashing (LSH)**: This is a hashing-based method that maps similar data points to the same hash buckets. It is efficient for high-dimensional data but may have a higher probability of false positives and false negatives. The **Annoy (Approximate Nearest Neighbors Oh Yeah)** algorithm is a popular LSH algorithm that uses random projection trees to index vectors. It constructs a binary tree structure where each node represents a random hyperplane. Annoy is simple to use and provides fast approximate nearest neighbor search.

- **Hierarchical navigable small world (HNSW)**: HNSW is a graph-based indexing algorithm that constructs a hierarchical graph structure to organize the vectors. It uses a combination of randomization and greedy search to build a navigable network, allowing for efficient nearest-neighbor search. HNSW is known for its high search accuracy and scalability.

- Apart from HNSW and KNN, there are other graph-based methods, like **Graph Neural Networks (GNNs)** and **Graph Convolutional Networks (GCNs)**, that leverage graph structures for similarity search.

These indexing algorithms have different trade-offs in terms of search speed, accuracy, and memory usage. The choice of algorithm depends on the specific requirements of the application and the characteristics of the vector data.

Vector libraries

Vector libraries, like Facebook (Meta) Faiss or Spotify Annoy, provide functionality for working with vector data. In the context of vector search, a vector library is specifically designed to store and perform similarity search on vector embeddings. These libraries use the **Approximate Nearest Neighbor (ANN)** algorithm to efficiently search through vectors and find the most similar ones. They typically offer different implementations of the ANN algorithm, such as clustering or tree-based methods, and allow users to perform vector similarity search for various applications.

Here's a quick overview of some open-source libraries for vector storage that shows their popularity in terms of GitHub stars over time (source: `star-history.com`):

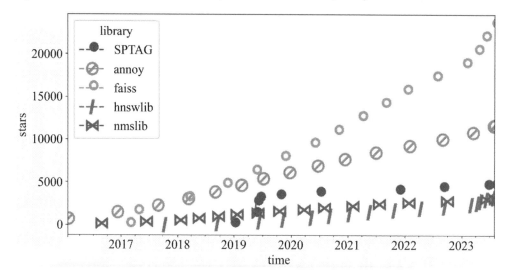

Figure 5.3: Star history for several popular open-source vector libraries

You can see that Faiss has been starred a lot by GitHub users. Annoy comes second. Others have not found the same popularity yet.

Let's quickly go through these:

- **Faiss (Facebook AI Similarity Search)** is a library developed by Meta (previously Facebook) that provides efficient similarity search and clustering of dense vectors. It offers various indexing algorithms, including PQ, LSH, and HNSW. Faiss is widely used for large-scale vector search tasks and supports both CPU and GPU acceleration.

- Annoy is a C++ library for approximate nearest neighbor search in high-dimensional spaces maintained and developed by Spotify implementing the Annoy algorithm. It is designed to be efficient and scalable, making it suitable for large-scale vector data. It works with a forest of random projection trees.

- hnswlib is a C++ library for approximate nearest-neighbor search using the HNSW algorithm. It provides fast and memory-efficient indexing and search capabilities for high-dimensional vector data.

- **nmslib (Non-Metric Space Library)** is an open-source library that provides efficient similarity search in non-metric spaces. It supports various indexing algorithms like HNSW, SW-graph, and SPTAG.

- SPTAG by Microsoft implements a distributed ANN. It comes with a k-d tree and relative neighborhood graph (SPTAG-KDT), as well as a balanced k-means tree and relative neighborhood graph (SPTAG-BKT).

Both nmslib and hnswlib are maintained by Leo Boytsov, who works as a senior research scientist at Amazon, and Yury Malkov. There are a lot more libraries. You can see an overview at `https://github.com/erikbern/ann-benchmarks`

Vector databases

A vector database is designed to handle vector embeddings, making it easier to search and query data objects. It offers additional features such as data management, metadata storage and filtering, and scalability. While vector storage focuses solely on storing and retrieving vector embeddings, a vector database provides a more comprehensive solution for managing and querying vector data. Vector databases can be particularly useful for applications that involve copious amounts of data and require flexible and efficient search capabilities across several types of vectorized data, such as text, images, audio, video, and more.

Vector databases can be used to store and serve machine learning models and their corresponding embeddings. The primary application is **similarity search** (also **semantic search**), where we can efficiently search through large volumes of text, images, or videos, identifying objects matching the query based on the vector representation. This is particularly useful in applications such as document search, reverse image search, and recommendation systems.

Other use cases for vector databases are continually expanding as the technology evolves; however, some common use cases for vector databases include:

- **Anomaly detection**: Vector databases can be used to detect anomalies in large datasets by comparing the vector embeddings of data points. This can be valuable in fraud detection, network security, or monitoring systems where identifying unusual patterns or behaviors is crucial.
- **Personalization**: Vector databases can be used to create personalized recommendation systems by finding similar vectors based on user preferences or behavior.
- **Natural Language Processing (NLP)**: Vector databases are widely used in NLP tasks such as sentiment analysis, text classification, and semantic search. By representing text as vector embeddings, it becomes easier to compare and analyze textual data.

These databases are popular because they are optimized for scalability and representing and retrieving data in high-dimensional vector spaces. Traditional databases are not designed to efficiently handle large-dimensional vectors, such as those used to represent images or text embeddings.

The characteristics of vector databases include:

- **Efficient retrieval of similar vectors:** Vector databases excel at finding close embeddings or similar points in a high-dimensional space. This makes them ideal for tasks like reverse image search or similarity-based recommendations.

- **Specialized for specific tasks:** Vector databases are designed to perform a specific task, such as finding close embeddings. They are not general-purpose databases and are tailored to handle substantial amounts of vector data efficiently.

- **Support for high-dimensional spaces:** Vector databases can handle vectors with thousands of dimensions, allowing for complex representations of data. This is crucial for tasks like natural language processing or image recognition.

- **Enable advanced search capabilities:** With vector databases, it becomes possible to build powerful search engines that can search for similar vectors or embeddings. This opens possibilities for applications like content recommendation systems or semantic search.

Overall, vector databases offer a specialized and efficient solution for handling large-dimensional vector data, enabling tasks like similarity search and advanced search capabilities.

The market for open-source software and databases is currently thriving due to several factors. Firstly, **artificial intelligence (AI)** and data management have become crucial for businesses, leading to a high demand for advanced database solutions.

In the database market, there is a history of new types of databases emerging and creating new market categories. These market creators often dominate the industry, attracting significant investments from **venture capitalists (VCs)**. For example, MongoDB, Cockroach, Neo4J, and Influx are all examples of successful companies that introduced innovative database technologies and achieved substantial market share. The popular Postgres has an extension for efficient vector search: pg_embedding. **HNSW** provides a faster and more efficient alternative to the pgvector extension with IVFFlat indexing.

Some examples of vector databases are listed in *Table 5.1*. I took the liberty of highlighting for each search engine the following perspectives:

- **Value proposition**: What is the unique feature that sets this vector search engine apart from others?
- **Business model**: The general type of the engine, whether it's a vector database, big data platform, or managed/self-hosted.
- **Indexing**: The algorithmic approach to similarity/vector search taken by this search engine and its unique capabilities.
- **License**: Whether it is open- or closed-source.

Database provider	Description	Business model	First released	License	Indexing	Organization
Chroma	Commercial open-source embedding store	(Partly open) SaaS	2022	Apache-2.0	HNSW	Chroma Inc
Qdrant	Managed/ self-hosted vector search engine and database with extended filtering support	(Partly open) SaaS	2021	Apache 2.0	HNSW	Qdrant Solutions GmbH
Milvus	Vector database built for scalable similarity search	(Partly open) SaaS	2019	BSD	IVF, HNSW, PQ, and more	Zilliz
Weaviate	Cloud-native vector database that stores both objects and vectors	Open SaaS	Started in 2018 as a traditional graph database, first released in 2019	BSD	Custom HNSW algorithm that supports CRUD	SeMI Technologies

Pinecone	Fast and scalable applications using embeddings from AI models	SaaS	First released in 2019	Propri-etary	Built on top of Faiss	Pinecone Systems Inc
Vespa	Commercial open-source vector database that supports vector search, lexical search, and search	Open SaaS	Originally a web search engine (all-theweb), acquired by Yahoo! in 2003, and later developed into and open-sourced as Vespa in 2017	Apache 2.0	HNSW, BM25	Yahoo!
Marqo	Cloud-native commercial open-source search and analytics engine	Open SaaS	2022	Apache 2.0	HNSW	S2Search Australia Pty Ltd

Table 5.1: Vector databases

In the preceding table, I've left out other aspects such as architecture, support for sharding, and in-memory processing. There are many vector database providers. I've omitted many solutions, such as FaissDB and Hasty.ai, and focused on a few ones that are integrated into LangChain.

For the open-source databases, the GitHub star histories give a good idea of their popularity and traction. Here's the plot over time (source: `star-history.com`):

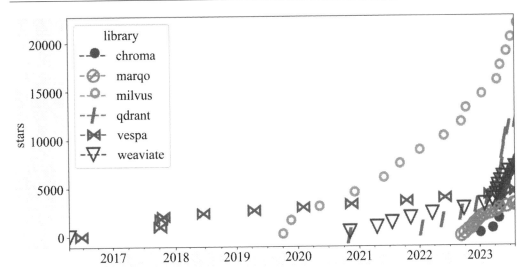

Figure 5.4: Star history of open-source vector databases on GitHub

You can see that milvus is immensely popular; however, other libraries such as qdrant, weviate, and chroma have been catching up.

In LangChain, vector storage can be implemented using the vectorstores module. This module provides various classes and methods for storing and querying vectors. Let's see an example of a vector store implementation in LangChain!

Chroma

This vector store is optimized for storing and querying vectors using Chroma as a backend. Chroma takes over for encoding and comparing vectors based on their angular similarity.

To use Chroma in LangChain, you need to follow these steps:

1. Import the necessary modules:

    ```
    from langchain.vectorstores import Chroma
    from langchain.embeddings import OpenAIEmbeddings
    ```

2. Create an instance of Chroma and provide the documents (splits) and the embedding method:

    ```
    vectorstore = Chroma.from_documents(documents=docs,
    embedding=OpenAIEmbeddings())
    ```

The documents (or splits, as seen in *Chapter 5, Building a Chatbot Like ChatGPT*) will be embedded and stored in the Chroma vector database. We'll discuss document loaders in another section of this chapter. However, for sake of completeness, you can get the docs argument for the preceding chroma vector store like this:

```python
from langchain.document_loaders import ArxivLoader
from langchain.text_splitter import
CharacterTextSplitter

loader = ArxivLoader(query="2310.06825")
documents = loader.load()
text_splitter = CharacterTextSplitter(chunk_size=1000,
chunk_overlap=0)
docs = text_splitter.split_documents(documents)
```

This will load and chunk up the paper about Mistal 7B. Please note that the download will be a PDF, and you'll need to have the pymupdf library installed.

3. We can query the vector store to retrieve similar vectors:

```python
similar_vectors = vector_store.query(query_vector, k)
```

Here, query_vector is the vector you want to find similar vectors to, and k is the number of similar vectors you want to retrieve.

In this section, we've learned a lot of the basics of embeddings and vector stores. We've also seen how to work with embeddings and documents in vector stores and vector databases. In practice, there are two building blocks for us to pick up if we want to build a chatbot, most importantly document loaders and retrievers, both of which we'll look at now.

Loading and retrieving in LangChain

LangChain implements a toolchain of different building blocks for building retrieval systems. In this section, we'll look at how we can put them together in a pipeline for building a chatbot with RAG. This includes data loaders, document transformers, embedding models, vector stores, and retrievers.

The relationship between them is illustrated in the diagram here (source: LangChain documentation):

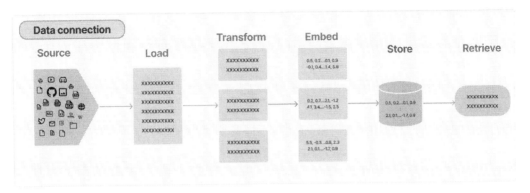

Figure 5.5: Vector stores and data loaders

In LangChain, we first load documents through data loaders. Then we can transform them and pass these documents to a vector store as embedding. We can then query the vector store or a retriever associated with the vector store. Retrievers in LangChain can wrap the loading and vector storage into a single step. We'll mostly skip transformations in this chapter; however, you'll find explanations with examples of data loaders, embeddings, storage mechanisms, and retrievers.

In LangChain, we can load our documents from many sources and in a bunch of formats through the integrated document loaders. You can use the LangChain integration hub to browse and select the appropriate loader for your data source. Once you have selected the loader, you can load the document using the specified loader.

Let's look at document loaders in LangChain! In the actual pipeline of implementing RAG, these come as the first step.

Document loaders

Document loaders are used to load data from a source as **Document** objects, which consist of text and associated metadata. There are several types of integrations available, such as document loaders for loading a simple `.txt` file (`TextLoader`), loading the text contents of a web page (`WebBaseLoader`), loading articles from Arxiv (`ArxivLoader`), or loading a transcript of a YouTube video (`YoutubeLoader`). For webpages, the `Diffbot` integration gives a clean extraction of the content. Other integrations exist for images such as providing image captions (`ImageCaptionLoader`).

Document loaders have a `load()` method that loads data from the configured source and returns it as documents. They may also have a `lazy_load()` method for loading data into memory as and when they are needed.

Here is an example of a document loader for loading data from a text file:

```
from langchain.document_loaders import TextLoader


loader = TextLoader(file_path="path/to/file.txt")
documents = loader.load()
```

The `documents` variable will contain the loaded documents, which can be accessed for further processing. Each document consists of `page_content` (the text content of the document) and `metadata` (associated metadata such as the source URL or title).

Similarly, we can load documents from Wikipedia:

```
from langchain.document_loaders import WikipediaLoader
loader = WikipediaLoader("LangChain")
documents = loader.load()
```

It's important to note that the specific implementation of document loaders may vary depending on the programming language or framework being used.

In LangChain, vector retrieval in agents or chains is done via retrievers, which access vector storage. Let's now see how retrievers work.

Retrievers in LangChain

Retrievers in LangChain are a type of component that is used to search and retrieve information from a given index stored in a vector store as a backend, such as Chroma, to index and search embeddings. Retrievers play a crucial role in answering questions over documents, as they are responsible for retrieving relevant information based on the given query.

Here are a few examples of retrievers:

- **BM25 retriever**: This retriever uses the BM25 algorithm to rank documents based on their relevance to a given query. It is a popular information retrieval algorithm that considers term frequency and document length.

- **TF-IDF retriever**: This retriever uses the TF-IDF (Term Frequency-Inverse Document Frequency) algorithm to rank documents based on the importance of terms in the document collection. It assigns higher weights to terms that are rare in the collection but occur frequently in a specific document.

- **Dense retriever**: This retriever uses dense embeddings to retrieve documents. It encodes documents and queries into dense vectors, and calculates the similarity between them using cosine similarity or other distance metrics.

- **kNN retriever**: This utilizes the well-known k-nearest neighbors algorithm to retrieve relevant documents based on their similarity to a given query.

These are just a few examples of retrievers available in LangChain. Each retriever has its own strengths and weaknesses, and the choice of retriever depends on the specific use case and requirements. For example, the purpose of an **Arxiv retriever** is to retrieve scientific articles from the Arxiv.org archive. It is a tool that allows users to search for and download scholarly articles in various fields such as physics, mathematics, computer science, and more.

The functionality of an Arxiv retriever includes specifying the maximum number of documents to be downloaded, retrieving relevant documents based on a query, and accessing the metadata information of the retrieved documents.

A **Wikipedia retriever** allows users to retrieve Wikipedia pages or documents from the website Wikipedia. The purpose of a Wikipedia retriever is to provide easy access to the vast amount of information available on Wikipedia and enable users to extract specific information or knowledge from it.

Let's see a few retrievers, what they are good for, and how we can customize a retriever.

kNN retriever

To use the kNN retriever, you need to create a new instance of the retriever and provide it with a list of texts. Here is an example of how to create a kNN retriever using embeddings from OpenAI:

```
from langchain.retrievers import KNNRetriever
from langchain.embeddings import OpenAIEmbeddings

words = ["cat", "dog", "computer", "animal"]
retriever = KNNRetriever.from_texts(words, OpenAIEmbeddings())
```

Once the retriever is created, you can use it to retrieve relevant documents by calling the get_ relevant_documents() method and passing a query string. The retriever will return a list of documents that are most relevant to the query.

Here is an example of how to use the kNN retriever:

```
result = retriever.get_relevant_documents("dog")
print(result)
```

This will output a list of documents that are relevant to the query. Each document contains the page content and metadata:

```
[Document(page_content='dog', metadata={}),
 Document(page_content='animal', metadata={}),
 Document(page_content='cat', metadata={}),
 Document(page_content='computer', metadata={})]
```

PubMed retriever

There are a few more specialized retrievers in LangChain, such as the one from PubMed. A **PubMed retriever** is a component in LangChain that helps to incorporate biomedical literature retrieval into their language model applications. PubMed contains millions of citations for biomedical literature from various sources.

In LangChain, the PubMedRetriever class is used to interact with the PubMed database and retrieve relevant documents based on a given query. The get_relevant_documents() method of the class takes a query as input and returns a list of relevant documents from PubMed.

Here's an example of how to use the PubMed retriever in LangChain:

```
from langchain.retrievers import PubMedRetriever
retriever = PubMedRetriever()
documents = retriever.get_relevant_documents("COVID")
for document in documents:
    print(document.metadata["Title"])
```

In this example, the get_relevant_documents() method is called with the query "COVID". The method then retrieves relevant documents related to the query from PubMed and returns them as a list. I am get the following titles as printed output:

```
The COVID-19 pandemic highlights the need for a psychological support in
systemic sclerosis patients.
```

```
Host genetic polymorphisms involved in long-term symptoms of COVID-19.
Association Between COVID-19 Vaccination and Mortality after Major
Operations.
```

Custom retrievers

We can implement our own custom retrievers in LangChain by creating a class that is inherited from the BaseRetriever abstract class. The class should implement the get_relevant_documents() method, which takes a query string as input and returns a list of relevant documents.

Here is an example of how a retriever can be implemented:

```
from langchain.schema import Document, BaseRetriever


class MyRetriever(BaseRetriever):
    def get_relevant_documents(self, query: str, **kwargs) ->
list[Document]:
        # Implement your retrieval logic here
        # Retrieve and process documents based on the query
        # Return a list of relevant documents

        relevant_documents = []

        # Your retrieval logic goes here...

        return relevant_documents
```

You can customize this method to perform any retrieval operations you need, such as querying a database or searching through indexed documents.

Once you have implemented your retriever class, you can create an instance of it and call the get_relevant_documents() method to retrieve relevant documents based on a query.

Now that we've learned about vector stores and retrievers, let's put all of this to use. Let's implement a chatbot with a retriever!

Implementing a chatbot

We'll implement a chatbot now. We'll assume you have the environment installed with the necessary libraries and the API keys as per the instructions in *Chapter 3, Getting Started with LangChain*.

To implement a simple chatbot in LangChain, you can follow this recipe:

1. Set up a document loader.

2. Store documents in a vector store.

3. Set up a chatbot with retrieval from the vector storage.

We'll generalize this with several formats and make this available through an interface in a web browser through Streamlit. You'll be able to drop in your document and start asking questions. In production, for a corporate deployment for customer engagement, you can imagine that these documents are already loaded in, and your vector storage can just be static.

Let's start with the document loader.

Document loader

As mentioned, we want to be able to read different formats:

```python
from typing import Any
from langchain.document_loaders import (
  PyPDFLoader, TextLoader,
  UnstructuredWordDocumentLoader,
  UnstructuredEPubLoader
)


class EpubReader(UnstructuredEPubLoader):
    def __init__(self, file_path: str | list[str], ** kwargs: Any):
        super().__init__(file_path, **kwargs, mode="elements",
strategy="fast")


class DocumentLoaderException(Exception):
    pass


class DocumentLoader(object):
    """Loads in a document with a supported extension."""
    supported_extentions = {
        ".pdf": PyPDFLoader,
        ".txt": TextLoader,
        ".epub": EpubReader,
        ".docx": UnstructuredWordDocumentLoader,
```

```
        ".doc": UnstructuredWordDocumentLoader
    }
```

This gives us interfaces to read PDF, text, EPUB, and Word documents with different extensions. We'll now implement the loader logic:

```python
import logging
import pathlib
from langchain.schema import Document

def load_document(temp_filepath: str) -> list[Document]:
    """Load a file and return it as a list of documents."""
    ext = pathlib.Path(temp_filepath).suffix
    loader = DocumentLoader.supported_extentions.get(ext)
    if not loader:
        raise DocumentLoaderException(
            f"Invalid extension type {ext}, cannot load this type of file"
        )

    loader = loader(temp_filepath)
    docs = loader.load()
    logging.info(docs)
    return docs
```

This doesn't handle many errors now, but this can be extended if needed. Now we can make this loader available from the interface and connect it to vector storage.

Vector storage

This step includes setting up embedding mechanisms, vector storage, and a pipeline to pass our documents through:

```python
from langchain.embeddings import HuggingFaceEmbeddings
from langchain.text_splitter import RecursiveCharacterTextSplitter
from langchain.vectorstores import DocArrayInMemorySearch
from langchain.schema import Document, BaseRetriever

def configure_retriever(docs: list[Document]) -> BaseRetriever:
    """Retriever to use."""
```

```
    text_splitter = RecursiveCharacterTextSplitter(chunk_size=1500, chunk_
overlap=200)
    splits = text_splitter.split_documents(docs)
    embeddings = HuggingFaceEmbeddings(model_name="all-MiniLM-L6-v2")
    vectordb = DocArrayInMemorySearch.from_documents(splits, embeddings)
    return vectordb.as_retriever(search_type="mmr", search_kwargs={"k": 2,
"fetch_k": 4})
```

We are splitting our documents in chunks. Then we've set up a small model from Hugging Face for embeddings and an interface to DocArray for taking splits, creating embeddings, and storing them. Finally, our retriever is looking up documents by maximum marginal relevance.

We are using DocArray as our in-memory vector storage. DocArray provides various features like advanced indexing, comprehensive serialization protocols, a unified Pythonic interface, and more. Further, it offers efficient and intuitive handling of multimodal data for tasks such as natural language processing, computer vision, and audio processing.

We can initialize DocArray with different distance metrics such as cosine and Euclidean – cosine is the default.

For the retriever, we have two main options:

- **Similarity-search**: We can retrieve document according to similarity.
- **Maximum Marginal Relevance (MMR)**: We can apply diversity-based re-ranking of documents during retrieval to get results that cover different perspectives or points of view from the documents retrieved so far.

In the similarity search, we can set a similarity score threshold. We've opted for MMR. This helps retrieve a wider breadth of relevant information from different perspectives, rather than just repetitive, redundant hits. MMR mitigates retrieval redundancy and mitigates the bias inherent in the document collection. We've set the k parameter to 2, which means we will get 2 documents back from retrieval.

Retrieval can be improved by **contextual compression**, a technique where retrieved documents are compressed, and irrelevant information is filtered out. Instead of returning the full documents as-is, contextual compression uses the context of the given query to extract and return only the relevant information. This helps to reduce the cost of processing and improve the quality of responses in retrieval systems.

The base compressor is responsible for compressing the contents of individual documents based on the context of the given query. It uses a language model, such as GPT-3, to perform the compression. The compressor can filter out irrelevant information and return only the relevant parts of the document.

The base retriever is the document storage system that retrieves the documents based on the query. It can be any retrieval system, such as a search engine or a database. When a query is made to the contextual compression retriever, it first passes the query to the base retriever to retrieve relevant documents. Then, it uses the base compressor to compress the contents of these documents based on the context of the query. Finally, the compressed documents, containing only the relevant information, are returned as the response.

We have a few options for contextual compression:

- `LLMChainExtractor`: This passes over the returned documents and extracts from each only the relevant content.
- `LLMChainFilter`: This is slightly simpler; it only filters only the relevant documents (rather than the content from the documents).
- `EmbeddingsFilter`: This applies a similarity filter based on the document and the query in terms of embeddings.

The first two compressors require an LLM to call, which means it can be slow and costly. Therefore, `EmbeddingsFilter` can be a more efficient alternative.

We can integrate compression here with a simple `switch` statement at the end (replacing the `return` statement):

```
if not use_compression:
    return retriever

embeddings_filter = EmbeddingsFilter(
    embeddings=embeddings, similarity_threshold=0.76
)
return ContextualCompressionRetriever(
    base_compressor=embeddings_filter,
    base_retriever=retriever
)
```

Please note that I've just made up a new variable, `use_compression`. We can feed the `use_compression` parameter through `configure_qa_chain()` to the `configure_retriever()` method (not shown here).

For our chosen compressor, `EmbeddingsFilter`, we need to include two more additional imports:

```
from langchain.retrievers.document_compressors import EmbeddingsFilter
from langchain.retrievers import ContextualCompressionRetriever
```

Now that we have the mechanism to create the retriever. We can set up the chat chain:

```
from langchain.chains import ConversationalRetrievalChain
from langchain.chains.base import Chain
from langchain.chat_models import ChatOpenAI
from langchain.memory import ConversationBufferMemory


def configure_chain(retriever: BaseRetriever) -> Chain:
    """Configure chain with a retriever."""
    # Setup memory for contextual conversation
    memory = ConversationBufferMemory(memory_key="chat_history", return_
messages=True)


    # Setup LLM and QA chain; set temperature Low to keep hallucinations
in check
    llm = ChatOpenAI(
        model_name="gpt-3.5-turbo", temperature=0, streaming=True
    )
    # Passing in a max_tokens_limit amount automatically
    # truncates the tokens when prompting your LLm!
    return ConversationalRetrievalChain.from_llm(
        llm, retriever=retriever, memory=memory, verbose=True, max_tokens_
limit=4000
    )
```

One final thing for the retrieval logic is taking the documents and passing them to the retriever setup:

```
import os
import tempfile
def configure_qa_chain(uploaded_files):
```

```
    """Read documents, configure retriever, and the chain."""
    docs = []
    temp_dir = tempfile.TemporaryDirectory()
    for file in uploaded_files:
        temp_filepath = os.path.join(temp_dir.name, file.name)
        with open(temp_filepath, "wb") as f:
            f.write(file.getvalue())
        docs.extend(load_document(temp_filepath))

    retriever = configure_retriever(docs=docs)
    return configure_chain(retriever=retriever)
```

Now that we have the logic of the chatbot, we need to set up the interface. As mentioned, we'll use **streamlit** again:

```
import streamlit as st
from langchain.callbacks import StreamlitCallbackHandler

st.set_page_config(page_title="LangChain: Chat with Documents", page_
icon="🦜")
st.title("🦜 LangChain: Chat with Documents")

uploaded_files = st.sidebar.file_uploader(
    label="Upload files",
    type=list(DocumentLoader.supported_extentions.keys()),
    accept_multiple_files=True
)
if not uploaded_files:
    st.info("Please upload documents to continue.")
    st.stop()

qa_chain = configure_qa_chain(uploaded_files)
assistant = st.chat_message("assistant")
user_query = st.chat_input(placeholder="Ask me anything!")

if user_query:
    stream_handler = StreamlitCallbackHandler(assistant)
    response = qa_chain.run(user_query, callbacks=[stream_handler])
    st.markdown(response)
```

This gives us a chatbot with retrieval that's usable via a visual interface, and also has drop-in functionality for custom documents that you need to ask questions about.

Figure 5.6: Chatbot interface with document loaders in different formats

You can see the full implementation on GitHub. You can play around with the chatbot to see how it works and when it doesn't.

It's important to note that LangChain has limitations on input size and cost. You may need to consider workarounds to handle larger knowledge bases or optimize the cost of API usage. Additionally, fine-tuning models or hosting the LLM in-house can be more complex and less accurate compared to using commercial solutions. We'll look at these use cases in *Chapter 8, Customizing LLMs and Their Output*.

Memory is a component in the LangChain framework that allows chatbots and language models to remember previous interactions and information. It is essential in applications like chatbots because it enables the system to maintain context and continuity in conversations. Let's have a look at memory and its mechanisms in LangChain.

Memory

Memory enables chatbots to retain information from previous interactions, maintaining continuity and conversational context. This is analogous to human recall, which allows coherent, meaningful dialogue. Without memory, chatbots struggle to comprehend references to prior exchanges, resulting in disjointed, unsatisfying conversations.

Specifically, memory facilitates accuracy by retaining contextual understanding across the entire dialogue. The chatbot can reference this holistic perspective of the conversation to respond appropriately. Memory also enhances personalization and faithfulness by consistently recognizing facts and details from past interactions.

By storing knowledge from message sequences, memory permits extracting insights to improve performance over time. Architectures like LangChain implement memory so chatbots can build on previous exchanges, answer follow-up questions, and sustain natural, logical dialogues.

Overall, memory is a crucial component for sophisticated chatbots, allowing them to learn from conversations and mimic the recall and contextual awareness that comes naturally to human interlocutors. Further advances in retention and reasoning with long-term memory could lead to more meaningful and productive human-AI interaction.

Conversation buffers

Here's a practical example in Python that demonstrates how to use the LangChain memory feature:

```python
from langchain.memory import ConversationBufferMemory
from langchain.chains import ConversationChain

# Creating a conversation chain with memory
memory = ConversationBufferMemory()
llm = ChatOpenAI(
    model_name="gpt-3.5-turbo", temperature=0, streaming=True
)

chain = ConversationChain(llm=llm, memory=memory)
# User inputs a message
user_input = "Hi, how are you?"
# Processing the user input in the conversation chain
response = chain.predict(input=user_input)
# Printing the response
print(response)
# User inputs another message
user_input = "What's the weather like today?"
# Processing the user input in the conversation chain
response = chain.predict(input=user_input)
# Printing the response
print(response)
# Printing the conversation history stored in memory
print(memory.chat_memory.messages)
```

In this example, we create a conversation chain with memory using `ConversationBufferMemory`, which is a simple wrapper that stores the messages in a variable. The user's inputs are processed using the `predict()` method of the conversation chain. The conversation chain retains the memory of previous interactions, allowing it to provide context-aware responses.

Instead of constructing the memory separately from the chain, we could have simplified things:

```
conversation = ConversationChain(
    llm=llm,
    verbose=True,
    memory=ConversationBufferMemory()
)
```

We are setting `verbose` to `True` to see the prompts.

After processing the user inputs, we print the response generated by the conversation chain. Additionally, we print the conversation history stored in memory using `memory.chat_memory.messages`. The `save_context()` method is used to store inputs and outputs. You can use the `load_memory_variables()` method to view the stored content. To get the history as a list of messages, a `return_messages` parameter is set to `True`. We'll see examples of this in this section.

`ConversationBufferWindowMemory` is a memory type provided by LangChain that keeps track of the interactions in a conversation over time. Unlike `ConversationBufferMemory`, which retains all previous interactions, `ConversationBufferWindowMemory` only keeps the last k interactions, where k is the window size specified. Here's a simple example of how to use `ConversationBufferWindowMemory` in LangChain:

```
from langchain.memory import ConversationBufferWindowMemory
memory = ConversationBufferWindowMemory(k=1)
```

In this example, the window size is set to 1, meaning that only the last interaction will be stored in memory.

We can use the `save_context()` method to save the context of each interaction. It takes two arguments: `user_input` and `model_output`. These represent the user's input and the corresponding model's output for a given interaction.

```
memory.save_context({"input": "hi"}, {"output": "whats up"})
memory.save_context({"input": "not much you"}, {"output": "not much"})
```

We can see the message with `memory.load_memory_variables({})`.

We can also customize the conversational memory in LangChain, which involves modifying the prefixes used for the AI and human messages, as well as updating the prompt template to reflect these changes.

To customize the conversational memory, you can follow these steps:

1. Import the necessary classes and modules from LangChain:

```python
from langchain.llms import OpenAI
from langchain.chains import ConversationChain
from langchain.memory import ConversationBufferMemory
from langchain.prompts.prompt import PromptTemplate
llm = OpenAI(temperature=0)
```

2. Define a new prompt template that includes the customized prefixes. You can do this by creating a `PromptTemplate` object with the desired template string:

```python
template = """The following is a friendly conversation between a
human and an AI. The AI is talkative and provides lots of specific
details from its context. If the AI does not know the answer to a
question, it truthfully says it does not know.

Current conversation:
{history}
Human: {input}
AI Assistant:"""
PROMPT = PromptTemplate(input_variables=["history", "input"],
template=template)
conversation = ConversationChain(
    prompt=PROMPT,
    llm=llm,
    verbose=True,
    memory=ConversationBufferMemory(ai_prefix="AI Assistant"),
)
```

In this example, the AI prefix is set to `AI Assistant` instead of the default `AI`.

Remembering conversation summaries

ConversationSummaryMemory is a type of memory in LangChain that generates a summary of the conversation as it progresses. Instead of storing all messages verbatim, it condenses the information, providing a summarized version of the conversation. This is particularly useful for extended conversations, where including all previous messages might exceed token limits.

To use ConversationSummaryMemory, first create an instance of it, passing the language model (llm) as an argument. Then, use the save_context() method to save the interaction context, which includes the user input and AI output. To retrieve the summarized conversation history, use the load_memory_variables() method.

Here's an example:

```
from langchain.memory import ConversationSummaryMemory
from langchain.llms import OpenAI

# Initialize the summary memory and the language model
memory = ConversationSummaryMemory(llm=OpenAI(temperature=0))
# Save the context of an interaction
memory.save_context({"input": "hi"}, {"output": "whats up"})
# Load the summarized memory
memory.load_memory_variables({})
```

Storing knowledge graphs

In LangChain, we can also extract information from the conversation as facts and store these by integrating a knowledge graph as the memory. This can enhance the capabilities of language models and enable them to leverage structured knowledge during text generation and inference.

A **knowledge graph** is a structured knowledge representation model that organizes information in the form of entities, attributes, and relationships. It represents knowledge as a graph, where entities are represented as nodes and relationships between entities are represented as edges. In a knowledge graph, entities can be any concept, object, or thing in the world, and attributes describe the properties or characteristics of these entities. Relationships capture the connections and associations between entities, providing contextual information and enabling semantic reasoning.

There's functionality in LangChain for knowledge graphs for retrieval; however, LangChain also provides memory components to automatically create a knowledge graph based on our conversation messages.

We'll instantiate the `ConversationKGMemory` class and pass your LLM instance as the `llm` parameter:

```
from langchain.memory import ConversationKGMemory
from langchain.llms import OpenAI


llm = OpenAI(temperature=0)
memory = ConversationKGMemory(llm=llm)
```

As the conversation progresses, we can save relevant information from the knowledge graph into the memory using the `save_context()` function of `ConversationKGMemory`.

Combining several memory mechanisms

LangChain also allows combining multiple memory strategies using the `CombinedMemory` class. This is useful when you want to maintain various aspects of the conversation history. For instance, one memory could be used to store the complete conversation log:

```
from langchain.llms import OpenAI
from langchain.prompts import PromptTemplate
from langchain.chains import ConversationChain
from langchain.memory import ConversationBufferMemory, CombinedMemory,
ConversationSummaryMemory


# Initialize language model (with desired temperature parameter)
llm = OpenAI(temperature=0)
# Define Conversation Buffer Memory (for retaining all past messages)
conv_memory = ConversationBufferMemory(memory_key="chat_history_lines",
input_key="input")
# Define Conversation Summary Memory (for summarizing conversation)
summary_memory = ConversationSummaryMemory(llm=llm, input_key="input")
# Combine both memory types
memory = CombinedMemory(memories=[conv_memory, summary_memory])
# Define Prompt Template
_DEFAULT_TEMPLATE = """The following is a friendly conversation between a
human and an AI. The AI is talkative and provides lots of specific details
from its context. If the AI does not know the answer to a question, it
truthfully says it does not know.
Summary of conversation:
{history}
```

```
Current conversation:
{chat_history_lines}
Human: {input}
AI:"""
PROMPT = PromptTemplate(input_variables=["history", "input", "chat_
history_lines"], template=_DEFAULT_TEMPLATE)
# Initialize the Conversation Chain
conversation = ConversationChain(llm=llm, verbose=True, memory=memory,
prompt=PROMPT)
# Start the conversation
conversation.run("Hi!")
```

In this example, we first instantiate the language model and the several types of memories we're using – `ConversationBufferMemory` for retaining the full conversation history and `ConversationSummaryMemory` for creating a summary of the conversation. We then combine these memories using `CombinedMemory`. We also define a prompt template that accommodates our memory usage and, finally, we create and run `ConversationChain` by providing our language model, memory, and prompt to it.

`ConversationSummaryBufferMemory` is used to keep a buffer of recent interactions in memory and compiles old interactions into a summary instead of completely flushing them out. The threshold for flushing interactions is determined by token length and not by the number of interactions.

To use this, the memory buffer needs to be instantiated with the LLM, and `max_token_limit`. `ConversationSummaryBufferMemory` offers a method called `predict_new_summary()`, which can be used directly to generate a conversation summary.

Long-term persistence

There are also different ways of storing conversations in dedicated backends. Zep, being one such example, provides a persistent backend to store, summarize, and search chat histories using vector embeddings and auto-token counting. This long-term memory with fast vector search and configurable summarization enables more capable conversational AI with context awareness.

A practical example of using Zep is to integrate it as the long-term memory for a chatbot or AI app. By using the `ZepMemory` class, developers can initialize a `ZepMemory` instance with the Zep server URL, API key, and a unique session identifier for the user. This allows the chatbot or AI app to store and retrieve chat history or other relevant information.

For example, in Python, you can initialize a ZepMemory instance as follows:

```python
from langchain.memory import ZepMemory
ZEP_API_URL = "http://localhost:8000"
ZEP_API_KEY = "<your JWT token>"
session_id = str(uuid4())

memory = ZepMemory(
    session_id=session_id,
    url=ZEP_API_URL,
    api_key=ZEP_API_KEY,
    memory_key="chat_history",
)
```

This sets up a ZepMemory instance that you can use in your chains. Please note that the URL and API key need to be set according to your setup. As mentioned, once the memory is set up, you can use it in your chatbot's chain or with your AI agent to store and retrieve chat history or other relevant information. Overall, Zep simplifies the process of persisting, searching, and enriching chatbot or AI app histories, allowing developers to focus on developing their AI applications rather than building memory infrastructure.

In the next section, we'll look at using moderation to make sure responses are adequate. Moderation is crucial for creating a safe, respectful, and inclusive environment for users, protecting brand reputation, and complying with legal obligations.

Moderating responses

The role of moderation in chatbots is to ensure that the bot's responses and conversations are appropriate, ethical, and respectful. It involves implementing mechanisms to filter out offensive or inappropriate content and discouraging abusive behavior from users. This is an important part of any application that we'd want to deploy for customers.

In the context of moderation, a constitution refers to a set of guidelines or rules that govern the behavior and responses of the chatbot. It outlines the standards and principles that the chatbot should adhere to, such as avoiding offensive language, promoting respectful interactions, and maintaining ethical standards. The constitution serves as a framework for ensuring that the chatbot operates within the desired boundaries and provides a positive user experience.

Moderation and having a constitution are important in chatbots for several reasons:

- **Ensuring ethical behavior**: Chatbots can interact with a wide range of users, including vulnerable individuals. Moderation helps ensure that the bot's responses are ethical, respectful, and do not promote harmful or offensive content.

- **Protecting users from inappropriate content**: Moderation helps prevent the dissemination of inappropriate or offensive language, hate speech, or any content that may be harmful or offensive to users. It creates a safe and inclusive environment for users to interact with the chatbot.

- **Maintaining brand reputation**: Chatbots often represent a brand or organization. By implementing moderation, the developer can ensure that the bot's responses align with the brand's values and maintain a positive reputation.

- **Preventing abusive behavior**: Moderation can discourage users from engaging in abusive or improper behavior. By implementing rules and consequences, such as the "two strikes" rule mentioned in the example, the developer can discourage users from using provocative language or engaging in abusive behavior.

- **Legal compliance**: Depending on the jurisdiction, there may be legal requirements for moderating content and ensuring that it complies with laws and regulations. Having a constitution or set of guidelines helps the developer adhere to these legal requirements.

You can add a moderation chain to an `LLMChain` instance or a `Runnable` instance to ensure that the generated output from the language model is not harmful.

If the content passed into the moderation chain is deemed harmful, there are a few ways to handle it. You can choose to throw an error in the chain and handle it in your application, or you can return a message to the user explaining that the text was harmful. The specific handling method depends on your application's requirements.

In LangChain, first, you would create an instance of the `OpenAIModerationChain` class, which is a pre-built moderation chain provided by LangChain. This chain is specifically designed to detect and filter out harmful content:

```
from langchain.chains import OpenAIModerationChain
moderation_chain = OpenAIModerationChain()
```

Next, you would create an instance of the LLMChain class or of a Runnable instance, which represents your language model chain. This is where you define your prompt and interact with the language model. We can do this using the LCEL syntax, which we've introduced in *Chapter 4*, *Building Capable Assistants*:

```
from langchain.prompts import PromptTemplate
from langchain.chat_models import ChatOpenAI
from langchain.schema import StrOutputParser

cot_prompt = PromptTemplate.from_template(
    "{question} \nLet's think step by step!"
)
llm_chain = cot_prompt | ChatOpenAI() | StrOutputParser()
```

This is a chain with a **Chain of Thought (CoT)** prompt, which includes the instruction to think step by step.

To append the moderation chain to the language model chain, you can use the SequentialChain class or the LCEL (which is recommended). This allows you to chain multiple chains together in a sequential manner:

```
chain = llm_chain | moderation_chain
```

Now, when you want to generate text using the language model, you would pass your input text through the moderation chain first, and then through the language model chain.

```
response = chain.invoke({"question": "What is the future of
programming?"})
```

The first chain will come up with a preliminary answer. Then, the moderation chain will evaluate this answer and filter out any harmful content. If the input text is deemed harmful, the moderation chain can either throw an error or return a message indicating that the text is not allowed. I've added an example for moderation to the chatbot app on GitHub.

Further, guardrails can be used to define the behavior of the language model on specific topics, prevent it from engaging in discussions on unwanted topics, guide the conversation along a predefined path, enforce a particular language style, extract structured data, and more.

In the context of LLMs, guardrails (rails for short) refer to specific ways of controlling the model's output. They provide a means to add programmable constraints and guidelines to ensure the output of the language model aligns with desired criteria.

Here are a few ways guardrails can be used:

- **Controlling topics**: Guardrails allow you to define the behavior of your language model or chatbot on specific topics. You can prevent it from engaging in discussions on unwanted or sensitive topics like politics.

- **Predefined dialogue paths**: Guardrails enable you to define a predefined path for the conversation. This ensures that the language model or chatbot follows a specific flow and provides consistent responses.

- **Language style**: Guardrails allow you to specify the language style that the language model or chatbot should use. This ensures that the output is in line with your desired tone, formality, or specific language requirements.

- **Structured data extraction**: Guardrails can be used to extract structured data from the conversation. This can be useful for capturing specific information or performing actions based on user inputs.

Overall, guardrails provide a way to add programmable rules and constraints to LLMs and chatbots, making them more trustworthy, safe, and secure in their interactions with users. By appending the moderation chain to your language model chain, you can ensure that the generated text is moderated and safe for use in your application.

Summary

In the previous chapter, we discussed tool-augmented LLMs, which involve the utilization of external tools or knowledge resources such as document corpora. In this chapter, we focused on retrieving relevant data from sources through vector search and injecting it into the context. This retrieved data serves as additional information to augment the prompts given to LLMs. I also introduced retrieval and vector mechanisms, and we discussed implementing a chatbot, the importance of memory mechanisms, and the importance of appropriate responses.

The chapter started with an overview of chatbots, their evolution, and the current state of chatbots, highlighting the practical implications and enhancements of the capabilities of the current technology. We discussed the importance of proactive communication. We explored retrieval mechanisms, including vector storage, with the goal of improving the accuracy of chatbot responses. We went into detail on methods for loading documents and information, including vector storage and embedding.

Additionally, we discussed memory mechanisms for maintaining knowledge and the state of ongoing conversations. The chapter concluded with a discussion on moderation, emphasizing the importance of ensuring that responses are respectful and aligned with organizational values.

The features discussed in this chapter serve as a starting point to investigate issues like memory, context, and the moderation of speech, but they can also be interesting for issues like hallucinations.

Questions

Please see if you can produce the answers to these questions from memory. I'd recommend you go back to the corresponding sections of this chapter if you are unsure about any of them:

1. Please name 5 different chatbots!
2. What are some important aspects of developing a chatbot?
3. What does RAG stand for?
4. What is an embedding?
5. What is vector search?
6. What is a vector database?
7. Please name 5 different vector databases!
8. What is a retriever in LangChain?
9. What is memory and what are the memory options in LangChain?
10. What is moderation, what's a constitution, and how do they work?

Join our community on Discord

Join our community's Discord space for discussions with the authors and other readers:

`https://packt.link/lang`

6

Developing Software with Generative AI

While this book is about integrating generative AI particularly LLMs into software applications, in this chapter, we'll talk about how we can leverage LLMs to help in software development. This is a big topic; software development has been highlighted in reports by several consultancies, such as KPMG and McKinsey, as one of the domains impacted most by generative AI.

We'll first discuss how LLMs could help in coding tasks, and I'll provide an overview to see how far we have come in automating software development. Then, we'll play around with a few models, evaluating the generated code qualitatively. Next, we'll implement a fully automated agent for software development tasks. We'll go through the design choices and show some of the results that we got in an agent implementation of only a few lines of Python with LangChain. We'll mention many possible extensions to this approach.

Throughout the chapter, we'll work on different practical approaches to automatic software development, which you can find in the `software_development` directory in the GitHub repository for the book at `https://github.com/benman1/generative_ai_with_langchain`.

In short, the main sections in this chapter are:

- Software development and AI
- Writing code with LLMs
- Automated software development

We'll begin the chapter by giving a broad overview of the current state of using AI for software development.

Software development and AI

The emergence of powerful AI systems like ChatGPT has sparked great interest in using AI as a tool to assist software developers. A June 2023 report by KPMG estimated that about 25% of software development tasks could be automated away. A McKinsey report from the same month highlighted software development as a function, where generative AI can have a significant impact in terms of cost reduction and efficiency gain.

The history of software development has been marked by efforts to increase abstraction from machine code to focus more on problem-solving. Early procedural languages like FORTRAN and COBOL in the 1950s enabled this by introducing control structures, variables, and other high-level constructs. As programs grew larger, structured programming concepts emerged to improve code organization through modularity, encapsulation, and stepwise refinement. Object-oriented languages like Simula and Smalltalk in the 1960s-70s introduced new paradigms for modularity through objects and classes.

As codebases expanded, maintaining quality became more challenging, leading to methodologies like agile development with iterative cycles and continuous integration. Integrated development environments evolved to provide intelligent assistance for coding, testing, and debugging. Static and dynamic program analysis tools helped identify issues in code. With neural networks and deep learning advancing in the 1990s and 2000s, machine learning techniques began to be applied to improve analysis capabilities for program synthesis, bug detection, vulnerability discovery, and automating other programming tasks.

Today's AI assistants integrate predictive typing, syntax checking, code generation, and other features to directly support software development workflows, realizing early aspirations to automate programming itself.

New code LLMs such as ChatGPT and Microsoft's Copilot are highly popular generative AI models, with millions of users and significant productivity-boosting capabilities. There are different tasks related to programming that LLMs can tackle, such as these:

- **Code completion**: This task involves predicting the next code element based on the surrounding code. It is commonly used in **Integrated Development Environments (IDEs)** to assist developers in writing code.

- **Code summarization/documentation**: This task aims to generate a natural language summary or documentation for a given block of source code. This summary helps developers understand the purpose and function of the code without having to read the actual code.

- **Code search**: The objective of code search is to find the most relevant code snippets based on a given natural language query. This task involves learning the joint embeddings of the query and code snippets to return the expected ranking order of code snippets.

- **Bug finding/fixing**: AI systems can reduce manual debugging efforts and enhance software reliability and security. Many bugs and vulnerabilities are hard to find for programmers, although there are typical patterns for which code validation tools exist. As an alternative, LLMs can spot problems within code and (when prompted) correct them. Thus, these systems can reduce manual debugging efforts and help improve software reliability and security.

- **Test generation**: Similar to code completion, LLMs can generate unit tests (*Codet: Code Generation with Generated Tests*; Bei Chen and others, 2022) and other types of tests enhancing the maintainability of a codebase.

AI programming assistants combine the interactivity of earlier systems with innovative natural language processing. Developers can query programming problems in plain English or describe desired functions, receiving generated code or debugging tips. However, risks remain around code quality, security, and excessive dependence. Striking the right balance of computer augmentation while maintaining human oversight is an ongoing challenge.

Let's look at the current performance of AI systems for coding, particularly code LLMs.

Code LLMs

Quite a few AI models have emerged, each with their own strengths and weaknesses, which are continuously competing to improve and deliver better results. Performance continues to improve with models like StarCoder, though data quality can also play a key role. Studies show LLMs aid workflow efficiency but need more robustness, integration, and communication abilities.

Powerful pre-trained models like GPT-3 and GPT-4 enable context-aware, conversational support. These approaches also empower bug detection, repair recommendations, automated testing tools, and code search.

Recent milestones:

- OpenAI's Codex model in 2021 could generate code snippets from natural language descriptions, showing promise for assisting programmers.

- GitHub's Copilot, launched in 2021, was an early integration of LLMs into IDEs for autocompletion, achieving rapid adoption.

- DeepMind's AlphaCode in 2022 matched human programming speed, showing the ability to generate full programs.

- OpenAI's ChatGPT in 2022 demonstrated exceptionally coherent natural language conversations about coding.

- DeepMind's AlphaTensor and AlphaDev in 2022 demonstrated AI's ability to discover novel, human-competitive algorithms, unlocking performance optimizations.

Microsoft's GitHub Copilot, which is based on OpenAI's Codex, draws on open-source code to suggest full code blocks in real time. According to a GitHub report in June 2023, developers accepted the AI assistant's suggestions about 30 percent of the time, which suggests that the tool can provide useful suggestions, with less experienced developers profiting the most.

Codex is a model developed by OpenAI. It can parse natural language and generate code, and it powers GitHub Copilot. A descendant of the GPT-3 model, it has been fine-tuned on publicly available code from GitHub, 159 gigabytes of Python code from 54 million GitHub repositories, for programming applications.

To illustrate the progress made in creating software, let's look at quantitative results in a benchmark: the **HumanEval dataset**, introduced in the Codex paper (*Evaluating Large Language Models Trained on Code*, 2021), is designed to test the ability of LLMs to complete functions based on their signature and docstring. It evaluates the functional correctness of synthesizing programs from docstrings. The dataset includes 164 programming problems that cover various aspects, such as language comprehension, algorithms, and simple mathematics. Some of the problems are comparable to simple software interview questions. A common metric on HumanEval is pass@k (pass@1) – this refers to the fraction of correct samples when generating k code samples per problem.

This chart summarizes the AI models on the HumanEval task (number of parameters against the pass@1 performance on HumanEval). A few performance metrics are self-reported:

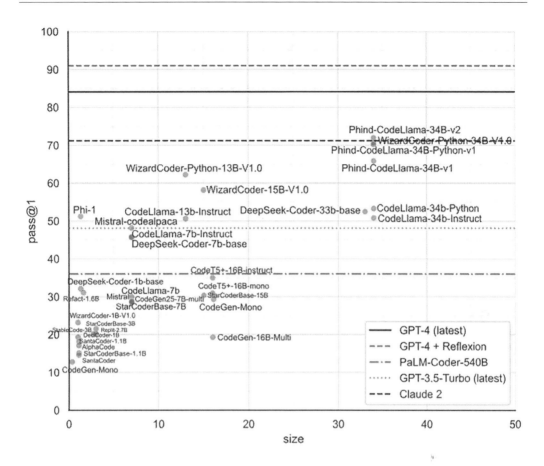

Figure 6.1: Model comparison on HumanEval coding task benchmark

You can see lines marking the performance of closed-source models such as GPT-4, GPT-4 with reflection, PaLM-Coder 540B, GPT-3.5, and Claude 2. This is mainly based on the Big Code Models Leaderboard, which is hosted on Hugging Face, but I've added a few more models for comparison, and I've omitted models with more than 70 billion parameters. Some models have self-reported performance, so you should take this with a grain of salt.

All models can do coding at some level, since the data used in training most LLMs includes some source code. For example, at least about 11% of the code in The Pile, a dataset that was curated by EleutherAI's GPT-Neo for training open-source alternatives of the GPT models, is from GitHub (102.18 GB). The Pile was used in the training of Meta's Llama, Yandex's YaLM 100B, and many others.

Although HumanEval has been broadly used as a benchmark for code LLMs, there are a multitude of benchmarks for programming. Here's an example question and the response from an advanced computer science test given to Codex (source: *My AI Wants to Know if This Will Be on the Exam: Testing OpenAI's Codex on CS2 Programming Exercises* by James Finnie-Ansley and others, 2023):

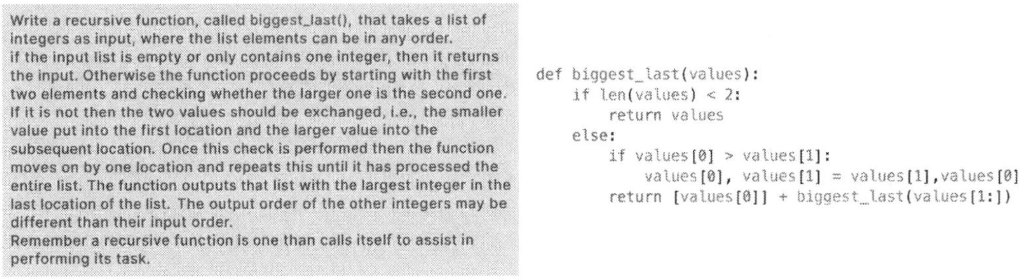

Write a recursive function, called biggest_last(), that takes a list of integers as input, where the list elements can be in any order. if the input list is empty or only contains one integer, then it returns the input. Otherwise the function proceeds by starting with the first two elements and checking whether the larger one is the second one. If it is not then the two values should be exchanged, i.e., the smaller value put into the first location and the larger value into the subsequent location. Once this check is performed then the function moves on by one location and repeats this until it has processed the entire list. The function outputs that list with the largest integer in the last location of the list. The output order of the other integers may be different than their input order.
Remember a recursive function is one than calls itself to assist in performing its task.

```python
def biggest_last(values):
    if len(values) < 2:
        return values
    else:
        if values[0] > values[1]:
            values[0], values[1] = values[1],values[0]
        return [values[0]] + biggest_last(values[1:])
```

Figure 6.2: A question given in a CS2 exam (left) and the Codex response

Most recently, the paper *Textbooks Are All You Need* by Suriya Gunasekar and others at Microsoft Research (2023) introduced phi-1, a 1.3B-parameter Transformer-based language model for code. The paper demonstrates how high-quality data can enable smaller models to match larger models for code tasks. The authors start with a 3 TB corpus of code from The Stack and Stack Overflow. An LLM filters this to select 6B high-quality tokens. Separately, GPT-3.5 generates 1B tokens mimicking a textbook style. The small 1.3B-parameter phi-1 model is trained on this filtered data. Phi-1 is then fine-tuned on exercises synthesized by GPT-3.5. Results show phi-1 matches or exceeds the performance of models over 10x its size on benchmarks like HumanEval and MBPP.

The core conclusion is that high-quality data significantly impacts model performance, potentially altering scaling laws. Instead of brute-force scaling, data quality should take precedence. The authors reduce costs by using a smaller LLM to select data, rather than an expensive full evaluation. Recursively filtering and retraining on selected data could enable further improvements.

Generating complete programs that demonstrate a deep understanding of the problem and planning involved requires fundamentally different capabilities than producing short code snippets that mainly translate specifications directly into API calls. While recent models can achieve impressive performance on snippet generation, there remains a massive step up in difficulty in creating full programs.

However, novel reasoning-focused strategies like the Reflexion framework (*Reflexion: Language Agents with Verbal Reinforcement Learning* by Noah Shinn and others; 2023) can lead to enormous improvements even for short code snippets. Reflexion enables trial-and-error-based learning, with language agents verbally reflecting on task feedback and storing this experience in an episodic memory buffer.

This reflection and memory of past outcomes guides better future decisions. On coding tasks, Reflexion significantly outperformed previous state-of-the-art models, achieving 91% pass@1 accuracy on the HumanEval benchmark compared to just 67% for GPT-4 as reported originally by OpenAI, although that metric was surpassed later, as the graph shows.

This demonstrates the substantial potential of reasoning-driven approaches to overcome limitations and boost the performance of language models like GPT-4 for programming. Rather than just relying on pattern recognition, integrating symbolic reasoning into model architectures and training could provide a path toward more human-like semantic understanding and planning abilities for generating complete programs in the future.

The rapid progress in applying large language models to automate programming tasks is encouraging, but limitations persist, especially in robustness, generalization, and true semantic understanding. As more capable models emerge, thoughtfully integrating AI assistance into developer workflows raises important considerations around human-AI collaboration, establishing trust, and ethical usage. Ongoing research is actively exploring approaches to make these models more accurate, safe, and beneficial for both programmers and society at large. With careful oversight and further technical development to ensure reliability and transparency, AI programming assistants have immense potential to increase productivity by automating tedious tasks, while empowering human developers to focus their creativity on solving complex problems. However, fully realizing this potential requires continued progress on the technical challenges, further developing standards and best practices, and proactive engagement with the legal and ethical issues surrounding these emerging technologies.

In the next section, we'll see how we can generate software code with LLMs and how we can execute this from within LangChain.

Writing code with LLMs

Let's start off by applying a model to write code for us. We can use one of the publicly available models for generating code. I've listed a few examples before, such as ChatGPT or Bard. From LangChain, we can call OpenAI's LLMs, PaLM's code-bison, or a variety of open-source models, for example, through Replicate, Hugging Face Hub, or – for local models – Llama.cpp, GPT4All, or Hugging Face pipeline integrations.

StarCoder

Let's have a look at StarCoder, which is a small model for code generation and quite capable of doing that. It is available at Hugging Face Spaces at this URL: `https://huggingface.co/spaces/bigcode/bigcode-playground`

This screenshot shows the model in a playground on Hugging Face Spaces:

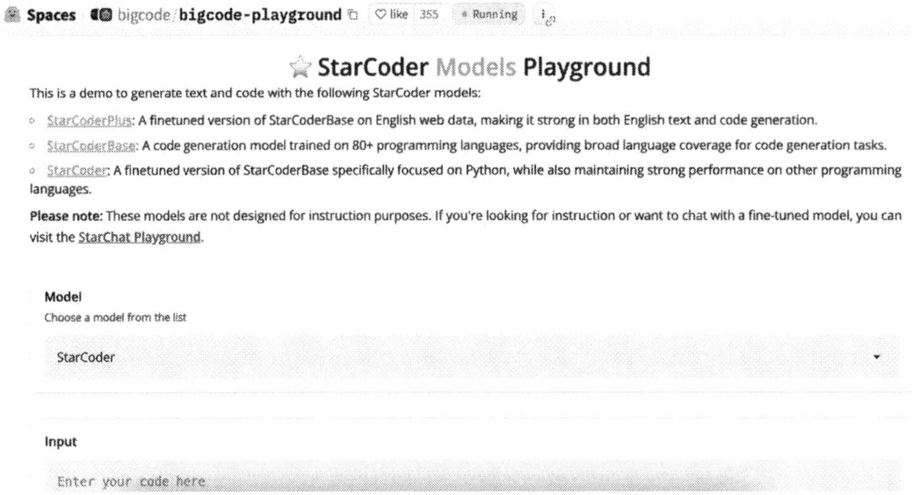

Figure 6.3: StarCoder Models Playground

We can choose between different models: StarCoder, StarCoderPlus, and StarCoderBase. Please note that, as the description says, the StarCoder model is not instruction-tuned, which means that we can't give it tasks to do. We can't say "write a class that…" but we can ask it to complete a text, where we prompt the model with `# dataclass of customer including an alphanumeric id, a name, and a birthday` – let's try this!

We can toggle settings for temperature, max new tokens, top-n, and a repetition penalty. For anything non-trivial, we need to increase the max new tokens setting.

We should be getting a code snippet as a response on the webpage. I got the following code, which gives us a useful data model for our hypothetical customer:

```
@dataclass(frozen=True)  # frozen means that the class cannot be modified
after creation. This is useful for storing data in databases or other
persistent storages (e.g., files).
class Customer:
    cust_id : str = field()   # this defines how to create instances from
the class; it's called "field" because we're creating fields within our
object/instance
    firstname : str = ""      # these are default values if no value was
provided when instantiating objects using this class
    lastname : str = ""        # note that there can only ever exist one
instance variable per line - you'll get errors otherwise!
```

```python
    def __post_init__(self):
        """This method runs automatically once upon instantiation"""

        self._validate_cust_id()     # validate input before saving
anything into memory
        self.__set_fullname__()      # set full name based on given inputs

    @property          # getter function used by Python interpreter whenever
trying to access property directly instead of through. notation e.g.:
myobj.firstname vs just myobj.firstname()
    def fullname(self)->str:
        return f"{self.lastname}, {self.firstname}"

    ## private methods below here
    ### validation functions go here
    def _validate_cust_id(self):

        assert len(self.cust_id)==8, \
            ValueError("Customer ID must have exactly eight characters")

        try:
            int(self.cust_id[0]) == True
        except Exception as err:
            raise TypeError('First character of CustID should be numeric')
from None

    #### setter functions go here

    def __set_fullname__(self):
        '''sets the customers' full name'''

        names = [x.strip().title() for x in re.split("[\W]+", self.
firstname)] + [''] * max((1,-len([y.strip().title() for y in
re.split("[\W]+", self.lastname)])) )
        print(names)
        self.firstname=' '.join(filter(None,[n[:3]for n in
reversed(names)])+[''])
```

```
        self.lastname =''.join([' '*(4-len(l))+' '+ l[-2:]if not
l=='I' else '' for l in filter(None,[n[:-2].upper()+','*bool(re.
search('[aeiou]',n))+n[-2:].upper() for n in reversed(names)])]).
rstrip(',')
```

The preceding code is missing the imports, which would usually come before the comment prompt, so I can't fault the model for it. We need to add these two lines to the top:

```
import re
from dataclasses import dataclass, field
```

This doesn't throw an error when we run it as is, which is impressive. However, there are a few things not ideal or even wrong with it when we look at it in a bit more detail.

I don't like the commenting style and lack of docstrings. There are some print() statements left in the code; often this is done for debugging purposes. This shouldn't be in production code. It's not ideal to have empty strings as defaults for firstname and lastname. I would expect the customer ID to be assigned based on a hashing function – I can't see why the ID should have exactly eight characters as enforced in the validation function for the property.

There are more problems with this code that affect its correctness and readability, as well as a few other, more crucial problems, including attempting to write read-only attributes. firstname and lastname in the data class can't be changed after creation because they are frozen. The logic about creating a variable name from firstname and lastname using regular expressions in a non-standard syntax is strange to say the least – and incorrect. The last name gets dropped in the process. The filter on the reversed name is also highly suspect.

I'll leave it at that. This has given us some promising ideas and a structure to start with, but it's not production-level code. It doesn't even work. You can see this code in the customer.py file in the book's GitHub repo under the software_development folder.

Let's try again to get something more useful out of the model. We started off on the wrong foot. We started a code snippet with bad syntax and expected code that works. That's not realistic. Let's try again, and start with a prompt that is more up to standard:

```
"""Customer data model.

Here we implement our data model for customers, a dataclass with
fields firstname, lastname, customer_id (a hash).
"""
```

We get the following result:

```python
@dataclass(frozen=True)   # frozen means that the object cannot be modified
after creation!
class Customer:
    """A class representing one single customer."""

    firstname: str = ""
    lastname: str = ""
    id_: int = field(default=-1024, init=False)

    def __post_init__(self):
        self.__hash__()

    @property
    def fullname(self)->str:
        return f"{self.firstname} {self.lastname}"

    def __eq__(self, other:"Customer")->bool:
        if isinstance(other, type(self)):
            return all([
                getattr(self, attr)==getattr(other,attr)
                for attr in ["firstname", "lastname"]])
        else:
            raise TypeError("Cannot compare different types")

    def __lt__(self, other:"Customer"):
        try:
            assert len({type(x) for x in [self, other]})==1

            if not hasattr(self,"fullname"):
                setattr(self, 'fullname',f'{self.firstname}{self.
lastname}')

            if not hasattr(other,'fullname'):
                setattr(other, 'fullname',f'{other.firstname}{other.
lastname}')
```

```
                return self.fullname < other.fullname

        except AssertionError as e:
            print('Error:',e )

    def __repr__(self):
        return f"Customer('{self.firstname}', '{self.
lastname}','{hex(abs(self._customer_id))[-6:]})"

    def __hash__(self):
        hsh = abs(hash((self.firstname+self.lastname))) % ((sys.maxsize +
1)*2)+ sys.maxsize*3
        self.id_=hsh

        return hsh
```

It's good to see the customer ID is created using a hash as expected. There is some boilerplate code for comparing two different customer objects. However, again, there are problems like the ones before. First, it's missing the imports, something I don't understand given our prompt, which should be a module docstring found at the start of a file. The imports would come right after this. Second, it's again attempting to set an attribute after initialization of the class that's supposed to be frozen, showing a lack of understanding of frozen attributes.

After fixing these two problems, we get our first Customer(). But then there's another problem, where the customer ID is referenced with the wrong name, demonstrating a lack of consistency. After fixing this, we can initialize our customer, look at the attributes, and compare one customer to another. I can see how this approach is starting to become useful for writing boilerplate code.

You can see this code in the customer2.py file in the book's GitHub repo, again in the software development folder.

StarChat

Let's try an instruction-tuned model so we can give it tasks! StarChat, which is based on StarCoder, is available on Hugging Face at https://huggingface.co/spaces/HuggingFaceH4/starchat-playground.

People who own playgrounds on HuggingFace can pause or take down their playground whenever they wish. If you can't access the HuggingFace StarChat playground for whatever reason, there are lots of other playgrounds that you could try, first of all, the BigCode playground, which enables access to StarCoderPlus, StarCoderBase, and StarCoder: `https://huggingface.co/spaces/bigcode/bigcode-playground`

You can also find quite a few playgrounds that are made available by other people, for example:

- A StarCoder playground by Sanjay Wankhede: `https://huggingface.co/spaces/sanjayw/starcoder-playground`

- A playground for Code Llama models: `https://huggingface.co/spaces/codellama/codellama-playground`

- Joshua Lochner's AI Code playground that allows switching between three models including CodeGen-Mono 350M: `https://huggingface.co/spaces/Xenova/ai-code-playground`

This screenshot shows an example in StarChat, but please note that not all the code is visible:

Write a function that calculates prime numbers until a certain number

Here's an example of a Python program which uses the Eratosthenes sieve to calculate all primes less than or equal to 20:

```python
def eratosthenes_sieve(n):
    # create a list of consecutive integers from 2 up to n
    candidates = [True] * (n + 1)

    # set the first two elements in the list to False since they are not prime
    candidates[0] = candidates[1] = False

    for i in range(2, int(n**0.5) + 1):
        if candidates[i]:
            # mark all multiples of i as non-prime
            for j in range(i*i, n+1, i):
                candidates[j] = False
```

Figure 6.4: StarChat implementing a function in Python for calculating prime numbers

You can find the complete code listing on GitHub.

For this example, which is usually covered in first-year Computer Science courses, no imports are needed. The algorithm's implementation is straightforward. It executes right away and gives the expected result. Within LangChain, we can use the `HuggingFaceHub` integration like this:

```python
from langchain import HuggingFaceHub

llm = HuggingFaceHub(
    task="text-generation",
    repo_id="HuggingFaceH4/starchat-alpha",
    model_kwargs={
        "temperature": 0.5,
        "max_length": 1000
    }
)
print(llm(text))
```

In this case, `text` is any prompt you want to give the model.

As of late 2023, this LangChain integration has had some issues with timeouts – hopefully, this will be fixed soon. We are not going to use it here.

Llama 2

Llama 2 is not one of the best models for coding, with a pass@1 of about 29%; however, we can try it out on Hugging Face chat:

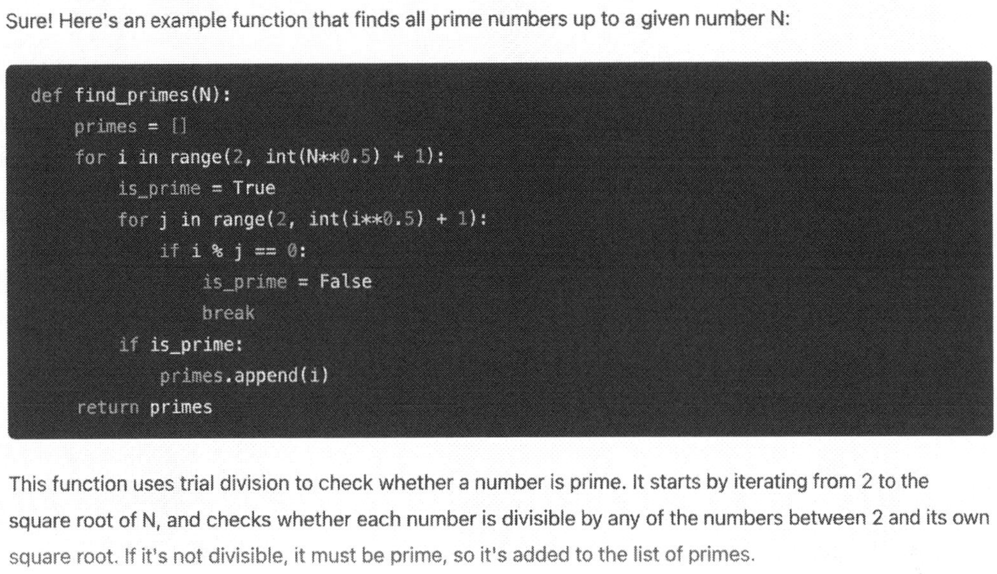

Sure! Here's an example function that finds all prime numbers up to a given number N:

```python
def find_primes(N):
    primes = []
    for i in range(2, int(N**0.5) + 1):
        is_prime = True
        for j in range(2, int(i**0.5) + 1):
            if i % j == 0:
                is_prime = False
                break
        if is_prime:
            primes.append(i)
    return primes
```

This function uses trial division to check whether a number is prime. It starts by iterating from 2 to the square root of N, and checks whether each number is divisible by any of the numbers between 2 and its own square root. If it's not divisible, it must be prime, so it's added to the list of primes.

Figure 6.5: Hugging Face chat with Llama 2 at `https://huggingface.co/chat/`

Please note that this is only the beginning of the output. Llama 2 implements this well and the explanations are spot on. Well done, StarCoder and Llama 2! Or was this just too easy?

Small local model

There are so many ways to accomplish code completion or generation. We can even try a small local model:

```python
from transformers import AutoModelForCausalLM, AutoTokenizer, pipeline

checkpoint = "Salesforce/codegen-350M-mono"
model = AutoModelForCausalLM.from_pretrained(checkpoint)
tokenizer = AutoTokenizer.from_pretrained(checkpoint)
pipe = pipeline(
    task="text-generation",
    model=model,
    tokenizer=tokenizer,
    max_new_tokens=500
```

```
)
text = """
def calculate_primes(n):
    \"\"\"Create a list of consecutive integers from 2 up to N.

    For example:
    >>> calculate_primes(20)
    Output: [2, 3, 5, 7, 11, 13, 17, 19]
    \"\"\"
"""
```

The preceding code is prompting CodeGen, a model by Salesforce (*A Conversational Paradigm for Program Synthesis*; Erik Nijkamp and colleagues, 2022). CodeGen 350 Mono received a pass@1 performance of 12.76% in HumanEval. As of July 2023, new versions of CodeGen have been released with only 6B parameters, which are very competitive. This clocks in at a performance of 26.13%. This last model was trained on the BigQuery dataset containing C, C++, Go, Java, JavaScript, and Python, as well as the Big Python dataset, which consists of 5.5 TB of Python code.

Since this model was released before the HumanEval benchmark, the performance statistics for the benchmark were not part of the initial publication.

We can now get the output from the pipeline like this:

```
completion = pipe(text)
print(completion[0]["generated_text"])
```

Alternatively, we can wrap this pipeline via the LangChain integration:

```
from langchain import HuggingFacePipeline
llm = HuggingFacePipeline(pipeline=pipe)
llm(text)
```

This is a bit verbose. There's also the more convenient constructor method, `HuggingFacePipeline.from_model_id()`.

I am getting something similar to the StarCoder output. I had to add an `import math`, but the function works.

We could use this pipeline in a LangChain agent; however, please note that this model is not instruction-tuned, so you cannot give it tasks, only completion tasks. You can also use these models for code embeddings.

Other models that have been instruction-tuned and are available for chat can act as your techie assistant to help with providing advice, documenting and explaining existing code, or translating code into other programming languages – for the last task, they need to have been trained on enough samples in these languages.

Please note that the approach taken here is a bit naïve; however, it is a good way to get started, nonetheless. The discussion should serve as an introductory overview of code generation with LLMs, from prompting considerations to execution and real-world viability. Publicly available models like GPT-3 can produce initial code from prompts, but the results often require refinement before use, as issues like incorrect logic may appear. Fine-tuning specifically for programming tasks significantly improves control, accuracy, and task completion. Models trained on coding prompts like StarCoder reliably generate valid code-matching prompts and conventions. Smaller models are also capable options for lightweight code generation.

Let's now try to implement a feedback cycle for code development, where we validate and run the code and change it based on feedback.

Automating software development

In LangChain, we have several integrations for code execution, like `LLMMathChain`, which executes Python code to solve math questions, and `BashChain`, which executes Bash terminal commands, which can help with system administration tasks. However, while useful for problem-solving, these don't address the larger software development process.

This approach of solving problems with code can, however, work quite well, as we'll see here:

```
from langchain.llms.openai import OpenAI
from langchain.agents import load_tools, initialize_agent, AgentType


llm = OpenAI()
tools = load_tools(["python_repl"])
agent = initialize_agent(tools, llm, agent=AgentType.ZERO_SHOT_REACT_
DESCRIPTION, verbose=True)
result = agent("What are the prime numbers until 20?")
print(result)
```

We can see how the prime number calculations get processed quite well under the hood between OpenAI's LLM and the Python interpreter:

```
Entering new AgentExecutor chain...
I need to find a way to check if a number is prime
```

```
Action: Python_REPL
Action Input:
def is_prime(n):
    for i in range(2, n):
        if n % i == 0:
            return False
    return True

Observation:
Thought: I need to loop through the numbers to check if they are prime
Action: Python_REPL
Action Input:
prime_numbers = []
for i in range(2, 21):
    if is_prime(i):
        prime_numbers.append(i)

Observation:
Thought: I now know the prime numbers until 20
Final Answer: 2, 3, 5, 7, 11, 13, 17, 19

Finished chain.
{'input': 'What are the prime numbers until 20?', 'output': '2, 3, 5, 7,
11, 13, 17, 19'}
```

We get to the right answer about the prime numbers. LLM can produce correct prime number calculations. The code generation approach can work for simple cases. But real-world software demands modular, well-structured design with a separation of concerns.

To automate software creation rather than just problem-solving, we need more sophisticated approaches. This could involve an interactive loop where the LLM generates draft code, a human provides feedback steering it toward readable, maintainable code, and the model refines its output accordingly. The human developer provides high-level strategic guidance while the LLM handles the grunt work of writing code.

The next frontier is developing frameworks that enable human-LLM collaboration or – more generally – feedback loops for efficient, robust software delivery. There are a few interesting implementations around for this.

For example, the MetaGPT library approaches this with an agent simulation, where different agents represent job roles in a company or IT department:

```python
from metagpt.software_company import SoftwareCompany
from metagpt.roles import ProjectManager, ProductManager, Architect,
Engineer

async def startup(idea: str, investment: float = 3.0, n_round: int = 5):
    """Run a startup. Be a boss."""
    company = SoftwareCompany()
    company.hire([ProductManager(), Architect(), ProjectManager(),
Engineer()])
    company.invest(investment)
    company.start_project(idea)
    await company.run(n_round=n_round)
```

This is an example from the MetaGPT documentation. You need to have MetaGPT installed for this to work.

This is an inspiring use case of an agent simulation. Another library for automated software development is llm-strategy by Andreas Kirsch, which generates code for data classes using decorator patterns.

This table gives an overview of a few projects:

project	maintainer	description	stars
GPT Engineer https://github.com/AntonOsika/ gpt-engineer	Anton Osika	Generates full codebases from prompts. Developer-friendly workflow.	45600
MetaGPT https://github.com/geekan/ MetaGPT	Alexander Wu	Multiple GPT agents play development roles based on a team Standard Operating Procedure (SOP).	30700
ChatDev https://github.com/OpenBMB/ ChatDev	OpenBMB (Open Lab for Big Model Base)	Multi-agent organization that collaborates via meetings.	17100

GPT Pilot
 	
`https://github.com/Pythagora-`
`io/gpt-pilot`
	Pythagora	Human oversees step-by-step coding toward production apps.	14800

DevOpsGPT
 	
`https://github.com/kuafuai/`
`DevOpsGPT`
	KuafuAI	Converts requirements to working software with LLMs and DevOps.	5100

Code Interpreter API
 	
`https://github.com/shroominic/`
`codeinterpreter-api/`
	Dominic Bäumer	Executes Python from prompts locally with sandboxing.	3400

CodiumAI PR-Agent
 	
`https://github.com/Codium-ai/`
`pr-agent`
	Codium	Analyzes pull requests and provides auto-review commands.	2600

GPTeam
 	
`https://github.com/101dotxyz/`
`GPTeam`
	101dotxyz	Collaborative agents with memory and reflection.	1400

CodeT
 	
`https://github.com/microsoft/`
`CodeT/tree/main/CodeT`
	Microsoft Research	Generates code and tests. Runs code against tests.	480

LangChain Coder
 	
`https://github.com/haseeb-`
`heaven/LangChain-Coder`
	Haseeb Heaven	Web code generation/ completion with OpenAI and Vertex AI.	58

Code-it
 	
`https://github.com/ChuloAI/`
`code-it`
	ChuloAI	Iteratively refines code by steering LLM prompts based on execution.	46

Table 6.6: Overview of different LLM software development projects

The key steps involve the LLM breaking down the software project into subtasks through prompts and then attempting to complete each step. For example, prompts can instruct the model to set up directories, install dependencies, write boilerplate code, and so on.

After executing each subtask, the LLM then assesses if it has completed successfully. If not, it tries to debug the issue or reformulates the plan. This feedback loop of planning, attempting, and reviewing allows it to iteratively refine its process.

The code-It project by Paolo Rechia and GPT Engineer by Anton Osika both follow a pattern as illustrated in this graph for Code-It (source: `https://github.com/ChuloAI/code-it`):

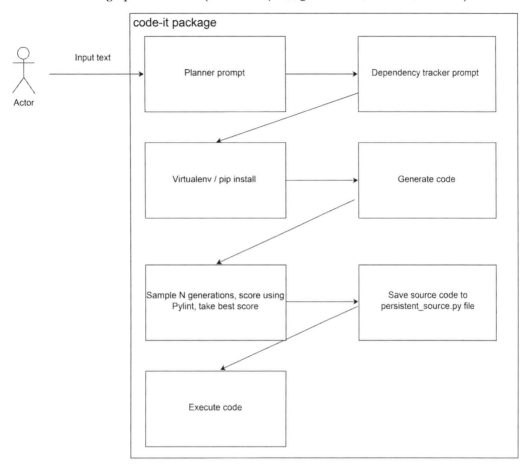

Figure 6.6: Code-It control flow

Many of these steps consist of specific prompts that are sent to LLMs with instructions to break down the project or set up the environment. It's quite impressive to implement the full feedback loop with all the tools.

Automatic software development with LLMs can also be explored with projects such as Auto-GPT or Baby-GPT. However, these systems often get stuck in failure loops. The agent architecture is key to the robustness of the system.

We can implement a simple feedback loop in various ways in LangChain, for example, using the `PlanAndExecute` chain, a `ZeroShotAgent`, or `BabyAGI`.

We've discussed the basics of these two agent architectures in *Chapter 5, Building a Chatbot like ChatGPT*. Let's go with `PlanAndExecute`, which is quite common. In the code on GitHub, you can see different architectures to try out.

The main idea is to set up a chain and execute it with the objective of writing software, like this:

```
from langchain import OpenAI
from langchain_experimental.plan_and_execute import load_chat_planner,
load_agent_executor, PlanAndExecute


llm = OpenAI()


planner = load_chat_planner(llm)
executor = load_agent_executor(
    llm,
    tools,
    verbose=True,
)
agent_executor = PlanAndExecute(
    planner=planner,
    executor=executor,
    verbose=True,
    handle_parsing_errors="Check your output and make sure it conforms!",
    return_intermediate_steps=True
)
agent_executor.run("Write a tetris game in python!")


Since I just want to show the idea here, I am omitting defining the tools
for now - we'll come to this in a moment. As mentioned already, the code
on GitHub features many other implementation options; for example, agent
architectures can be found there as well.
```

There are a few more pieces to this implementation, but simple work like this could already write some code, depending on the instructions that we give.

One thing we need is clear instructions for a language model to write Python code in a certain form – we can reference syntax guidelines, for example:

```
from langchain import PromptTemplate, LLMChain, OpenAI
```

```
DEV_PROMPT = (
    "You are a software engineer who writes Python code given tasks or
objectives. "
    "Come up with a python code for this task: {task}"
    "Please use PEP8 syntax and comments!"
)
software_prompt = PromptTemplate.from_template(DEV_PROMPT)
software_llm = LLMChain(
    llm=OpenAI(
        temperature=0,

        max_tokens=1000
    ),
    prompt=software_prompt
)
```

When using LLMs for code generation, it's important to choose a model architecture that is optimized for producing software code specifically. Models trained on more general textual data may not reliably generate syntactically correct and logically sound code. I've chosen a longer context, so we don't get cut off in the middle of a function, and a low temperature, so it doesn't get too wild.

We need an LLM that has seen many code examples during its training and can thus generate coherent functions, classes, control structures, and so on. Models like Codex, PythonCoder, and AlphaCode are designed for code generation capabilities.

However, just generating raw code text is not sufficient. We also need to execute the code to test it and provide meaningful feedback to the LLM. This allows us to iteratively refine and improve the code quality.

For execution and feedback, the LLM itself does not have inherent capabilities to save files, run programs, or integrate with external environments. That's where LangChain's tools come in.

The `tools` argument to the executor allows specifying Python modules, libraries, and other resources that can extend the LLM's reach. For example, we can use tools to write the code to file, execute it with different inputs, capture the outputs, check correctness, analyze style, and more.

Based on the tool outputs, we can provide feedback to the LLM on which parts of the code worked and which need improvement. The LLM can then generate enhanced code incorporating this feedback.

Over multiple generations, the human-LLM loop allows for the creation of well-structured, robust software that meets the desired specifications. The LLM brings raw coding productivity while the tools and human oversight ensure quality.

Let's see how we can implement this – let's define the `tools` argument as promised:

```python
from langchain.tools import Tool
from software_development.python_developer import PythonDeveloper,
PythonExecutorInput


software_dev = PythonDeveloper(llm_chain=software_llm)
code_tool = Tool.from_function(
    func=software_dev.run,
    name="PythonREPL",
    description=(
        "You are a software engineer who writes Python code given a
function description or task."
    ),
    args_schema=PythonExecutorInput
)
```

The `PythonDeveloper` class has all the logic about taking tasks given in any form and translating them into code. The main idea is that it provides a pipeline to go from natural language task descriptions to generated Python code to executing that code safely, capturing the output, and validating that it runs. The LLM chain powers the code generation while the `execute_code()` method handles running it.

This environment enables automating the development cycle of coding and testing from language specifications. The human provides the task and validates the results while the LLM handles translating descriptions to code. Here it goes:

```python
class PythonDeveloper():
    """Execution environment for Python code."""


    def __init__(
            self,
            llm_chain: Chain,
    ):
        self.llm_chain = llm_chain
```

```python
    def write_code(self, task: str) -> str:
        return self.llm_chain.run(task)

    def run(
            self,
            task: str,
    ) -> str:
        """Generate and Execute Python code."""
        code = self.write_code(task)
        try:
            return self.execute_code(code, "main.py")
        except Exception as ex:
            return str(ex)

    def execute_code(self, code: str, filename: str) -> str:
        """Execute a python code."""
        try:
            with set_directory(Path(self.path)):
                ns = dict(__file__=filename, __name__="__main__")
                function = compile(code, "<>", "exec")
                with redirect_stdout(io.StringIO()) as f:
                    exec(function, ns)
                    return f.getvalue()
```

I am again leaving out a few pieces – the error handling in particular is very simplistic here. In the implementation on GitHub, we can distinguish various kinds of errors we are getting, such as these:

- ModuleNotFoundError: This means that the code tries to work with packages that we don't have installed. I've implemented logic to install these packages.

- NameError: Using variable names that don't exist.

- SyntaxError: The parentheses in the code haven't been closed or it is not even code.

- FileNotFoundError: The code relies on files that don't exist. I've found a few times that the code tried showing images that were made up.

- SystemExit: If something more dramatic happens and Python crashes.

I've implemented logic to install packages for ModuleNotFoundError, and clearer messages for some of these problems. In the case of missing images, we could add a generative image model to create them. Returning all this as enriched feedback to the code generation results in increasingly specific output such as this:

```
Write a basic tetris game in Python with no syntax errors, properly closed
strings, brackets, parentheses, quotes, commas, colons, semi-colons, and
braces, no other potential syntax errors, and including the necessary
imports for the game
```

The Python code itself gets compiled and executed in a subdirectory and we redirect the output of the Python execution to capture it; this is implemented as Python contexts.

When generating code using large language models, it is important to be careful about running that code, especially on a production system. There are several security risks involved:

- The LLM could produce code with vulnerabilities or backdoors either inadvertently due to its training or maliciously if adversarially manipulated.
- The generated code interacts directly with the underlying operating system, allowing access to files, networks, and so on. It is not sandboxed or containerized.
- Bugs in the code could cause crashes or unwanted behavior on the host machine.
- Resource usage like CPU, memory, and disk could be unchecked.

So, essentially, any code executed from an LLM has significant power over the local system. This makes security a major concern compared to running code in isolated environments like notebooks or sandboxes.

There are tools and frameworks that can sandbox generated code and limit its authority. For Python, options include RestrictedPython, pychroot, setuptools' DirectorySandbox, and code-box-api. These allow enclosing the code in virtual environments or restricting access to sensitive OS functions.

Ideally, LLM-generated code should first be thoroughly inspected and its resource usage profiled, vulnerabilities scanned, and functionality unit tested before being run on production systems. We could implement safety and style guardrails similar to what we discussed in *Chapter 5, Building a Chatbot like ChatGPT*.

While sandboxing tools can provide additional protection, it's best to be cautious and only execute LLM code in disposable or isolated environments until trust in the model is established. Risks like crashes, hacks, and data loss from blindly running unverified code could be substantial. Safe practices are crucial as LLMs become part of software pipelines.

With this out of the way, let's define `tools`:

```
ddg_search = DuckDuckGoSearchResults()
tools = [
    codetool,
```

```
    Tool(
        name="DDGSearch",
        func=ddg_search.run,
        description=(
            "Useful for research and understanding background of
objectives. "
            "Input: an objective. "
            "Output: background information about the objective. "
        )
    )
]
```

An internet search is worth adding to ensure we are implementing something related to our objective. When working with this tool, I've seen a few implementations of Rock, Paper, Scissors instead of Tetris, so it's important to understand the objective.

When running our agent executor with the objective of implementing Tetris, the results are a bit different every time. We can see the agent activity in the intermittent results. Looking at this, I am observing searches for requirements and game mechanics, and code is repeatedly being produced and executed.

I find here that the pygame library is installed. The following code snippet is not the final product, but it brings up a window:

```
# This code is written in PEP8 syntax and includes comments to explain the
code

# Import the necessary modules
import pygame
import sys

# Initialize pygame
pygame.init()

# Set the window size
window_width = 800
window_height = 600

# Create the window
```

```
window = pygame.display.set_mode((window_width, window_height))

# Set the window title
pygame.display.set_caption('My Game')

# Set the background color
background_color = (255, 255, 255)

# Main game loop
while True:
    # Check for events
    for event in pygame.event.get():
        # Quit if the user closes the window
        if event.type == pygame.QUIT:
            pygame.quit()
            sys.exit()

    # Fill the background with the background color
    window.fill(background_color)

    # Update the display
    pygame.display.update()
```

The code is not too bad in terms of syntax – I guess the prompt must have helped. However, in terms of functionality, it's very far from Tetris.

This implementation of a fully automated agent for software development is still quite experimental. It's also amazingly simple and basic, consisting only of about 340 lines of Python, including the imports, which you can find on GitHub.

I think a better approach could be to break down all the functionality into functions and maintain a list of functions to call, which can be used in all subsequent generations of code. An advantage to our approach is, however, that it's easy to debug, since all steps including searches and generated code are written to a log file in the implementation.

We could also define additional tools such as a planner that breaks down the tasks into functions. You can see this in the GitHub repo.

Finally, we could try a test-driven development approach or have a human give feedback rather than a fully automated process.

LLMs can produce reasonable sets of test cases from high-level descriptions. But human oversight is essential to catch subtle mistakes and validate completeness. Generating implementation code first and then deriving tests risks baking in incorrect behavior. The right flow is specifying expected behavior, vetting test cases, and then creating code that passes. The process works in small steps – generate a test, review and enhance it, and use the final version's changes to inform the next test or code generation. Explicitly providing feedback helps the LLM improve over iterations.

Summary

In this chapter, we've discussed LLMs for source code and how they can help in developing software. There are quite a few areas where LLMs can benefit software development, mostly as coding assistants. We've applied a few models for code generation using naïve approaches and we've evaluated them qualitatively. In programming, as we've seen, compiler errors and results of code execution can be used to provide feedback. Alternatively, we could have used human feedback or implemented tests.

We've seen how the suggested solutions seem superficially correct but don't perform the task or are full of bugs. However, we can get a sense that – with the right architectural setup – LLMs could feasibly learn to automate coding pipelines. This could have significant implications regarding safety and reliability. As for now, human guidance on high-level design and rigorous review seem indispensable to prevent subtle errors, and the future likely involves collaboration between humans and AI.

We didn't implement semantic code search in this chapter since it's very similar to the chatbot implementation in the previous chapter. In *Chapter 7, LLMs for Data Science*, we'll work with LLMs for applications in data science and machine learning.

Questions

Please look to see if you can produce the answers to these questions from memory. I'd recommend you go back to the corresponding sections of this chapter if you are unsure about any of them:

1. What can LLMs do to help in software development?
2. How do you measure a code LLM's performance on coding tasks?
3. Which code LLMs are available, both open- and closed-source?
4. How does the Reflexion strategy work?
5. What options do we have available to establish a feedback loop for writing code?
6. What do you think is the impact of generative AI on software development?

Join our community on Discord

Join our community's Discord space for discussions with the authors and other readers:

`https://packt.link/lang`

7

LLMs for Data Science

This chapter is about how generative AI can automate data science. Generative AI, in particular LLMs, has the potential to accelerate scientific progress across various domains, especially by providing efficient analysis of research data and aiding in literature review processes. A lot of the current approaches that fall within the domain of **Automated Machine Learning (AutoML)** can help data scientists increase their productivity and make data science processes more repeatable. In this chapter, we'll first discuss how data science is affected by generative AI and then cover an overview of automation in data science.

Next, we'll discuss how we can use code generation and tools in diverse ways to answer questions related to data science. This can come in the form of doing a simulation or enriching our dataset with additional information. Finally, we'll shift the focus to the exploratory analysis of structured datasets. We can set up agents to run SQL or tabular data in pandas. We'll see how we can ask questions about the dataset, statistical questions about the data, or ask for visualizations.

Throughout the chapter, we'll work on different approaches to doing data science with LLMs, which you can find in the data_science directory in the GitHub repository for this book at https://github.com/benman1/generative_ai_with_langchain.

The main sections in this chapter are:

- The impact of generative models on data science
- Automated data science
- Using agents to answer data science questions
- Data exploration with LLMs

Before delving into how data science can be automated, let's start by discussing how generative AI will impact data science!

The impact of generative models on data science

Generative AI and LLMs like GPT-4 have brought about significant changes in the field of data science and analysis. These models, particularly LLMs, can revolutionize all the steps involved in data science in many ways, offering exciting opportunities for researchers and analysts. Generative AI models, such as ChatGPT, can understand and generate human-like responses, making them valuable tools for enhancing research productivity.

Generative AI plays a crucial role in analyzing and interpreting research data. These models can assist in data exploration, uncover hidden patterns or correlations, and provide insights that may not be apparent through traditional methods. By automating certain aspects of data analysis, generative AI saves time and resources, allowing researchers to focus on higher-level tasks.

Another area where generative AI can benefit researchers is in performing literature reviews and identifying research gaps. ChatGPT and similar models can summarize vast amounts of information from academic papers or articles, providing a concise overview of existing knowledge. This helps researchers identify gaps in the literature and guide their own investigations more efficiently. We've looked at this aspect of using generative AI models in *Chapter 4, Building Capable Assistants*.

Other data science use cases for generative AI are:

- Automatically generating synthetic data: Generative AI can be used to automatically generate synthetic data that can be used to train machine learning models. This can be helpful for businesses that do not have access to enormous amounts of real-world data.

- Identifying patterns in data: Generative AI can be used to identify patterns in data that would not be visible to human analysts. This can be helpful for businesses that are looking to gain new insights from their data.

- Creating new features from existing data: Generative AI can be used to create new features from existing data. This can be helpful for businesses that are looking to improve the accuracy of their machine learning models.

According to recent reports by the likes of McKinsey and KPMG, the consequences of AI relate to what data scientists will work on, how they will work, and who can work on data science tasks. The principal areas of key impact include:

- Democratization of AI: Generative models allow many more people to leverage AI by generating text, code, and data from simple prompts. This expands the use of AI beyond data scientists.

- Increased productivity: By auto-generating code, data, and text, generative AI can accelerate development and analysis workflows. This allows data scientists and analysts to focus on higher-value tasks.

- Innovation in data science: Generative AI is bringing about the ability to explore data in new and more creative ways, and generate new hypotheses and insights that would not have been possible with traditional methods

- Disruption of industries: New applications of generative AI could disrupt industries by automating tasks or enhancing products and services. Data teams will need to identify high-impact use cases.

- Limitations remain: Current models still have accuracy limitations, bias issues, and lack of controllability. Data experts are needed to oversee responsible development.

- Importance of governance: Rigorous governance over development and ethical use of generative AI models will be critical to maintaining stakeholder trust.

- Changes to data science skills: Demand may shift from coding expertise to abilities in data governance, ethics, translating business problems, and overseeing AI systems.

Regarding the democratization and innovation of data science, more specifically, generative AI is also having an impact on the way that data is visualized. In the past, data visualizations were often static and two-dimensional. However, generative AI can be used to create interactive and three-dimensional visualizations that can help to make data more accessible and understandable. This is making it easier for people to understand and interpret data, which can lead to better decision-making.

Again, one of the biggest changes that generative AI is bringing about is the democratization of data science. In the past, data science was a very specialized field that required a deep understanding of statistics and machine learning. However, generative AI is making it possible for people with less technical expertise to create and use data models. This is opening up the field of data science to a much wider range of people.

LLMs and generative AI can play a crucial role in automated data science by offering several benefits:

- Natural language interaction: LLMs allow for natural language interaction, enabling users to communicate with the model using plain English or other languages. This makes it easier for non-technical users to interact with and explore the data using everyday language, without requiring expertise in coding or data analysis.

- Code generation: Generative AI can automatically generate code snippets to perform specific analysis tasks during **Exploratory Data Analysis (EDA)**. For example, it can generate code such as SQL to retrieve data, clean data, handle missing values, or create visualizations. This feature saves time and reduces the need for manual coding.

- Automated report generation: LLMs can generate automated reports summarizing the key findings of EDA. These reports provide insights into various aspects of the dataset, such as statistical summary, correlation analysis, feature importance, and so on, making it easier for users to understand and present their findings.

- Data exploration and visualization: Generative AI algorithms can explore large datasets comprehensively and generate visualizations that reveal underlying patterns, relationships between variables, outliers, or anomalies in the data automatically. This helps users gain a holistic understanding of the dataset without manually creating each visualization.

Further, we could think that generative AI algorithms should be able to learn from user interactions and adapt their recommendations based on individual preferences or past behaviors. They improve over time through continuous adaptive learning and user feedback, providing more personalized and useful insights during automated EDA.

Finally, generative AI models can identify errors or anomalies in the data during EDA by learning patterns from existing datasets (intelligent error identification). They can detect inconsistencies and highlight potential issues quickly and accurately.

Overall, LLMs and generative AI can enhance automated EDA by simplifying user interaction, generating code snippets, identifying errors/anomalies efficiently, automating report generation, facilitating comprehensive data exploration, visualization creation, and adapting to user preferences for more effective analysis of large and complex datasets.

However, while these models offer immense potential to enhance research and aid in literature review processes, they should not be treated as infallible sources. As we've seen earlier, LLMs work by analogy and struggle with reasoning and math. Their strength is creativity, not accuracy, and therefore, researchers must exercise critical thinking and ensure that the outputs generated by these models are accurate, unbiased, and aligned with rigorous scientific standards.

One notable example is Microsoft's Fabric, which incorporates a chat interface powered by generative AI. This allows users to ask data-related questions using natural language and receive instant answers without having to wait in a data request queue. By leveraging LLMs like OpenAI models, Fabric enables real-time access to valuable insights.

Fabric stands out among other analytics products due to its comprehensive approach. It addresses various aspects of an organization's analytics needs and provides role-specific experiences for different teams involved in the analytics process, such as data engineers, warehousing professionals, scientists, analysts, and business users.

With the integration of Azure OpenAI Service at every layer, Fabric harnesses generative AI's power to unlock the full potential of data. Features like Copilot in Microsoft Fabric provide conversational language experiences, allowing users to create dataflows, generate code or entire functions, build machine learning models, visualize results, and even develop custom conversational language experiences.

ChatGPT (and Fabric in extension) often produces incorrect SQL queries. This is fine when used by analysts who can check the validity of the output but a total disaster as a self-service analytics tool for non-technical business users. Therefore, organizations must ensure that they have reliable data pipelines in place and employ data quality management practices while using Fabric for analysis.

While the possibilities of generative AI in data analytics are promising, caution must be exercised. The reliability and accuracy of LLMs should be verified using first-principles reasoning and rigorous analysis. While these models have shown their potential in ad hoc analysis, idea generation during research, and summarizing complex analyses, they may not always be suitable as self-service analytical tools for non-technical users due to the need for validation by domain experts.

Automated data science

Data science is a field that combines computer science, statistics, and business analytics to extract knowledge and insights from data. Data scientists use a variety of tools and techniques to collect, clean, analyze, and visualize data. They then use this information to help businesses make better decisions. The responsibilities of a data scientist are wide-ranging and often involve multiple steps that vary depending on the specific role and industry. Tasks include data collecting, cleaning, analyzing, and visualizing. Data scientists are also tasked with building predictive models to help in decision-making processes. All the tasks mentioned are crucial to data science but can be time-consuming and complex.

Automating various aspects of the data science workflow allows data scientists to focus more on creative problem-solving while enhancing productivity. Recent tools are making different stages of the process more efficient by enabling faster iterations and less manual coding for common workflows. Some of the tasks for data science overlap with those of a software developer that we talked about in *Chapter 6, Developing Software with Generative AI*, namely, writing and deploying software, although with a narrower focus, on models.

Data science platforms like KNIME, H2O, and RapidMiner provide unified analytics engines to preprocess data, extract features, and build models. LLMs integrated into these platforms, such as GitHub Copilot or Jupyter AI, can generate code for data processing, analysis, and visualization based on natural language prompts. Jupyter AI allows conversing with a virtual assistant to explain code, identify errors, and create notebooks.

This screenshot from the documentation shows the chat feature, the Jupyternaut chat (Jupyter AI):

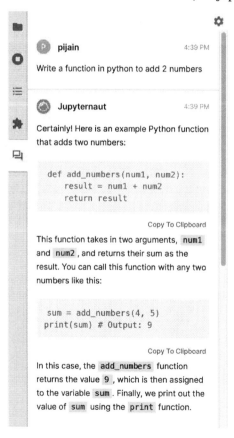

Figure 7.1: Jupyter AI – Jupyternaut chat

It should be plain to see that having a chat like that at your fingertips to ask questions, create simple functions, or change existing functions can be a boon to data scientists.

Overall, automated data science can accelerate analytics and ML application development. It allows data scientists to focus on higher-value and creative aspects of the process. Democratizing data science for business analysts is also a key motivation behind automating these workflows. In the following sections, we'll investigate different tasks in turn, and we'll highlight how generative AI can contribute to improving the workflow and create efficiency gains in areas such as data collection, visualization and **EDA**, preprocessing and feature engineering, and finally, AutoML. Let's look at each of these areas in more detail.

Data collection

Automated data collection is the process of collecting data without human intervention. Automatic data collection can be a valuable tool for businesses. It can help businesses to collect data more quickly and efficiently, and it can free up human resources to focus on other tasks.

In the context of data science or analytics, we refer to **ETL (extract, transform, and load)** as the process that not only takes data from one or more sources (data collection) but also prepares it for specific use cases.

There are many ETL tools, including commercial ones such as AWS Glue, Google Dataflow, Amazon **Simple Workflow Service (SWF)**, dbt, Fivetran, Microsoft SSIS, IBM InfoSphere DataStage, Talend Open Studio, or open-source tools such as Airflow, Kafka, and Spark. In Python, there are many more tools (too many to list them all), such as pandas for data extraction and processing, and even celery and joblib, which can serve as ETL orchestration tools.

In LangChain, there's an integration with Zapier, which is an automation tool that can be used to connect different applications and services. This can be used to automate the process of data collection from a variety of sources. LLMs offer an accelerated way to gather and process data, notably excelling in the organization of unstructured datasets.

The best tool for automatic data collection will depend on the specific needs of the business. Businesses should consider the type of data they need to collect, the volume of data they need to collect, and the budget they have available.

Visualization and EDA

EDA involves manually exploring and summarizing data to understand its various aspects before performing machine learning tasks. It helps in identifying patterns, detecting inconsistencies, testing assumptions, and gaining insights. However, with the advent of large datasets and the need for efficient analysis, automated EDA has become important.

Automated EDA and visualization refer to the process of using software tools and algorithms to automatically analyze and visualize data, without significant manual intervention. These tools provide several benefits. They can speed up the data analysis process, reducing the time spent on tasks like data cleaning, handling missing values, outlier detection, and feature engineering. These tools also enable the more efficient exploration of complex datasets by generating interactive visualizations that provide a comprehensive overview of the data.

The use of generative AI in data visualization adds another dimension to automated EDA by generating new visualizations based on user prompts, making the visualization and interpretation of data even more accessible.

Preprocessing and feature extraction

Automated data preprocessing can include tasks such as data cleaning, data integration, data transformation, and feature extraction. It is related to the transform step in ETL, so there's a lot of overlap in tools and techniques. Automated feature engineering, on the other hand, is becoming essential to leveraging the full power of ML algorithms on complex real-world data. This includes removing errors and inconsistencies from the data and converting it into a format compatible with the analytical tools that will be used.

During preprocessing and feature engineering, LLMs automate the cleaning, integration, and transformation of data. The adoption of these models promises to streamline processes, thereby improving privacy management by minimizing human handling of sensitive information during these stages. While boosting flexibility and performance in preprocessing tasks, there remains a challenge in ensuring the safety and interpretability of automatically engineered features, which may not be as transparent as manually created ones. The gains in efficiency must not undermine the need for checks against introducing inadvertent biases or errors through automation.

AutoML

AutoML frameworks represent a noteworthy leap in the evolution of machine learning. By streamlining the complete model development cycle, including tasks such as data cleaning, feature selection, model training, and hyperparameter tuning, AutoML frameworks significantly economize on the time and effort customarily expended by data scientists. These frameworks not only enhance the pace but also potentially elevate the quality of machine learning models.

The basic idea of AutoML is illustrated in this diagram from the GitHub repo of the **mljar** AutoML library (source: `https://github.com/mljar/mljar-supervised`):

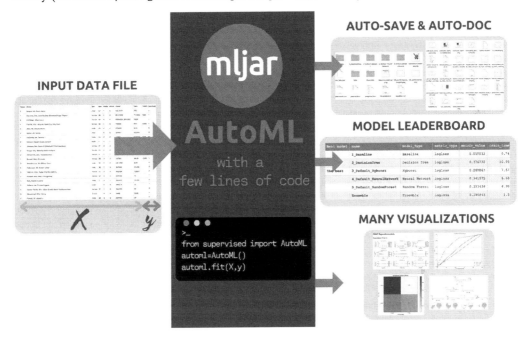

Figure 7.2: How AutoML works

Key to the value offered by AutoML systems is their contributory effect on ease of use and productivity growth. Within typical developer environments, these systems enable the rapid identification and productionizing of machine learning models, simplifying both comprehension and deployment processes. The genesis of these frameworks can be traced back to innovations like Auto-WEKA. As one of the early broad-framework attempts, developed at the University of Waikato, it was penned in Java to automate the process for tabular data within the Weka machine learning suite.

Since the release of Auto-Weka, the landscape has vastly diversified with powerful frameworks such as auto-sklearn, autokeras, NASLib, Auto-PyTorch, TPOT, Optuna, AutoGluon, and Ray (tune). Spawning across various programming languages, these frameworks lend themselves to an eclectic array of machine learning tasks. More contemporary AutoML advancements have harnessed neural architecture search techniques to encapsulate vast portions of the ML pipeline, including unstructured data types like images, video, and audio. Solutions like Google AutoML, Azure AutoML, and H2O's offering are at the forefront of this revolution, delivering capabilities that extend ML accessibility to individuals beyond expert data scientists.

These modern solutions are equipped to adeptly deal with structured formats such as tables and time series. By conducting elaborate hyperparameter searches, their performance can meet or even surpass manual interventions. Frameworks such as PyCaret facilitate training multiple models concurrently with minimal code while maintaining a focus on time series data through specialized projects like Nixtla's StatsForecast and MLForecast.

The attributes characterizing AutoML frameworks are manifold: they provide deployment capacities wherein certain solutions enable direct production embedding, especially cloud-based ones; others necessitate exportation in formats compatible with platforms like TensorFlow. The diversity in the data types handled is another facet, with a concentrated focus on tabular datasets alongside deep learning frameworks catering to assorted data varieties. Several frameworks highlight explainability as a paramount feature – this is particularly pertinent where regulations or reliability are at stake in industries like healthcare and finance. Monitoring post-deployment is another operational feature to ensure sustained model performance over time.

Despite recent advancements, users are confronted with typical drawbacks associated with such automated systems. A "black-box" scenario emerges quite frequently yielding difficulties in comprehending the internal workings, which can impede problem debugging within AutoML models. Moreover, while their impact through time savings and democratization of ML practices makes machine learning more accessible for those without extensive experience, their efficacy in automating ML tasks can face limitations due to inherent task complexities.

AutoML has been revitalized with the inclusion of LLMs, as they bring automation to tasks such as feature selection, model training, and hyperparameter tuning. The impact on privacy is considerable; AutoML systems that utilize generative models can create synthetic data, reducing reliance on personal data repositories. In terms of safety, automated systems must be designed with failsafe mechanisms to prevent the propagation of errors across successive layers of ML workflows. The flexibility offered by AutoML through LLM integration improves competitive performance by making it possible for non-experts to achieve expert-level model tuning.

With respect to ease of use, while AutoML with integrated LLMs offers simplified interfaces for model development pipelines, users must grapple with complex choices regarding model selection and evaluation.

As we'll see in the next couple of sections, LLMs and tools can significantly accelerate data science workflows, reduce manual effort, and open up new analysis opportunities. As we've seen with Jupyter AI (Jupyternaut chat) – and in *Chapter 6, Developing Software with Generative AI* – there's a lot of potential to increase efficiency by creating software with generative AI (code LLMs). This is a good starting point for the practical part of this chapter as we investigate the use of generative AI in data science. Let's start to use agents to run code or call other tools to answer questions!

Using agents to answer data science questions

Tools like `LLMMathChain` can be utilized to execute Python for answering computational queries. We've already seen different agents with tools before.

For instance, by chaining LLMs and tools, one can calculate mathematical powers and obtain results effortlessly:

```
from langchain import OpenAI, LLMMathChain


llm = OpenAI(temperature=0)
llm_math = LLMMathChain.from_llm(llm, verbose=True)


llm_math.run("What is 2 raised to the 10th power?")
```

We should see something like this:

```
> Entering new LLMMathChain chain...
What is 2 raised to the 10th power?
2**10
numexpr.evaluate("2**10")
Answer: 1024
> Finished chain.
[2]:'Answer: 1024'
```

Such capabilities, while adept at delivering straightforward numerical answers, are not as straightforward to integrate into conventional EDA workflows. Other chains, like CPAL (**CPALChain**) and PAL (**PALChain**), can tackle more complex reasoning challenges, mitigating the risks of generative models producing implausible content; yet their practical applications remain elusive in real-world scenarios.

With `PythonREPLTool`, we can create simple visualizations of toy data or train with synthetic data, which can be nice for illustration or bootstrapping a project. This is an example from the LangChain documentation:

```python
from langchain.agents.agent_toolkits import create_python_agent
from langchain.tools.python.tool import PythonREPLTool
from langchain.llms.openai import OpenAI
from langchain.agents.agent_types import AgentType
agent_executor = create_python_agent(
    llm=OpenAI(temperature=0, max_tokens=1000),
    tool=PythonREPLTool(),
    verbose=True,
    agent_type=AgentType.ZERO_SHOT_REACT_DESCRIPTION,
)
agent_executor.run(
    """Understand, write a single neuron neural network in PyTorch.
Take synthetic data for y=2x. Train for 1000 epochs and print every 100
epochs.
Return prediction for x = 5"""
)
```

This demonstrates constructing a single-neuron neural network using PyTorch, training it with synthetic data, and making predictions – all performed directly on the user's machine. However, caution is advised as executing Python code without safeguards can pose security risks.

We get this output back, which includes a prediction:

```
Entering new AgentExecutor chain...
I need to write a neural network in PyTorch and train it on the given data
Action: Python_REPL
Action Input:
import torch
model = torch.nn.Sequential(
    torch.nn.Linear(1, 1)
)
loss_fn = torch.nn.MSELoss()
optimizer = torch.optim.SGD(model.parameters(), lr=0.01)
# Define the data
x_data = torch.tensor([[1.0], [2.0], [3.0], [4.0]])
```

```
y_data = torch.tensor([[2.0], [4.0], [6.0], [8.0]])
for epoch in range(1000):  # Train the model
    y_pred = model(x_data)
    loss = loss_fn(y_pred, y_data)
    if (epoch+1) % 100 == 0:
        print(f'Epoch {epoch+1}: {loss.item():.4f}')
    optimizer.zero_grad()
    loss.backward()
    optimizer.step()

# Make a prediction
x_pred = torch.tensor([[5.0]])
y_pred = model(x_pred)

Observation: Epoch 100: 0.0043
Epoch 200: 0.0023
Epoch 300: 0.0013
Epoch 400: 0.0007
Epoch 500: 0.0004
Epoch 600: 0.0002
Epoch 700: 0.0001
Epoch 800: 0.0001
Epoch 900: 0.0000
Epoch 1000: 0.0000

Thought: I now know the final answer
Final Answer: The prediction for x = 5 is y = 10.00.
```

Through iterative training displayed in verbose logs, users witness the progressive reduction of loss over epochs until a satisfactory prediction is attained. Despite this showcasing how a neural network learns and predicts over time, scaling this approach in practice would necessitate more sophisticated engineering efforts.

LLMs and tools can be useful if we want to enrich our data with category or geographic information. For example, if our company offers flights from Tokyo, and we want to know the distances of our customers from Tokyo, we can use WolframAlpha as a tool. Here's a simplistic example:

```
from langchain.agents import load_tools, initialize_agent
from langchain.llms import OpenAI
```

```
from langchain.chains.conversation.memory import ConversationBufferMemory
llm = OpenAI(temperature=0)
tools = load_tools(['wolfram-alpha'])
memory = ConversationBufferMemory(memory_key="chat_history")
agent = initialize_agent(tools, llm, agent="conversational-react-
description", memory=memory, verbose=True)
agent.run(
    """How far are these cities to Tokyo?
* New York City
* Madrid, Spain
* Berlin
""")
```

Please make sure you've set the OPENAI_API_KEY and WOLFRAM_ALPHA_APPID environment variables as discussed in *Chapter 3, Getting Started with LangChain*. Here's the output:

```
> Entering new AgentExecutor chain...

AI: The distance from New York City to Tokyo is 6760 miles. The distance
from Madrid, Spain to Tokyo is 8,845 miles. The distance from Berlin,
Germany to Tokyo is 6,845 miles.

> Finished chain.

The distance from New York City to Tokyo is 6760 miles. The distance from
Madrid, Spain to Tokyo is 8,845 miles. The distance from Berlin, Germany
to Tokyo is 6,845 miles.
```

By combining LLMs with external tools like WolframAlpha, it's possible to perform more challenging data enrichment, such as calculating distances between cities, such as from Tokyo to New York City, Madrid, or Berlin. Such integrations could significantly enhance the utility of datasets used in various business applications. Nonetheless, these examples address relatively straightforward queries; deploying such implementations on a larger scale demands more extensive engineering strategies beyond those discussed.

However, we can give agents datasets to work with, and here is where it can get immensely powerful when we connect more tools. Let's ask and answer questions about structured datasets!

Data exploration with LLMs

Data exploration is a crucial and foundational step in data analysis, allowing researchers to gain a comprehensive understanding of their datasets and uncover significant insights. With the emergence of LLMs like ChatGPT, researchers can harness the power of natural language processing to facilitate data exploration.

As we mentioned earlier, generative AI models such as ChatGPT have the ability to understand and generate human-like responses, making them valuable tools for enhancing research productivity. Asking our questions in natural language and getting responses in digestible pieces and shapes can be a great boost to analysis.

LLMs can help explore textual data and other forms of data, such as numerical datasets or multimedia content. Researchers can leverage ChatGPT's capabilities to ask questions about statistical trends in numerical datasets or even query visualizations for image classification tasks.

Let's load up a dataset and work with that. We can quickly get a dataset from scikit-learn:

```
from sklearn.datasets import load_iris
df = load_iris(as_frame=True)["data"]
```

The Iris dataset is well known – it's a toy dataset, but it will help us illustrate the capabilities of using generative AI for data exploration. We'll use a DataFrame in the following example. We can create a pandas DataFrame agent now and we'll see how easy it is to get simple stuff done!

```
from langchain.agents import create_pandas_dataframe_agent
from langchain import PromptTemplate
from langchain.llms.openai import OpenAI

PROMPT = (
    "If you do not know the answer, say you don't know.\n"
    "Think step by step.\n"
    "\n"
    "Below is the query.\n"
    "Query: {query}\n"
)
prompt = PromptTemplate(template=PROMPT, input_variables=["query"])
llm = OpenAI()
agent = create_pandas_dataframe_agent(llm, df, verbose=True)
```

I've included instructions for the model to indicate uncertainty and to follow a step-by-step thought process, with the aim of reducing hallucinations. Now we can query our agent against the DataFrame:

```
agent.run(prompt.format(query="What's this dataset about?"))
```

We get the answer `This dataset is about the measurements of some type of flower`, which is correct.

Let's show how to get a visualization:

```
agent.run(prompt.format(query="Plot each column as a barplot!"))
```

Here is the plot:

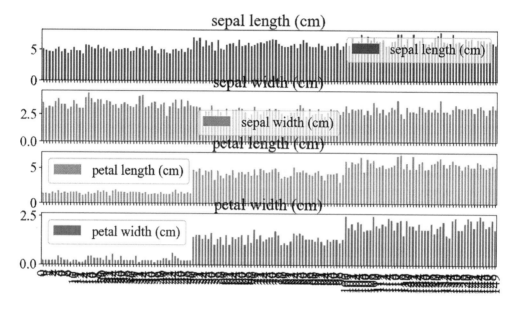

Figure 7.3: Iris dataset barplots

The plot is not perfect. The output can be finicky and depends on the llm model parameter and on the instructions. In this case, I used `df.plot.bar(rot=0, subplots=True)`. We might want to introduce more tweaks, for example, to padding between the panels, the font size, or the placement of the legend, to make this really nice.

We can also ask to see the distributions of the columns visually, which will give us this neat plot:

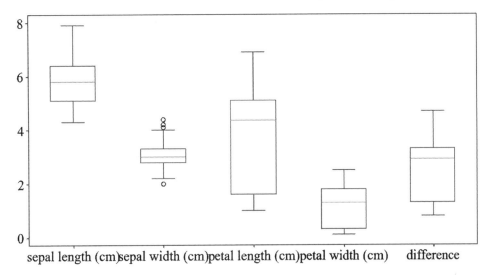

Figure 7.4: Iris dataset boxplots

We can request the plot to use other plotting backends, such as Seaborn; however, please note that these have to be installed.

We can also ask more questions about the dataset, like which row has the biggest difference between petal length and petal width. We get the answer with the intermediate steps as follows (shortened):

```
df['difference'] = df['petal length (cm)'] - df['petal width (cm)']
df.loc[df['difference'].idxmax()]
Observation: sepal length (cm)      7.7
sepal width (cm)        2.8
petal length (cm)       6.7
petal width (cm)        2.0
difference              4.7
Name: 122, dtype: float64
Thought: I now know the final answer
Final Answer: Row 122 has the biggest difference between petal length and
petal width.
```

I think that's worth a pat on the back, LLM!

We could extend this example by adding more instructions to the prompt about plotting, such as the sizes of plots.

It's a bit harder to implement the same plotting logic in a Streamlit app, because we need to use the plotting functionality in corresponding Streamlit functions, for example, st.bar_chart(). However, this can be done as well. You can find explanations for this on the Streamlit blog (*Building a Streamlit and scikit-learn app with ChatGPT*).

What about statistical tests?

```
agent.run(prompt.format(query="Validate the following hypothesis
statistically: petal width and petal length come from the same
distribution."))
```

We get this response:

```
Thought: I should use a statistical test to answer this question.
Action: python_repl_ast
Action Input: from scipy.stats import ks_2samp
Observation:
Thought: I now have the necessary tools to answer this question.
Action: python_repl_ast
Action Input: ks_2samp(df['petal width (cm)'], df['petal length (cm)'])
Observation: KstestResult(statistic=0.6666666666666666,
pvalue=6.639808432803654e-32, statistic_location=2.5, statistic_sign=1)
Thought: I now know the final answer
Final Answer: The p-value of 6.639808432803654e-32 indicates that the two
variables come from different distributions.
```

That checks off the statistical test! We can ask complex questions about the dataset with simple prompts in plain English.

There's also the PandasAI library, which uses LangChain under the hood and provides similar functionality. Here's an example from the documentation with an example dataset:

```
import pandas as pd
from pandasai.llm import OpenAI
from pandasai.schemas.df_config import Config
from pandasai import SmartDataframe

df = pd.DataFrame({
```

```
    "country": ["United States", "United Kingdom", "France", "Germany",
"Italy", "Spain", "Canada", "Australia", "Japan", "China"],
    "gdp": [19294482071552, 2891615567872, 2411255037952, 3435817336832,
1745433788416, 1181205135360, 1607402389504, 1490967855104, 4380756541440,
14631844184064],
    "happiness_index": [6.94, 7.16, 6.66, 7.07, 6.38, 6.4, 7.23, 7.22,
5.87, 5.12]
})
smart_df = SmartDataframe(df, config=Config(llm=OpenAI()))
print(smart_df.chat("Which are the 5 happiest countries?"))
```

This will give us the requested result similar to before when we were using LangChain directly. Please note that PandasAI is not part of the setup for the book, so you'll have to install it separately if you want to use it.

For data in SQL databases, we can connect with a SQLDatabaseChain. The LangChain documentation shows this example:

```
from langchain.llms import OpenAI
from langchain.utilities import SQLDatabase
from langchain_experimental.sql import SQLDatabaseChain
db = SQLDatabase.from_uri("sqlite:///../../../../notebooks/Chinook.db")
llm = OpenAI(temperature=0, verbose=True)
db_chain = SQLDatabaseChain.from_llm(llm, db, verbose=True)
db_chain.run("How many employees are there?")
```

We are connecting to a database first. Then we can ask questions about the data in natural language. This can also be quite powerful. An LLM will create the queries for us. I would expect this to be particularly useful when we don't know about the schema of the database. The SQLDatabaseChain can also check queries and autocorrect them if the use_query_checker option is set.

By following the outlined steps, we have leveraged the impressive natural language processing capabilities of LLMs for data exploration. Through loading a dataset, such as the Iris dataset from scikit-learn, we can use an LLM-powered agent to query about data specifics in accessible, everyday language. The creation of a pandas DataFrame agent enabled simple analysis tasks and visualization requests, demonstrating the AI's capacity to produce plots and specific data insights.

We can not only inquire about the nature of the dataset verbally but also command the agent to generate visual representations such as barplots and boxplots for **EDA**. Although these visualizations might require additional fine-tuning for aesthetic refinement, they established a groundwork for analysis. When delving into more nuanced requests, such as identifying disparities between two data attributes, the agent adeptly added new columns and located pertinent numerical differences, showing its practical utility in drawing actionable conclusions.

Efforts extended beyond mere visualization as the application of statistical tests was also explored through concise English prompts, resulting in articulate interpretations of statistical operations like KS-tests performed by the agent.

The capabilities of integrations aren't limited to static datasets but extend to dynamic SQL databases where an LLM can automate query generation, even offering autocorrection for syntactical errors in SQL statements. This capability particularly shines when schemas are unfamiliar.

Summary

Beginning with an examination of AutoML frameworks, this chapter highlighted the value these systems bring to the entirety of the data science pipeline, facilitating each stage from data preparation to model deployment. We then considered how the integration of LLMs can further elevate productivity and make data science more approachable for both technical and non-technical stakeholders.

Diving into code generation, we saw parallels with software development, as discussed in *Chapter 6, Developing Software with Generative AI*, observing how tools and functions generated by LLMs can respond to queries or enhance datasets through augmentation techniques. This included leveraging third-party tools like WolframAlpha to add external data points to existing datasets. Our exploration then shifted toward the use of LLMs for data exploration, building upon the techniques for ingesting and analyzing voluminous textual data detailed in *Chapter 4, Building Capable Assistants*, on question answering. Here, our focus turned to structured datasets, examining how SQL databases or tabular information could be effectively analyzed through LLM-powered exploratory processes.

To sum up our exploration, it is clear that AI technologies, illustrated by platforms such as ChatGPT plugins and Microsoft Fabric, hold transformative potential for data analysis. However, despite the remarkable strides in enabling and enhancing the work of data scientists through these AI tools, the current state of AI technology isn't at a point where it can supplant human experts but rather augments their capabilities and broadens their analytical toolset.

In the next chapter, we'll focus on conditioning techniques to improve the performance of LLMs through prompting and fine-tuning.

Questions

Please have a look to see if you can come up with the answers to these questions from memory. I recommend you go back to the corresponding sections of this chapter if you are unsure about any of them:

1. What steps are involved in data science?
2. Why would we want to automate data science/analysis?
3. How can generative AI help data scientists?
4. What kind of agents and tools can we use to answer simple questions?
5. How can we get an LLM to work with data?

Join our community on Discord

Join our community's Discord space for discussions with the authors and other readers:

```
https://packt.link/lang
```

8

Customizing LLMs and Their Output

This chapter is about techniques and best practices to improve the reliability and performance of LLMs in certain scenarios, such as complex reasoning and problem-solving tasks. This process of adapting a model for a certain task or making sure that our model output corresponds to what we expect is called conditioning. In this chapter, we'll discuss fine-tuning and prompting as methods for conditioning.

Fine-tuning involves training the pre-trained base model on specific tasks or datasets relevant to the desired application. This process allows the model to adapt, becoming more accurate and contextually relevant for the intended use case.

On the other hand, by providing additional input or context at inference time, LLMs can generate text tailored to a particular task or style. **Prompt engineering** is significant in unlocking LLM reasoning capabilities, and prompt techniques form a valuable toolkit for researchers and practitioners working with LLMs. We'll discuss and implement advanced prompt engineering strategies like few-shot learning, tree-of-thought, and self-consistency.

Throughout the chapter, we'll work on fine-tuning and prompting with LLMs. You can find the corresponding code in the GitHub repository for the book at `https://github.com/benman1/generative_ai_with_langchain`

The main sections in this chapter are:

- Conditioning LLMs
- Fine-tuning
- Prompt engineering

Let's start by discussing conditioning, why it's important, and how we can achieve it.

Conditioning LLMs

Pre-training an LLM on diverse data to learn patterns of language results in a base model that has a broad understanding of diverse topics. While base models such as GPT-4 can generate impressive text on a wide range of topics, conditioning them can enhance their capabilities in terms of task relevance, specificity, and coherence, and can guide the model's behavior to be in line with what is considered ethical and appropriate. In this chapter, we'll focus on fine-tuning and prompt techniques as two methods of conditioning.

Conditioning refers to a collection of methods used to direct the model's generation of outputs. This includes not only prompt crafting but also more systemic techniques, such as fine-tuning the model on specific datasets to adapt its responses to certain topics or styles persistently.

Conditioning techniques enable LLMs to comprehend and execute complex instructions, delivering content that closely matches our expectations. This ranges from off-the-cuff interactions to systematic training that orients a model's behavior toward reliable performance in specialist domains, like legal consultation or technical documentation. Furthermore, part of conditioning includes implementing safeguards to avert the production of malicious or harmful content, such as incorporating filters or training the model to avoid certain types of problematic outputs, thereby better aligning it with desired ethical standards.

Alignment refers to the process and goal of training and modifying LLMs so that their general behavior, decision-making processes, and outputs conform to broader human values, ethical principles, and safety considerations.

The two terms are not synonymous; while conditioning can include fine-tuning and is focused on influencing the model through various techniques at different layers of interaction, alignment is concerned with the fundamental and holistic calibration of the model's behavior to human ethics and safety standards.

Conditioning can be applied at different points in a model's life cycle. One strategy involves fine-tuning the model on data that represents the intended use case to help the model specialize in that area. This method depends on the availability of such data and the ability to integrate it into the training process. Another method involves conditioning the model dynamically at the time of inference, where the input prompt is tailored with additional context to shape the desired output. This approach offers flexibility but can add complexity to the model's operation in live environments.

In the next section, I will summarize key methods for conditioning such as fine-tuning and prompt engineering, discuss the rationale, and examine their relative pros and cons.

Methods for conditioning

With the advent of large pre-trained language models like GPT-3, there has been growing interest in techniques to adapt these models for downstream tasks. As LLMs continue to develop, they will become even more effective and useful for a broader range of applications, and we can expect future advancements in fine-tuning and prompting techniques to help go even further in complex tasks that involve reasoning and tool use.

Several approaches have been proposed for conditioning. Here is a table summarizing the different techniques:

Stage	Technique	Examples
Training	Data curation	Training on diverse data
	Objective function	Careful design of training objective
	Architecture and training process	Optimizing model structure and training
Fine-tuning	Task specialization	Training on specific datasets/tasks
Inference-time conditioning	Dynamic inputs	Prefixes, control codes, and context examples
Human oversight	Human-in-the-loop	Human review and feedback

Table 8.1: Steering generative AI outputs

Combining these techniques provides developers with more control over the behavior and outputs of generative AI systems. The ultimate goal is to ensure that human values are incorporated at all stages, from training to deployment, to create responsible and aligned AI systems.

In this chapter, we emphasize fine-tuning and prompting, as they stand out for their effectiveness and prevalence in the conditioning of LLMs. Fine-tuning involves adjusting all parameters of a pre-trained model through additional training on specialized tasks. This method is aimed at enhancing model performance for particular objectives and is known to yield robust results. However, fine-tuning can be resource-intensive, presenting a trade-off between high performance and computational efficiency. To address these limitations, we explore strategies like adapters and **Low-Rank Adaptation (LoRA)**, which introduce elements of sparsity or implement partial freezing of parameters to lighten the burden.

Prompt-based techniques, on the other hand, offer a way to dynamically condition LLMs at inference time. Through careful crafting of input prompts and subsequent optimization and evaluations, these methods can steer the behavior of LLMs in desired directions without the need for heavy retraining. Prompts can be carefully designed to elicit specific behaviors or to encapsulate particular knowledge areas, providing a versatile and resource-savvy approach to model conditioning.

Moreover, we delve into the transformative role of **Reinforcement Learning with Human Feedback (RLHF)** within fine-tuning processes, where human feedback serves as a critical guide for the model's learning trajectory. RLHF has exhibited the potential to profoundly improve the capabilities of language models like GPT-3, making fine-tuning an even more impactful technique. By integrating RLHF, we harness the nuanced understanding of human evaluators to further refine the model behavior, ensuring outputs that are not only relevant and accurate but also align with user intent and expectations.

All these different techniques for conditioning facilitate the development of LLMs that are both high-performing and aligned with desired outcomes across various applications. Let's start off by discussing the reasons why InstructGPT, which was trained through RLHF, has had such a transformative impact.

Reinforcement learning with human feedback

In their March 2022 paper, Ouyang and others from OpenAI demonstrated using RLHF with **Proximal Policy Optimization (PPO)** to align LLMs, like GPT-3, with human preferences.

RLHF is an online approach that fine-tunes LMs using human preferences. It has three main steps:

1. **Supervised pre-training**: The LM is first trained via standard supervised learning on human demonstrations.

2. **Reward model training**: A reward model is trained on human ratings of LM outputs to estimate a reward.

3. **RL fine-tuning**: The LM is fine-tuned via reinforcement learning to maximize the expected reward from the reward model using an algorithm like PPO.

The main change, RLHF, allows incorporating nuanced human judgments into language model training through a learned reward model. As a result, human feedback can steer and improve language model capabilities beyond standard supervised fine-tuning. This new model can be used to follow instructions that are given in natural language, and it can answer questions in a way that's more accurate and relevant than GPT-3. InstructGPT outperformed GPT-3 on user preference, truthfulness, and harm reduction, despite having 100x fewer parameters.

Starting in March 2022, OpenAI started releasing the GPT-3.5 series models, upgraded versions of GPT-3, which include fine-tuning with RLHF.

InstructGPT opened up new avenues to improve language models by incorporating reinforcement learning from human feedback methods beyond traditional fine-tuning approaches. RL training can be unstable and computationally expensive; notwithstanding, its success inspired further research into refining RLHF techniques, reducing data requirements for alignment, and developing more powerful and accessible models for a wide range of applications.

Low-rank adaptation

As LLMs become larger, it becomes difficult to train them on consumer hardware, and deploying them for each specific task becomes expensive. There are a few methods that reduce computational, memory, and storage costs while improving performance in low-data and out-of-domain scenarios.

Parameter-Efficient Fine-Tuning (PEFT) methods enable the use of small checkpoints for each task, making the models more portable. This small set of trained weights can be added on top of the LLM, allowing the same model to be used for multiple tasks without replacing the entire model.

Low-Rank Adaptation (LoRA) is a type of PEFT, where the pre-trained model weights are frozen. It introduces trainable rank decomposition matrices into each layer of the Transformer architecture to reduce the number of trainable parameters. LoRA achieves comparable model quality compared to fine-tuning while having fewer trainable parameters and higher training throughput.

The QLORA method is an extension of LoRA, which enables efficient fine-tuning of large models by backpropagating gradients through a frozen 4-bit quantized model into learnable low-rank adapters. This allows you to fine-tune a 65B parameter model on a single GPU. QLORA models achieve 99% of ChatGPT performance on Vicuna, using innovations like new data types and optimizers. QLORA reduces the memory requirements to fine-tune a 65B parameter model from >780 GB to <48 GB, without affecting runtime or predictive performance.

Quantization refers to techniques to reduce the numerical precision of weights and activations in neural networks like LLMs. The main purpose of quantization is to reduce the memory footprint and computational requirements of large models.

Some key points about the quantization of LLMs:

- It involves representing weights and activations using fewer bits than a standard single-precision floating point (FP32). For example, weights could be quantized to 8-bit integers.

- This allows you to shrink a model size by up to 4x and improve throughput on specialized hardware.

- Quantization typically has a minor impact on model accuracy, especially with re-training.

- Common quantization methods include scalar, vector, and product quantization, which quantize weights separately or in groups.

- Activations can also be quantized by estimating their distribution and binning appropriately.

- Quantization-aware training adjusts weights during training to minimize quantization loss.

- LLMs like BERT and GPT-3 have been shown to work well with 4–8-bit quantization via fine-tuning.

In the next section, we'll discuss methods to condition LLMs at inference time, which include prompt engineering.

Inference-time conditioning

One commonly used approach is **conditioning at inference time** (an output generation phase), where specific inputs or conditions are provided dynamically to guide the output generation process. LLM fine-tuning may not always be feasible or beneficial in certain scenarios:

- **Limited fine-tuning services:** When models are only accessible through APIs that lack or have restricted fine-tuning capabilities

- **Insufficient data:** In cases where there is a lack of data for fine-tuning, either for the specific downstream task or relevant application domain

- **Dynamic data:** In cases of applications with frequently changing data, such as news-related platforms, fine-tuning models frequently becomes challenging, leading to potential drawbacks

- **Context-sensitive applications**: Dynamic and context-specific applications like personalized chatbots cannot perform fine-tuning based on individual user data

For conditioning at inference time, most commonly, we provide a textual prompt or instruction at the beginning of the text generation process. This prompt can be a few sentences or even a single word, acting as an explicit indication of the desired output.

Some common techniques for inference-time conditioning include:

- **Prompt tuning**: Providing natural language guidance for intended behavior. Sensitive to prompt design.
- **Prefix tuning**: Prepending trainable vectors to LLM layers.
- **Constraining tokens**: Forcing inclusion/exclusion of certain words
- **Metadata**: Providing high-level info like genre, target audience, and so on

Prompts can facilitate generating text that adheres to specific themes, styles, or even mimics a particular author's writing style. These techniques involve providing contextual information during inference time, such as for in-context learning or retrieval augmentation.

An example of prompt tuning is prefixing prompts, where instructions like "Write a child-friendly story about..." are prepended to the prompt. For example, in chatbot applications, conditioning the model with user messages helps it generate responses that are personalized and pertinent to the ongoing conversation.

Further examples include prepending relevant documents to prompts to assist LLMs with writing tasks (for example, news reports, Wikipedia pages, and company documents), or retrieving and prepending user-specific data (financial records, health data, and emails) before prompting an LLM to ensure personalized answers. By conditioning LLM outputs on contextual information at runtime, these methods can guide models without relying on traditional fine-tuning processes.

Often, demonstrations are part of the instructions for reasoning tasks, where few-shot examples are provided to induce the desired behavior. Powerful LLMs, such as GPT-3, can solve tasks without further training through prompting techniques. In this approach, the problem to be solved is presented to the model as a text prompt, with some text examples of similar problems and their solutions. The model must provide a completion of the prompt via inference. **Zero-shot prompting** involves no solved examples, while few-shot prompting includes a small number of examples of similar (problem and solution) pairs.

It has been shown that prompting provides easy control over large frozen models like GPT-4 and allows steering model behavior without extensive fine-tuning.

Prompting enables conditioning models on new knowledge with low overhead, but careful prompt engineering is needed for the best results. This is what we'll discuss as part of this chapter.

In prefix tuning, continuous task-specific vectors are trained and supplied to models at inference time. Similar ideas have been proposed for adapter approaches, such as parameter **Efficient Transfer Learning (PELT)** or **Ladder Side-Tuning (LST)**.

Conditioning at inference time can also happen during sampling, such as grammar-based sampling, where the output can be constrained to be compatible with certain well-defined patterns, such as a programming language syntax.

In the next section, we'll fine-tune a small open-source LLM (OpenLLaMa) for **Question Answering (QA)** with PEFT and quantization, and we'll deploy it on Hugging Face.

Fine-tuning

As we discussed in the first section of this chapter, the goal of model fine-tuning for LLMs is to optimize a model to generate outputs that are more specific to a task and context than the original foundation model.

The need for fine-tuning arises because pre-trained LMs are designed to model general linguistic knowledge, not specific downstream tasks. Their capabilities manifest only when adapted to applications. Fine-tuning allows pre-trained weights to be updated for target datasets and objectives. This enables knowledge transfer from the general model while customizing it for specialized tasks.

In general, there are three advantages of fine-tuning that are immediately obvious to users of these models:

- **Steerability**: The capability of models to follow instructions (instruction-tuning)
- **Reliable output-formatting**: This is important, for example, for API calls/function calling)
- **Custom tone**: This makes it possible to adapt the output style as appropriate to the task and audience.
- **Alignment**: The output of models should correspond to core values, for example, concerning safety, security, and privacy considerations.

The idea of fine-tuning pre-trained neural networks originated in computer vision research in the early 2010s. Howard and Ruder (2018) demonstrated the effectiveness of fine-tuning models like ELMo and ULMFit on downstream tasks. The seminal BERT model (Devlin and others., 2019) established fine-tuning of pre-trained transformers as the de facto approach in NLP.

In this section, we'll fine-tune a model for question answering. This recipe is not specific to Lang-Chain, but we'll point out a few customizations, where LangChain could be applicable. You can find the code in the notebooks directory in the GitHub repository for the book.

As a first step, we'll set up fine-tuning with libraries and environment variables.

Setup for fine-tuning

Fine-tuning consistently achieves strong results across tasks but requires extensive computational resources. Therefore, it's a good idea to do fine-tuning in an environment where we can access powerful GPUs and memory resources. We'll run this on Google Colab instead of the local environment, where we can run fine-tuning of LLMs free of charge (with only a few restrictions).

 Google Colab is a computation environment that provides different means for hardware acceleration of computation tasks such as **Tensor Processing Units** (**TPUs**) and **Graphical Processing Units** (**GPUs**). These are available both in free and professional tiers. For the task in this section, the free tier is sufficient. You can sign into a Colab environment at this URL: https://colab.research.google.com/

Please make sure you set your Google Colab machine settings in the top menu to TPU or GPU to make sure you have sufficient resources to run the following code and that the training doesn't take too long. We'll install all required libraries in the Google Colab environment – I am adding the versions of these libraries that I've used to make our fine-tuning repeatable:

- peft: PEFT (version 0.5.0)
- trl: Proximal Policy Optimization (0.6.0)
- bitsandbytes: k-bit optimizers and matrix multiplication routines, needed for quantization (0.41.1)
- accelerate: train and use PyTorch models with multi-GPU, TPU, and mixed-precision (0.22.0)
- transformers: Hugging Face transformers library with backends in JAX, PyTorch, and TensorFlow (4.32.0)
- datasets: community-driven open-source library of datasets (2.14.4)
- sentencepiece: Python wrapper for fast tokenization (0.1.99)
- wandb: for monitoring the training progress on Weights and Biases (0.15.8)
- langchain for loading the model back as a LangChain LLM after training (0.0.273)

We can install these libraries from the Colab notebook as follows:

```
!pip install -U accelerate bitsandbytes datasets transformers peft trl
sentencepiece wandb langchain huggingface_hub
```

To download and train models from Hugging Face, we need to authenticate with the platform. Please note that if you want to push your model to Hugging Face later, you need to generate a new API token with write permissions on Hugging Face: `https://huggingface.co/settings/tokens`

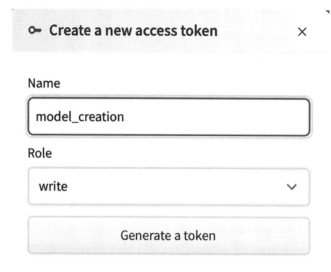

Figure 8.1: Creating a new API token on Hugging Face write permissions

We can authenticate from the notebook like this:

```
from huggingface_hub import notebook_login
notebook_login()
```

When prompted, paste your Hugging Face access token.

 A note of caution before we start: when executing the code, you need to log in to different services, so make sure you pay attention when running the notebook!

Weights and Biases (W&B) is an MLOps platform that can help developers monitor and document ML training workflows from end to end. As mentioned earlier, we will use W&B to get an idea of how well the training is working and if the model is improving over time. For W&B, we need to name the project; alternatively, we can use `wandb`'s `init()` method:

```
import os
os.environ["WANDB_PROJECT"] = "finetuning"
```

To authenticate with W&B, you need to create a free account with them at `https://www.wandb.ai`. You can find your API key on the **Authorize** page: `https://wandb.ai/authorize`.

Again, we need to paste in our API token.

If the previous training run is still active – this could be from a previous execution of the notebook if you are running it a second time – let's make sure we start a new one! This will ensure that we get new reports and a dashboard on W&B:

```
import wandb
if wandb.run is not None:
    wandb.finish()
```

Next, we'll need to choose a dataset against which we want to optimize. We can use lots of different datasets here that are appropriate for coding, storytelling, tool use, SQL generation, **grade-school math questions (GSM8k)**, or many other tasks. Hugging Face provides a wealth of datasets, which can be viewed at this URL: `https://huggingface.co/datasets`. These cover a lot of different and even the most niche tasks.

We can also customize our own dataset. For example, we can use LangChain to set up training data. There are quite a few methods available for filtering that could help reduce redundancy in the dataset. It would have been appealing to show data collection as a practical recipe in this chapter. However, because of the complexity, it is out of the scope of the book.

It might be harder to filter for quality from web data, but there are a lot of possibilities. For code models, we could apply code validation techniques to score segments as a quality filter. If the code comes from GitHub, we can filter by stars or by stars by repo owner.

For texts in natural language, quality filtering is not trivial. Search engine placement could serve as a popularity filter, since it's often based on user engagement with the content. Further, knowledge distillation techniques could be tweaked as a filter by fact density and accuracy.

In this recipe, we are fine-tuning for question-answering performance with the Squad V2 dataset. You can see a detailed dataset description on Hugging Face: `https://huggingface.co/spaces/evaluate-metric/squad_v2`:

```
from datasets import load_dataset
dataset_name = "squad_v2"
dataset = load_dataset(dataset_name, split="train")
eval_dataset = load_dataset(dataset_name, split="validation")
```

We are taking both training and validation splits. The Squad V2 dataset has a part that's supposed to be used in training and another one in validation, as we can see in the output of load_dataset(dataset_name):

```
DatasetDict({
    train: Dataset({
        features: ['id', 'title', 'context', 'question', 'answers'],
        num_rows: 130319
    })
    validation: Dataset({
        features: ['id', 'title', 'context', 'question', 'answers'],
        num_rows: 11873
    })
})
```

We'll use the validation splits for early stopping. Early stopping will allow us to stop training when the validation error begins to degrade.

The Squad V2 dataset is composed of various features, which we can see here:

```
{'id': Value(dtype='string', id=None),
 'title': Value(dtype='string', id=None),
 'context': Value(dtype='string', id=None),
 'question': Value(dtype='string', id=None),
 'answers': Sequence(feature={'text': Value(dtype='string', id=None),
 'answer_start': Value(dtype='int32', id=None)}, length=-1, id=None)}
```

The basic idea in training is prompting the model with a question and comparing the answer to the dataset. In the next section, we'll use this setup to fine-tune an open-source LLM.

Open-source models

We want a small model that we can run locally at a decent token rate. LLaMa-2 models require signing a license agreement with your email address and getting confirmed (which, to be fair, can be very fast), as it comes with restrictions for commercial use. LLaMa derivatives such as OpenLLaMa have performed quite well, as can be evidenced on the HF leaderboard: https://huggingface.co/spaces/HuggingFaceH4/open_llm_leaderboard

OpenLLaMa version 1 cannot be used for coding tasks, because of the tokenizer. Therefore, let's use v2! We'll use a 3B parameter model, which we'll be able to use even on older hardware:

```
model_id = "openlm-research/open_llama_3b_v2"
new_model_name = f"openllama-3b-peft-{dataset_name}"
```

We can use even smaller models such as EleutherAI/gpt-neo-125m, which can also give a particularly good compromise between resource use and performance.

Let's load the model:

```
import torch
from transformers import AutoModelForCausalLM, BitsAndBytesConfig

bnb_config = BitsAndBytesConfig(
    load_in_4bit=True,
    bnb_4bit_quant_type="nf4",
    bnb_4bit_compute_dtype=torch.float16,
)

device_map="auto"

base_model = AutoModelForCausalLM.from_pretrained(
    model_id,
    quantization_config=bnb_config,
    device_map="auto",
    trust_remote_code=True,
)
base_model.config.use_cache = False
```

The Bits and Bytes configuration makes it possible to quantize our model in 8, 4, 3, or even 2 bits with a much-accelerated inference and lower memory footprint, without incurring a big cost in terms of performance.

We are going to store model checkpoints on Google Drive; you need to confirm your login to your Google account:

```
from google.colab import drive
drive.mount('/content/gdrive')
```

 We'll need to authenticate with Google for this to work.

We can set our output directory for model checkpoints and logs to our Google Drive:

```
output_dir = "/content/gdrive/My Drive/results"
```

If you don't want to use Google Drive, just set this to a directory on your computer.

For training, we need to set up a tokenizer:

```
from transformers import AutoTokenizer
tokenizer = AutoTokenizer.from_pretrained(model_id, trust_remote_
code=True)
tokenizer.pad_token = tokenizer.eos_token
tokenizer.padding_side = "right"
```

Now, we'll define our training configuration. We'll set up LORA and other training arguments:

```
from transformers import TrainingArguments, EarlyStoppingCallback
from peft import LoraConfig
# More info: https://github.com/huggingface/transformers/pull/24906
base_model.config.pretraining_tp = 1

peft_config = LoraConfig(
    lora_alpha=16,
    lora_dropout=0.1,
    r=64,
    bias="none",
    task_type="CAUSAL_LM",
)
training_args = TrainingArguments(
    output_dir=output_dir,
    per_device_train_batch_size=4,
    gradient_accumulation_steps=4,
    learning_rate=2e-4,
    logging_steps=10,
    max_steps=2000,
    num_train_epochs=100,
    evaluation_strategy="steps",
    eval_steps=5,
    save_total_limit=5,
    push_to_hub=False,
```

```
        load_best_model_at_end=True,
        report_to="wandb"
)
```

A few comments to explain some of these parameters are in order. The push_to_hub argument means that we can push the model checkpoints to the HuggingSpace Hub regularly during training. For this to work, you need to set up the HuggingSpace authentication (with write permissions, as mentioned). If we opt for this, as output_dir, we can use new_model_name. This will be the repository name under which the model will be available here on Hugging Face: https://huggingface.co/models.

Alternatively, as I've done here, you can save your model locally or in the cloud, for example, in Google Drive in a directory. I've set max_steps and num_train_epochs very high, because I've noticed that training can still improve after many steps. Early stepping and a high number of maximum training steps should help to get the model to provide higher performance. For early stopping, we need to set evaluation_strategy as "steps" and load_best_model_at_end=True.

eval_steps is the number of update steps between two evaluations. save_total_limit=5 means that only the last five models are saved. Finally, report_to="wandb" means that we'll send training stats, some model metadata, and hardware information to W&B, where we can look at graphs and dashboards for each run.

The training can then use our configuration:

```
from trl import SFTTrainer

trainer = SFTTrainer(
    model=base_model,
    train_dataset=dataset,
    eval_dataset=eval_dataset,
    peft_config=peft_config,
    dataset_text_field="question",  # this depends on the dataset!
    max_seq_length=512,
    tokenizer=tokenizer,
    args=training_args,
    callbacks=[EarlyStoppingCallback(early_stopping_patience=200)]
)
trainer.train()
```

The training can take quite a while, even running on a TPU device. Frequent evaluation slows the training down by a lot. If you disable the early stopping, you can make this much faster.

We should see some statistics as the training progresses, but it's nicer to show the graph of performance, as we can see on W&B:

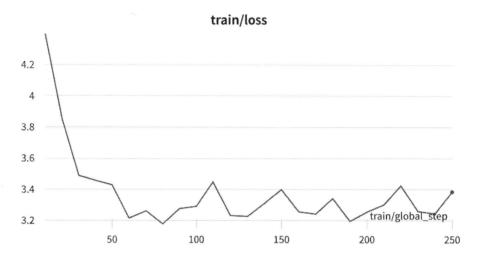

Figure 8.2: Fine-tuning training loss over time (steps)

After training is done, we can save the final checkpoint on disk for re-loading:

```
trainer.model.save_pretrained(
    os.path.join(output_dir, "final_checkpoint"),
)
```

We can now share our final model with friends to brag about the performance we've achieved by manually pushing to Hugging Face:

```
trainer.model.push_to_hub(
    repo_id=new_model_name
)
```

We can now load the model back using a combination of our Hugging Face username and the repository name (the new model name). Let's quickly show how to use this model in LangChain. Usually, the peft model is stored as an adapter, not as a full model; therefore, the loading is a bit different:

```
from peft import PeftModel, PeftConfig
from transformers import AutoModelForCausalLM, AutoTokenizer, pipeline
```

```
from langchain.llms import HuggingFacePipeline

model_id = 'openlm-research/open_llama_3b_v2'
config = PeftConfig.from_pretrained("benji1a/openllama-3b-peft-squad_v2")
model = AutoModelForCausalLM.from_pretrained(model_id)
model = PeftModel.from_pretrained(model, "benji1a/openllama-3b-peft-squad_
v2")
tokenizer = AutoTokenizer.from_pretrained(model_id, trust_remote_
code=True)
tokenizer.pad_token = tokenizer.eos_token
pipe = pipeline(
    "text-generation",
    model=model,
    tokenizer=tokenizer,
    max_length=256
)
llm = HuggingFacePipeline(pipeline=pipe)
```

We've done everything so far on Google Colab, but we could equally execute this locally; just note that you need to have the huggingface peft library installed!

Commercial models

So far, we've shown how to fine-tune and deploy an open-source LLM. Some commercial models can be fine-tuned on custom data as well. For example, both OpenAI's GPT-3.5 and Google's PaLM model offer this capability. This has been integrated with a few Python libraries.

With the Scikit-LLM library, this is only a few lines of code. We won't go through a full recipe in this section, but please look at the Scikit-LLM library or the documentation of different cloud LLM providers to find all the details. The Scikit-LLM library is not part of the setup that we discussed in *Chapter 3, Getting Started with LangChain*, so you'd have to install it manually. I've also not included the training data, X_train. You'd have to come up with a training dataset yourself.

Fine-tuning a PaLM model for text classification can be done like this:

```
from skllm.models.palm import PaLMClassifier
clf = PaLMClassifier(n_update_steps=100)
clf.fit(X_train, y_train) # y_train is a list of labels
labels = clf.predict(X_test)
```

Similarly, you can fine-tune the GPT-3.5 model for text classification like this:

```
from skllm.models.gpt import GPTClassifier
clf = GPTClassifier(
        base_model = "gpt-3.5-turbo-0613",
        n_epochs = None, # int or None. When None, will be determined
automatically by OpenAI
        default_label = "Random", # optional
)
clf.fit(X_train, y_train) # y_train is a list of labels
labels = clf.predict(X_test)
```

Interestingly, in the fine-tuning available on OpenAI, all inputs are passed through a moderation system to make sure that the inputs are compatible with safety standards.

This concludes fine-tuning. LLMs can be deployed and queried without any task-specific tuning. By prompting, we can accomplish few-shot learning or even zero-shot learning, as we'll discuss in the next section.

Prompt engineering

Prompts are the instructions and examples we provide to language models to steer their behavior. They are important for steering the behavior of LLMs because they allow you to align the model outputs to human intentions without expensive retraining. Carefully engineered prompts can make LLMs suitable for a wide variety of tasks beyond what they were originally trained for. Prompts act as instructions that demonstrate to the LLM what the desired input-output mapping is.

Prompts consist of three main components:

- **Instructions** that describe the task requirements, goals, and format of input/output. They explain the task to the model unambiguously.
- **Examples** that demonstrate the desired input-output pairs. They provide diverse demonstrations of how different inputs should map to outputs.
- **Input** that the model must act on to generate the output.

The following figure shows a few examples of prompting different language models (source: *Pretrain, Prompt, and Predict - A Systematic Survey of Prompting Methods in Natural Language Processing* by Liu and colleagues, 2021):

Figure 8.3: Prompt examples, particularly knowledge probing in close form, and summarization

Prompt engineering, also known as in-context learning, refers to techniques to steer LLM behavior through carefully designed prompts, without changing the model weights. The goal is to align the model outputs with human intentions for a given task. Prompt tuning, on the other hand, provides intuitive control over model behavior but is sensitive to the precise wording and design of prompts, suggesting the need for carefully crafted guidelines to achieve desired results. But what do good prompts look like?

The most important first step is to start simple and work iteratively. Begin with concise, straightforward instructions and build up complexity gradually as needed. Break complex tasks down into simpler sub-tasks. This avoids overwhelming the model initially. Be as specific, descriptive, and detailed as possible about the exact task and desired format of the output. Providing relevant examples is highly effective in demonstrating the required reasoning chains or output styles.

For complex reasoning tasks, prompting the model to explain its step-by-step thought process leads to increased accuracy. Techniques like chain-of-thought prompting guide the model to reason explicitly. Providing few-shot examples further demonstrates the desired reasoning format. Problem decomposition prompts that break down complex problems into smaller, more manageable sub-tasks also improve reliability by enabling a more structured reasoning process. Sampling multiple candidate responses and picking the most consistent one helps reduce errors and inconsistencies, compared to relying on a single-model output.

Instead of focusing on what not to do, clearly specify the desired actions and outcomes. Direct, unambiguous instructions work best. Avoid imprecise or vague prompts. Start simple, be specific, provide examples, prompt for explanations, decompose problems, and sample multiple responses – these are some best practices to steer LLMs effectively using careful prompt engineering. With iteration and experimentation, prompts can be optimized to improve reliability, even for complex tasks, and achieve a performance often comparable to fine-tuning.

After learning about best practices, let's look at a few prompt techniques, from simple to increasingly more advanced!

Prompt techniques

Basic prompting methods include zero-shot prompting with just the input text, and few-shot prompting with a few demonstration examples showing the desired input-output pairs. Researchers have identified biases like majority label bias and recency bias that contribute to variability in few-shot performance. Careful prompt design through example selection, ordering, and formatting can help mitigate these issues.

More advanced prompting techniques include instruction prompting, where the task requirements are described explicitly rather than just demonstrated. Self-consistency sampling generates multiple outputs and selects the one that aligns best with the examples. **Chain-of-Thought (CoT)** prompting generates explicit reasoning steps, leading to the final output. This is especially beneficial for complex reasoning tasks. CoT prompts can be manually written or generated automatically via methods like **augment-prune-select**.

This table gives a brief overview of a few methods of prompting compared to fine-tuning:

Technique	Description	Key Idea	Performance Considerations
Zero-Shot Prompting	No examples provided; rely on the model's training	Leverages the model's pre-training	Works for simple tasks, but struggles with complex reasoning
Few-Shot Prompting	Provides a few demos of input and desired output	Shows desired reasoning format	Tripled accuracy on grade-school math

CoT	Prefix responses with intermediate reasoning steps	Gives the model space to reason before answering	Quadrupled accuracy on a math dataset
Least-to-Most Prompting	Prompts the model for simpler subtasks first	Decomposes a problem into smaller pieces	Boosted accuracy from 16% to 99.7% on some tasks
Self-Consistency	Picks the most frequent answer from multiple samples	Increases redundancy	Gained 1–24 percentage points across benchmarks
Chain-of-Density	Iteratively creates dense summaries by adding entities	Generates rich, concise summaries	Improves information density in summaries
Chain-of-Verification (CoV)	Verifies an initial response by generating and answering questions	Mimics human verification	Enhances robustness and confidence
Active Prompting	Picks uncertain samples for human labeling as examples	Finds effective few-shot examples	Improves few-shot performance
Tree-of-Thought	Generates and automatically evaluates multiple responses	Allows backtracking through reasoning paths	Finds an optimal reasoning route
Verifiers	Trains a separate model to evaluate responses	Filters out incorrect responses	Lifted grade-school math accuracy by ~20 percentage points
Fine-Tuning	Fine-tunes on an explanation dataset generated via prompting	Improves the model's reasoning abilities	73% accuracy on a commonsense QA dataset

Table 8.2: Prompting techniques for LLMs compared to fine-tuning

Some prompting techniques incorporate external information retrieval to provide missing context to the LLM before generating the output. For open-domain QA, relevant paragraphs can be retrieved via search engines and incorporated into the prompt. For closed-book QA, few-shot examples with an evidence-question-answer format work better than a QA format.

In the next few subsections, we'll go through a few of the aforementioned techniques. LangChain provides tools to enable advanced prompt engineering strategies like zero-shot prompting, few-shot learning, chain-of-thought, self-consistency, and tree-of-thought. All these techniques described here enhance the accuracy, consistency, and reliability of LLMs' reasoning capabilities on complex tasks by providing clearer instructions, fine-tuning with targeted data, employing problem breakdown strategies, incorporating diverse sampling approaches, integrating verification mechanisms, and adopting probabilistic modeling frameworks.

You can find all the examples from this section in the `prompting` directory in the GitHub repository for the book. Let's start with the vanilla strategy: we just ask for a solution.

Zero-shot prompting

Zero-shot prompting, as opposed to few-shot prompting, involves feeding task instructions directly to an LLM without providing any demonstrations or examples. This prompt tests the capabilities of the pre-trained model to understand and follow the instructions:

```
from langchain import PromptTemplate
from langchain.chat_models import ChatOpenAI
model = ChatOpenAI()
prompt = PromptTemplate(input_variables=["text"], template="Classify the
sentiment of this text: {text}")
chain = prompt | model
print(chain.invoke({"text": "I hated that movie, it was terrible!"}))
```

This outputs the sentiment classification prompt with the input text, without any examples:

```
content='The sentiment of this text is negative.' additional_kwargs={}
example=False
```

Few-shot learning

Few-shot learning presents the LLM with just a few input-output examples relevant to the task, without explicit instructions. This allows the model to infer the intentions and goals purely from demonstrations. Carefully selected, ordered, and formatted examples can improve the model's inference abilities. However, few-shot learning can be prone to biases and variability across trials. Adding explicit instructions can make the intentions more transparent to the model and improve robustness. Overall, prompts combine the strengths of instructions and examples to maximize steering of the LLM for the task at hand.

The `FewShotPromptTemplate` allows you to show the model just a few demonstration examples of the task to prime it, without explicit instructions.

Let's extend the previous example for sentiment classification with few-shot prompting. In this example, we want an LLM to categorize customer feedback into Positive, Negative, or Neutral. We provide it with a few examples:

```
examples = [{
    "input": "I absolutely love the new update! Everything works
seamlessly.",
    "output": "Positive",
    },{
    "input": "It's okay, but I think it could use more features.",
    "output": "Neutral",
    }, {
    "input": "I'm disappointed with the service, I expected much better
performance.",
    "output": "Negative"
}]
```

We can use these examples in a prompt like this:

```
from langchain.prompts import FewShotPromptTemplate, PromptTemplate
from langchain.chat_models import ChatOpenAI
example_prompt = PromptTemplate(
    template="{input} -> {output}",
    input_variables=["input", "output"],
)
prompt = FewShotPromptTemplate(
    examples=examples,
    example_prompt=example_prompt,
    suffix="Question: {input}",
    input_variables=["input"]
)
print((prompt | ChatOpenAI()).invoke({"input": " This is an excellent book
with high quality explanations."}))
```

We should get the following output:

```
content='Positive' additional_kwargs={} example=False
```

You can expect the LLM to use these examples to guide its classification of the new sentence. The few-shot method primes the model without extensive training, relying instead on its pre-trained knowledge and the context provided by the examples.

To choose examples tailored to each input, `FewShotPromptTemplate` can accept a `SemanticSim ilarityExampleSelector`, based on embeddings rather than hardcoded examples. The `Semant icSimilarityExampleSelector` automatically finds the most relevant examples for each input.

For many tasks, standard few-shot prompting works well, but there are many other techniques and extensions when dealing with more complex reasoning tasks.

Chain-of-thought prompting

CoT prompting aims to encourage reasoning by getting the model to provide intermediate steps, leading to the definitive answer. This is done by prefixing the prompt with instructions to show its thinking.

There are two variants of CoT, zero-shot and few-shot. In zero-shot CoT, we just add the instruction "Let's think step by step!" to the prompt.

When asking an LLM to reason through a problem, it is often more effective to have it explain its reasoning before stating the final answer. This encourages the LLM to logically think through the problem first, rather than just guessing the answer and trying to justify it afterward. Asking an LLM to explain its thought process aligns well with its core capabilities.

For example:

```
from langchain.chat_models import ChatOpenAI
from langchain.prompts import PromptTemplate

reasoning_prompt = "{question}\nLet's think step by step!"
prompt = PromptTemplate(
  template=reasoning_prompt,
  input_variables=["question"]
)
model = ChatOpenAI()
chain = prompt | model
print(chain.invoke({
    "question": "There were 5 apples originally. I ate 2 apples. My friend
gave me 3 apples. How many apples do I have now?",
}))
```

After running this, we get the reasoning process together with the result:

```
content='Step 1: Originally, there were 5 apples.\nStep 2: I ate 2
apples.\nStep 3: So, I had 5 - 2 = 3 apples left.\nStep 4: My friend gave
me 3 apples.\nStep 5: Adding the apples my friend gave me, I now have 3 +
3 = 6 apples.' additional_kwargs={} example=False
```

The preceding approach is also called **zero-shot chain-of-thought**.

Few-shot chain-of-thought prompting is a few-shot prompt, where the reasoning is explained as part of the example solutions, with the idea to encourage an LLM to explain its reasoning before deciding.

If we go back to the few-shot examples from earlier, we can extend them as follows:

```
examples = [{
    "input": "I absolutely love the new update! Everything works
seamlessly.",
    "output": "Love and absolute works seamlessly are examples of positive
sentiment. Therefore, the sentiment is positive",
    },{
    "input": "It's okay, but I think it could use more features.",
    "output": "It's okay is not an endorsement. The customer further
thinks it should be extended. Therefore, the sentiment is neutral",
    }, {
    "input": "I'm disappointed with the service, I expected much better
performance.",
    "output": "The customer is disappointed and expected more. This is
negative"
}]
```

In these examples, the reasons for the decision are explained. This encourages the LLM to give a similar result explaining its reasoning.

It has been shown that CoT prompting can lead to more accurate results; however, this performance boost was found to be proportional to the size of the model, and the improvements were negligible or even negative in smaller models.

Self-consistency

With self-consistency prompting, the model generates multiple candidate answers to a question. These are then compared against each other, and the most consistent or frequent answer is selected as the final output. A good example of self-consistency prompting with LLMs is in the context of fact verification or information synthesis, where accuracy is paramount.

In the first step, we'll create multiple solutions to a question or a problem:

```python
from langchain import PromptTemplate, LLMChain
from langchain.chat_models import ChatOpenAI
solutions_template = """
Generate {num_solutions} distinct answers to this question:
{question}

Solutions:
"""
solutions_prompt = PromptTemplate(
    template=solutions_template,
    input_variables=["question", "num_solutions"]
)
solutions_chain = LLMChain(
    llm=ChatOpenAI(),
    prompt=solutions_prompt,
    output_key="solutions"
)
```

For the second step, we want to count the different answers. We can use an LLM again:

```python
consistency_template = """
For each answer in {solutions}, count the number of times it occurs.
Finally, choose the answer that occurs most.

Most frequent solution:
"""
consistency_prompt = PromptTemplate(
    template=consistency_template,
    input_variables=["solutions"]
)
consistency_chain = LLMChain(
    llm=ChatOpenAI(),
    prompt=consistency_prompt,
    output_key="best_solution"
)
```

Let's put these two chains together with a `SequentialChain`:

```
from langchain.chains import SequentialChain
answer_chain = SequentialChain(
    chains=[solutions_chain, consistency_chain],
    input_variables=["question", "num_solutions"],
    output_variables=["best_solution"]
)
```

Let's ask a simple question and check the answer:

```
print(answer_chain.run(
    question="Which year was the Declaration of Independence of the United
States signed?",
    num_solutions="5"
))
```

We should get a response like this:

```
1776 is the year in which the Declaration of Independence of the United
States was signed. It occurs twice in the given answers (3 and 4).
```

We should get the right response based on the vote; however, of the five responses we produced, three were wrong.

This approach leverages the model's ability to reason and utilize internal knowledge while reducing the risk of outliers or incorrect information, by focusing on the most recurring answer, thus improving the overall reliability of the response given by the LLM.

Tree-of-thought

In **Tree-of-Thought (ToT)** prompting, we generate multiple problem-solving steps or approaches for a given prompt and then use the AI model to critique them. The critique will be based on the model's judgment of the solution's suitability to the problem.

There is actually an implementation now of ToT in the LangChain experimental package; however, let's walk through an instructive step-by-step example of implementing ToT using LangChain.

First, we'll define our four chain components with `PromptTemplates`. We need a solution template, an evaluation template, a reasoning template, and a ranking template.

Let's first generate solutions:

```
solutions_template = """
Generate {num_solutions} distinct solutions for {problem}. Consider
factors like {factors}.

Solutions:
"""
solutions_prompt = PromptTemplate(
    template=solutions_template,
    input_variables=["problem", "factors", "num_solutions"]
)
```

Let's ask the LLM to evaluate these solutions:

```
evaluation_template = """
Evaluate each solution in {solutions} by analyzing pros, cons,
feasibility, and probability of success.

Evaluations:
"""
evaluation_prompt = PromptTemplate(
    template=evaluation_template,
    input_variables=["solutions"]
)
```

After this step, we want to reason a bit more about them:

```
reasoning_template = """
For the most promising solutions in {evaluations}, explain scenarios,
implementation strategies, partnerships needed, and handling potential
obstacles.

Enhanced Reasoning:
"""
reasoning_prompt = PromptTemplate(
    template=reasoning_template,
    input_variables=["evaluations"]
)
```

Finally, we can rank these solutions given our reasoning so far:

```python
ranking_template = """
Based on the evaluations and reasoning, rank the solutions in {enhanced_
reasoning} from most to least promising.

Ranked Solutions:
"""
ranking_prompt = PromptTemplate(
    template=ranking_template,
    input_variables=["enhanced_reasoning"]
)
```

Next, we create chains from these templates before we put the chains all together:

```python
from langchain.chains.llm import LLMChain
from langchain.chat_models import ChatOpenAI

solutions_chain = LLMChain(
    llm=ChatOpenAI(),
    prompt=solutions_prompt,
    output_key="solutions"
)
evalutation_chain = LLMChain(
    llm=ChatOpenAI(),
    prompt=evaluation_prompt,
    output_key="evaluations"
)
reasoning_chain = LLMChain(
    llm=ChatOpenAI(),
    prompt=reasoning_prompt,
    output_key="enhanced_reasoning"
)
ranking_chain = LLMChain(
    llm=ChatOpenAI(),
    prompt=ranking_prompt,
    output_key="ranked_solutions"
)
```

Please note how each output_key corresponds to an input_key in the prompt of the following chain. Finally, we connect these chains into a SequentialChain:

```
from langchain.chains import SequentialChain
tot_chain = SequentialChain(
    chains=[solutions_chain, evalutation_chain, reasoning_chain, ranking_
chain],
    input_variables=["problem", "factors", "num_solutions"],
    output_variables=["ranked_solutions"]
)
print(tot_chain.run(
    problem="Prompt engineering",
    factors="Requirements for high task performance, low token use, and few
calls to the LLM",
    num_solutions=3
))
```

Let's run our tot_chain and see the printed output:

```
1. Train or fine-tune language models using datasets that are relevant to
the reasoning task at hand.
2. Develop or adapt reasoning algorithms and techniques to improve the
performance of language models in specific reasoning tasks.
3. Evaluate existing language models and identify their strengths and
weaknesses in reasoning.
4. Implement evaluation metrics to measure the reasoning performance of
the language models.
5. Iteratively refine and optimize the reasoning capabilities of the
language models based on evaluation results.


It is important to note that the ranking of solutions may vary depending
on the specific context and requirements of each scenario.
```

I wholeheartedly agree with the suggestions. They show the strengths of ToT. A lot of these topics are part of this chapter, while some will come up in *Chapter 9, Generative AI in Production*, where we'll discuss evaluating LLMs and their performance.

This allows us to leverage the LLM at each stage of the reasoning process. The ToT approach helps avoid dead ends by fostering exploration. If you want to see more examples, in the LangChain cookbook, you can find a ToT for playing sudoku.

Prompt design is highly significant for unlocking LLM reasoning capabilities, and it offers the potential for future advancements in models and prompting techniques. These principles and techniques form a valuable toolkit for researchers and practitioners working with LLMs.

Summary

Conditioning allows steering generative AI to improve performance, safety, and quality. In this chapter, the focus is on conditioning through fine-tuning and prompting. In fine-tuning, the language model is trained on many examples of tasks formulated as natural language instructions, along with appropriate responses. This is often done through reinforcement learning with human feedback; however, other techniques have been developed that have been shown to produce competitive results with lower resource footprints. In the first recipe of this chapter, we implemented fine-tuning of a small open-source model for question answering.

There are many techniques for prompting that can improve the reliability of LLMs in complex reasoning tasks, including step-by-step prompting, alternate selection, inference prompts, problem decomposition, sampling multiple responses, and employing separate verifier models. These methods have been shown to enhance accuracy and consistency in reasoning tasks. LangChain provides building blocks to unlock advanced prompting strategies like few-shot learning, CoT, ToT, and others, as we've shown in the examples.

In *Chapter 9, Generative AI in Production*, we'll talk about the productionization of generative AI and critical issues related to it, such as evaluating LLM apps, deploying them to a server, and monitoring them.

Questions

I'd recommend that you go back to the corresponding sections of this chapter if you are unsure about any of the answers to these questions:

1. What is conditioning, and what is alignment?
2. What are the different methods of conditioning, and how can we distinguish them?
3. What is instruction tuning, and what is its importance?
4. Name a few fine-tuning methods.
5. What is quantization?
6. What is few-shot learning?
7. What is CoT prompting?
8. How does ToT work?

Join our community on Discord

Join our community's Discord space for discussions with the authors and other readers:

`https://packt.link/lang`

9

Generative AI in Production

As we've discussed in this book, LLMs have gained significant attention in recent years due to their ability to generate human-like text. From creative writing to conversational chatbots, these generative AI models have diverse applications across industries. However, taking these complex neural network systems from research to real-world deployment comes with significant challenges.

So far, we've talked about models, agents, and LLM apps as well as different use cases, but there are many issues that become important when deploying these apps into production to engage with customers and to make decisions that can have a significant financial impact. This chapter explores the practical considerations and best practices for productionizing generative AI, specifically LLM apps. Before we deploy an application, performance and regulatory requirements need to be ensured, it needs to be robust at scale, and finally monitoring has to be in place. Maintaining rigorous testing, auditing, and ethical safeguards is essential for trustworthy deployment. We'll discuss evaluation and observability, and cover a broad range of topics that encompass the governance and lifecycle management of operationalized AI and decision models, including generative AI models.

While getting an LLM app ready for production, offline evaluation provides a preliminary understanding of a model's abilities in a controlled setting, and when in production, observability offers continuing insights into its performance in live environments. We'll discuss a few tools for either case and I'll give examples. We'll also discuss the deployment of LLM applications and give an overview of available tools and examples for deployment.

Throughout the chapter, we'll work on practical examples with LLM apps, which you can find in the GitHub repository for the book at `https://github.com/benman1/generative_ai_with_langchain`.

The main sections of this chapter are:

- How to get LLM apps ready for production

- How to evaluate LLM apps

- How to deploy LLM apps

- How to observe LLM apps

Let's start with an overview of what it means and involves to get an LLM app ready for production!

How to get LLM apps ready for production

Deploying LLM applications to production is intricate, encompassing robust data management, ethical foresight, efficient resource allocation, diligent monitoring, and alignment with behavioral guidelines. Practices to ensure deployment readiness involve:

- **Data management:** Rigorous attention to data quality is critical to avoid biases that can emanate from imbalanced or inappropriate training data. Substantial efforts in data curation and ongoing scrutiny of model outputs are required to mitigate emerging biases.

- **Ethical deployment and compliance:** LLM applications are potentially capable of generating harmful content, thus necessitating strict review processes, safety guidelines, and compliance with regulations such as HIPAA, especially in sensitive sectors such as healthcare.

- **Resource management:** The resource demands of LLMs call for an infrastructure that is both efficient and environmentally sustainable. Innovation in infrastructure helps to reduce costs and address environmental concerns tied to the energy demands of LLMs.

- **Performance management:** Models must be continually monitored for data drift—where changes in input data patterns can alter model performance—and performance degradation over time. Detecting these deviations necessitates prompt retraining or model adjustments.

- **Interpretability:** To build trust and offer insight into the decision-making processes of LLMs, interpretability tools are increasingly important for users who need clarity on how model decisions are reached.

- **Data security:** Protecting sensitive information within LLM processes is essential for privacy and compliance. Strong encryption measures and stringent access controls bolster security measures.

- **Model behavior standards**: Models must align with ethical guidelines beyond basic functional performance—ensuring outputs are constructive (helpful), innocuous (harmless), and trustworthy (honest). This results in stability and societal acceptance.

- **Hallucination mitigation**: Hallucinations refer to instances where LLMs inadvertently generate or recall sensitive personal information from their training data corpus in the outputs, despite no prompting for such details in the input source—highlighting critical privacy concerns and the need for mitigation strategies.

Essential recommendations for deploying LLM apps encompass an array of practices aimed at mitigating technical challenges, improving performance, and ensuring ethical integrity. First and foremost, it's crucial to develop standardized datasets with relevant benchmarks to test and measure model capabilities, including the detection of regressions and alignment with defined goals.

Metrics should be task-specific to gauge the model's proficiency accurately. There also needs to be a robust framework that includes ethical guidelines, safety protocols, and review processes to prevent the generation and dissemination of harmful content. Human reviewers serve as an essential checkpoint in content validation and bring ethical discernment to AI outputs, ensuring adherence across all contexts.

A forward-thinking UX can foster a transparent relationship with users while reinforcing sensible use. This can include anticipating inaccuracies, such as disclaimers on limitations, attributions, and collecting rich user feedback.

To explain outputs, we should invest in interpretability methods that explain how generative AI models arrive at their decisions. Visualizing attention mechanisms or analyzing feature importance can peel back the layers of complexity, which is particularly crucial for high-stakes industries such as healthcare or finance.

We discussed hallucinations in *Chapter 4, Building Capable Assistants*. Mitigation techniques include external retrieval and tool augmentation to provide pertinent context, as we discussed in *Chapter 5, Building a Chatbot like ChatGPT*, and *Chapter 6, Developing Software with Generative AI*, in particular. There is a danger of models recalling private information, and ongoing advances in methods spanning data filtering, architecture adjustments, and inference techniques show promise in mitigating these problems.

For security, we can strengthen role-based access policies, employ stringent data encryption standards, adopt anonymization best practices where feasible, and ensure continuous verification through compliance audits. Security is a huge topic in the context of LLMs, however, we'll focus on evaluation, observability, and deployment in this chapter.

We need to optimize infrastructure and resource usage by employing distributed techniques such as data parallelism or model parallelism to facilitate workload distribution across multiple processing units. We can employ techniques such as model compression or other computer architectural optimizations for more efficient deployment regarding inference speed and latency management. Techniques such as model quantization, discussed in *Chapter 8, Customizing LLMs and Their Output*, or model distillation can also help reduce the resource footprint of the model. Further, storing model outputs can reduce latency and costs for repeated queries.

With insightful planning and preparation, generative AI promises to transform industries from creative writing to customer service. But thoughtfully navigating the complexities of these systems remains critical as they continue to permeate increasingly diverse domains. This chapter aims to provide a practical guide to some of the pieces that we haven't covered in this book so far, aiming to help you build impactful and responsible generative AI applications. We cover strategies for data curation, model development, infrastructure, monitoring, and transparency.

Before we continue our discussion, a few words on terminology are in order. Let's start by introducing MLOps and similar terms, and define what they mean and imply.

Terminology

MLOps is a paradigm that focuses on deploying and maintaining machine learning models in production reliably and efficiently. It combines the practices of DevOps with machine learning to transition algorithms from experimental systems to production systems. MLOps aims to increase automation, improve the quality of production models, and address business and regulatory requirements.

LLMOps is a specialized sub-category of MLOps. It refers to the operational capabilities and infrastructure necessary for fine-tuning and operationalizing LLMs as part of a product. While it may not be drastically different from the concept of MLOps, the distinction lies in the specific requirements connected to handling, refining, and deploying massive language models such as GPT-3, which houses 175 billion parameters.

The term **LMOps** is more inclusive than LLMOps as it encompasses various types of language models, including both LLMs and smaller generative models. This term acknowledges the expanding landscape of language models and their relevance in operational contexts.

Foundational Model Orchestration (FOMO) specifically addresses the challenges faced when working with foundation models, that is, models trained on broad data that can be adapted to a wide range of downstream tasks. It highlights the need for managing multi-step processes, integrating with external resources, and coordinating the workflows involving these models.

The term **ModelOps** focuses on the governance and lifecycle management of AI and decision models as they are deployed. Even more broadly, **AgentOps** involves the operational management of LLMs and other AI agents, ensuring their appropriate behavior, managing their environment and resource access, and facilitating interactions between agents while addressing concerns related to unintended outcomes and incompatible objectives.

While FOMO emphasizes the unique challenges of working specifically with foundational models, LMOps provides a more inclusive and comprehensive coverage of a wider range of language models beyond just the foundational ones. LMOps acknowledges the versatility and increasing importance of language models in various operational use cases, while still falling under the broader umbrella of MLOps. Finally, AgentOps explicitly highlights the interactive nature of agents consisting of generative models operating with certain heuristics and includes tools.

The emergence of all of these very specialized terms underscores the rapid evolution of the field; however, their long-term prevalence is unclear. MLOps is widely used and often encompasses the many more specialized terms we just covered. Therefore, we'll stick to MLOps for the remainder of this chapter.

Before productionizing any LLM app, we should first evaluate its output, so we should start with this. We will focus on the evaluation methods provided by LangChain.

How to evaluate LLM apps

The crux of LLM deployment lies in the meticulous curation of training data to preempt biases, implementing human-led annotation for data enhancement, and establishing automated output monitoring systems. Evaluating LLMs either as standalone entities or in conjunction with an agent chain is crucial to ensure they function correctly and produce reliable results, and this is an integral part of the ML lifecycle. The evaluation process determines the performance of the models in terms of effectiveness, reliability, and efficiency.

The goal of evaluating LLMs is to understand their strengths and weaknesses, enhancing accuracy and efficiency while reducing errors, thereby maximizing their usefulness in solving real-world problems. This evaluation process typically occurs offline during the development phase. Offline evaluations provide initial insights into model performance under controlled test conditions and include aspects such as hyperparameter tuning and benchmarking against peer models or established standards. They offer a necessary first step toward refining a model before deployment.

While human assessments are sometimes seen as the gold standard, they are hard to scale and require careful design to avoid bias from subjective preferences or authoritative tones. There are many standardized benchmarks such as MBPP to test basic programming skills, while GSM8K is utilized for multi-step mathematical reasoning. API-Bank evaluates models' aptitudes for making decisions about API calls. ARC puts models' question-answering abilities up against complex integrations of information, whereas HellaSwag assesses common-sense reasoning in physical situations using adversarial filtering.

HumanEval focuses on code generation's functional correctness over syntactic similarity. MMLU assesses language understanding across a wide range of subjects at varying depths, indicating proficiency in specialized domains. SuperGLUE takes GLUE a step further with more challenging tasks to monitor the fairness and comprehension of language models. TruthfulQA brings a unique angle by benchmarking the truthfulness of LLM responses, foregrounding the significance of veracity.

Benchmarks such as MATH demand high-level reasoning capability evaluations. GPT-4's performance on this benchmark varies with prompting method sophistication, from few-shot prompts to reinforcement learning with reward modeling approaches. Notably, dialog-based fine-tuning can sometimes detract from capabilities assessed by measures such as MMLU.

Evaluations can provide insights into how well an LLM generates outputs that are relevant, accurate, and helpful. Tests such as FLAN and FLASK stress behavioral dimensions, thus prioritizing responsible AI systems deployment. This chart compares several open and closed source models on the FLASK benchmark (source: *"FLASK: Fine-grained Language Model Evaluation based on Alignment Skill Sets"* by Ye and colleagues, 2023; https://arxiv.org/abs/2307.10928):

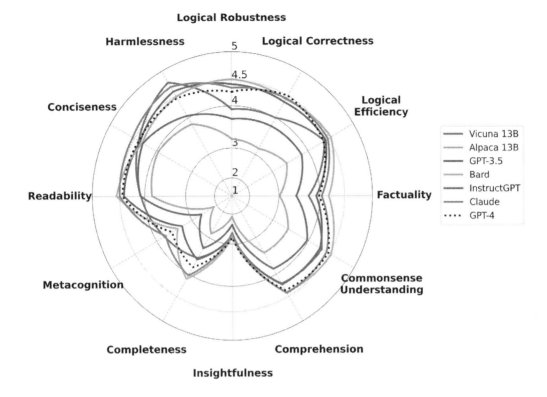

Figure 9.1: Result of an evaluation with Claude as an evaluating language model

In the result reported in the chart, Claude is the LLM evaluating all outputs. This skews results in favor of Claude and models similar to it. Often, GPT-3.5 or GPT-4 are used as evaluators, which shows the OpenAI models emerging as winners.

In LangChain, there are various ways to evaluate the outputs of LLMs, including comparing chain outputs, pairwise string comparisons, string distances, and embedding distances. The evaluation results can be used to determine the preferred model based on the comparison of outputs. Confidence intervals and p-values can also be calculated to assess the reliability of the evaluation results.

LangChain provides several tools for evaluating the outputs of LLMs. A common approach is to compare the outputs of different models or prompts using `PairwiseStringEvaluator`. This prompts an evaluator model to choose between two model outputs for the same input and aggregates the results to determine an overall preferred model.

Other evaluators allow assessing model outputs based on specific criteria such as correctness, relevance, and conciseness. The `CriteriaEvalChain` can score outputs on custom or predefined principles without needing reference labels. Configuring the evaluation model is also possible by specifying a different chat model such as ChatGPT as the evaluator.

You can follow the code in this section online under the `monitoring_and_evaluation` folder in the book's GitHub project. Let's compare outputs of different prompts or LLMs with the `PairwiseStringEvaluator`, which prompts an LLM to select the preferred output given a specific input.

Comparing two outputs

This evaluation requires an evaluator, a dataset of inputs, and two or more LLMs, chains, or agents to compare. The evaluation aggregates the results to determine the preferred model.

The evaluation process involves several steps:

1. **Create the evaluator**: Load the evaluator using the `load_evaluator()` function, specifying the type of evaluator (in this case, `pairwise_string`).

2. **Select the dataset**: Load a dataset of inputs using the `load_dataset()` function.

3. **Define models to compare**: Initialize the LLMs, chains, or agents to compare using the necessary configurations. This involves initializing the language model and any additional tools or agents required.

4. **Generate responses**: Generate outputs for each of the models before evaluating them. This is typically done in batches to improve efficiency.

5. **Evaluate pairs**: Evaluate the results by comparing the outputs of different models for each input. This is often done using a random selection order to reduce positional bias.

Here's an example from the documentation for pairwise string comparisons:

```
from langchain.evaluation import load_evaluator
evaluator = load_evaluator("labeled_pairwise_string")
evaluator.evaluate_string_pairs(
    prediction="there are three dogs",
    prediction_b="4",
    input="how many dogs are in the park?",
    reference="four",
)
```

The output from the evaluator should look as follows:

```
    {'reasoning': "Both assistants provided a direct answer to the user's
question. However, Assistant A's response is incorrect as it stated there
are three dogs in the park, while the reference answer indicates there are
four. On the other hand, Assistant B's response is accurate and matches
the reference answer. Therefore, considering the criteria of correctness
and accuracy, Assistant B's response is superior. \n\nFinal Verdict:
[[B]]",
'value': 'B',
'score': 0

}
```

The evaluation result includes a score between 0 and 1, indicating the effectiveness of each agent, sometimes along with reasoning that outlines the evaluation process and justifies the score. In this specific example against the reference, both results are factually incorrect based on the input. We could remove the reference and let an LLM judge the outputs instead.

Comparing against criteria

LangChain provides several predefined evaluators for different evaluation criteria. These evaluators can be used to assess outputs based on specific rubrics or criteria sets. Some common criteria include conciseness, relevance, correctness, coherence, helpfulness, and controversiality.

CriteriaEvalChain allows you to evaluate model outputs against custom or predefined criteria. It provides a way to verify whether an LLM or chain's output complies with a defined set of criteria. You can use this evaluator to assess correctness, relevance, conciseness, and other aspects of the generated outputs.

CriteriaEvalChain can be configured to work with or without reference labels. Without reference labels, the evaluator relies on the LLM's predicted answer and scores it based on the specified criteria. With reference labels, the evaluator compares the predicted answer to the reference label and determines its compliance with the criteria.

The evaluation LLM used in LangChain, by default, is GPT-4. However, you can configure the evaluation LLM by specifying other chat models, such as ChatAnthropic or ChatOpenAI, with the desired settings (for example, temperature). The evaluators can be loaded with a custom LLM by passing the LLM object as a parameter to the load_evaluator() function.

LangChain supports both custom criteria and predefined principles for evaluation. Custom criteria can be defined using a dictionary of `criterion_name: criterion_description` pairs. These criteria can be used to assess outputs based on specific requirements or rubrics.

Here's a simple example:

```
custom_criteria = {
    "simplicity": "Is the language straightforward and unpretentious?",
    "clarity": "Are the sentences clear and easy to understand?",
    "precision": "Is the writing precise, with no unnecessary words or
details?",
    "truthfulness": "Does the writing feel honest and sincere?",
    "subtext": "Does the writing suggest deeper meanings or themes?",
}
evaluator = load_evaluator("pairwise_string", criteria=custom_criteria)


evaluator.evaluate_string_pairs(
    prediction="Every cheerful household shares a similar rhythm of joy;
but sorrow, in each household, plays a unique, haunting melody.",
    prediction_b="Where one finds a symphony of joy, every domicile of
happiness resounds in harmonious,"
    " identical notes; yet, every abode of despair conducts a dissonant
orchestra, each"
    " playing an elegy of grief that is peculiar and profound to its own
existence.",
    input="Write some prose about families.",
)
```

We can get a very nuanced comparison of the two outputs, as this result shows:

```
{'reasoning': 'Response A is simple, clear, and precise. It uses
straightforward language to convey a deep and sincere message about
families. The metaphor of music is used effectively to suggest deeper
meanings about the shared joys and unique sorrows of families.\n\nResponse
B, on the other hand, is less simple and clear. The language is more
complex and pretentious, with phrases like "domicile of happiness" and
"abode of despair" instead of the simpler "household" used in Response A.
The message is similar to that of Response A, but it is less effectively
conveyed due to the unnecessary complexity of the language.\n\nTherefore,
based on the criteria of simplicity, clarity, precision, truthfulness,
```

```
and subtext, Response A is the better response.\n\n[[A]]', 'value': 'A',
'score': 1}
```

Alternatively, you can use the predefined principles available in LangChain, such as those from Constitutional AI. These principles are designed to evaluate the ethical, harmful, and sensitive aspects of the outputs. The use of principles in evaluation allows for a more focused assessment of the generated text.

String and semantic comparisons

LangChain supports string comparison and distance metrics for evaluating LLM outputs. String distance metrics such as Levenshtein and Jaro provide a quantitative measure of similarity between predicted and reference strings. Embedding distances using models such as SentenceTransformers calculates semantic similarity between the generated and expected texts.

Embedding distance evaluators can use embedding models, such as those based on GPT-4 or Hugging Face embeddings, to compute vector distances between the predicted and reference strings. This measures the semantic similarity between the two strings and can provide insights into the quality of the generated text.

Here's a quick example from the documentation:

```
from langchain.evaluation import load_evaluator
evaluator = load_evaluator("embedding_distance")
evaluator.evaluate_strings(prediction="I shall go", reference="I shan't
go")
```

The evaluator returns the score 0.0966466944859925. You can change the embeddings used with the embeddings parameter in the load_evaluator() call.

This often gives better results than older string distance metrics, but these are also available and allow for simple unit testing and assessment of accuracy. String comparison evaluators compare predicted strings against reference strings or inputs.

String distance evaluators use distance metrics, such as the Levenshtein or Jaro distance, to measure the similarity or dissimilarity between predicted and reference strings. This provides a quantitative measure of how similar the predicted string is to the reference string.

Finally, there's an agent trajectory evaluator, where the evaluate_agent_trajectory() method is used to evaluate the input, prediction, and agent trajectory.

We can also use LangSmith, a companion project for LangChain that aims to facilitate the passage of LLM apps from prototype to production, to compare our performance against a dataset. Let's step through an example!

Running evaluations against datasets

As we've mentioned, comprehensive benchmarking and evaluation, including testing, are critical for safety, robustness, and intended behavior. We can run evaluations against benchmark datasets in LangSmith as we'll see now. First, please make sure you create an account on LangSmith here: `https://smith.langchain.com/`.

You can obtain an API key and set it as `LANGCHAIN_API_KEY` in your environment. We can also set environment variables for project ID and tracing:

```
import os
os.environ["LANGCHAIN_TRACING_V2"] = "true"
os.environ["LANGCHAIN_PROJECT"] = "My Project"
```

This configures LangChain to log traces. If we don't tell LangChain the project ID, it will log against the `default` project. After this setup, when we run our LangChain agent or chain, we'll be able to see the traces on LangSmith.

Let's log a run!

```
from langchain.chat_models import ChatOpenAI

llm = ChatOpenAI()
llm.predict("Hello, world!")
```

We can find all these runs on LangSmith. LangSmith lists all runs so far on the LangSmith project page: `https://smith.langchain.com/projects`

We can also find all runs via the LangSmith API:

```
from langsmith import Client
client = Client()
runs = client.list_runs()
print(runs)
```

We can list runs from a specific project or by `run_type`, for example, `chain`. Each run comes with inputs and outputs, as `runs[0].inputs` and `runs[0].outputs`, respectively.

We can create a dataset from existing agent runs with the `create_example_from_run()` function – or from anything else. Here's how to create a dataset with a set of questions:

```
questions = [
    "A ship's parts are replaced over time until no original parts remain.
Is it still the same ship? Why or why not?",  # The Ship of Theseus
Paradox
    "If someone lived their whole life chained in a cave seeing only
shadows, how would they react if freed and shown the real world?",  #
Plato's Allegory of the Cave
    "Is something good because it is natural, or bad because it is
unnatural? Why can this be a faulty argument?",  # Appeal to Nature
Fallacy
    "If a coin is flipped 8 times and lands on heads each time, what
are the odds it will be tails next flip? Explain your reasoning.",  #
Gambler's Fallacy
    "Present two choices as the only options when others exist. Is the
statement \"You're either with us or against us\" an example of false
dilemma? Why?",  # False Dilemma
    "Do people tend to develop a preference for things simply because they
are familiar with them? Does this impact reasoning?",  # Mere Exposure
Effect
    "Is it surprising that the universe is suitable for intelligent life
since if it weren't, no one would be around to observe it?",  # Anthropic
Principle
    "If Theseus' ship is restored by replacing each plank, is it still the
same ship? What is identity based on?",  # Theseus' Paradox
    "Does doing one thing really mean that a chain of increasingly
negative events will follow? Why is this a problematic argument?",  #
Slippery Slope Fallacy
    "Is a claim true because it hasn't been proven false? Why could this
impede reasoning?",  # Appeal to Ignorance
]
shared_dataset_name = "Reasoning and Bias"
ds = client.create_dataset(
    dataset_name=shared_dataset_name, description="A few reasoning and
cognitive bias questions",
```

```
)
for q in questions:
    client.create_example(inputs={"input": q}, dataset_id=ds.id)
```

We can then define an LLM agent or chain on the dataset like this:

```
from langchain.chat_models import ChatOpenAI
from langchain.chains import LLMChain
llm = ChatOpenAI(model="gpt-4", temperature=0.0)
def construct_chain():
    return LLMChain.from_string(
        llm,
        template="Help out as best you can.\nQuestion: {input}\nResponse:
",
    )
```

To run an evaluation on a dataset, we can either specify an LLM or – for parallelism – use a constructor function to initialize the model or LLM app for each input. Now, to evaluate the performance against our dataset, we need to define an evaluator as we saw in the previous section:

```
from langchain.smith import RunEvalConfig
evaluation_config = RunEvalConfig(
    evaluators=[
        RunEvalConfig.Criteria({"helpfulness": "Is the response
helpful?"}),
        RunEvalConfig.Criteria({"insightful": "Is the response carefully
thought out?"})
    ]
)
```

As seen, the criteria are defined by a dictionary that includes a criterion as a key and a question to check for as the value.

We'll pass a dataset together with the evaluation configuration with evaluators to run_on_ dataset() to generate metrics and feedback:

```
from langchain.smith import run_on_dataset
results = run_on_dataset(
  client=client,
  dataset_name=shared_dataset_name,
  dataset=dataset,
```

```
llm_or_chain_factory=construct_chain,
evaluation=evaluation_config
)
```

Similarly, we could pass a dataset and evaluators to `run_on_dataset()` to generate metrics and feedback asynchronously.

We can view the evaluator feedback in the LangSmith UI to identify areas for improvement:

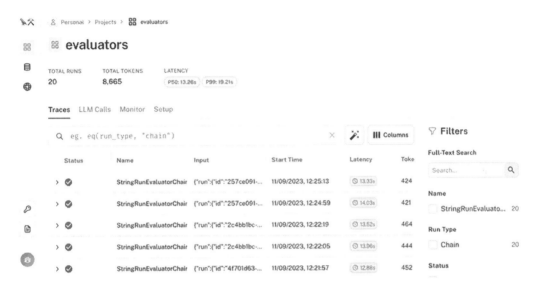

Figure 9.2: Evaluators in LangSmith

We can click on any of these evaluations to see some detail, for example, for the careful thinking evaluator, we get this prompt that includes the original answer from the LLM:

```
You are assessing a submitted answer on a given task or input based on a
set of criteria. Here is the data:
[BEGIN DATA]
***
[Input]: Is something good because it is natural, or bad because it is
unnatural? Why can this be a faulty argument?
***
[Submission]: The argument that something is good because it is natural,
or bad because it is unnatural, is often referred to as the "appeal to
nature" fallacy. This argument is faulty because it assumes that what is
natural is automatically good or beneficial, and what is unnatural is
automatically bad or harmful. However, this is not always the case. For
```

```
example, many natural substances can be harmful or deadly, such as certain
plants or animals. Conversely, many unnatural things, such as modern
medicine or technology, can greatly benefit our lives. Therefore, whether
something is natural or unnatural is not a reliable indicator of its value
or harm.
***
[Criteria]: insightful: Is the response carefully thought out?
***
[END DATA]
Does the submission meet the Criteria? First, write out in a step by step
manner your reasoning about each criterion to be sure that your conclusion
is correct. Avoid simply stating the correct answers at the outset. Then
print only the single character "Y" or "N" (without quotes or punctuation)
on its own line corresponding to the correct answer of whether the
submission meets all criteria. At the end, repeat just the letter again by
itself on a new line.
```

We get this evaluation:

```
The criterion is whether the response is insightful and carefully thought
out.

The submission provides a clear and concise explanation of the "appeal to
nature" fallacy, demonstrating an understanding of the concept. It also
provides examples to illustrate why this argument can be faulty, showing
that the respondent has thought about the question in depth. The response
is not just a simple yes or no, but a detailed explanation that shows
careful consideration of the question.

Therefore, the submission does meet the criterion of being insightful and
carefully thought out.
```

A way to improve performance for a few types of problems is to use few-shot prompting. LangSmith can help us with this as well. You can find more examples of this in the LangSmith documentation.

We haven't discussed data annotation queues, a new feature in LangSmith that addresses a critical gap that emerges after prototyping. Each log can be filtered by attributes such as errors to focus on problematic cases, or manually reviewed and annotated with labels or feedback and edited as needed. Edited logs can be added to a dataset for uses including fine-tuning the model.

This concludes the topic of evaluation here. Now that we've evaluated our agent, let's say we are happy with the performance and have decided to deploy it! What should we do next?

How to deploy LLM apps

Given the increasing use of LLMs in various sectors, it's imperative to understand how to effectively deploy models and apps into production. Deployment services and frameworks can help to scale the technical hurdles. There are lots of different ways to productionize LLM apps or applications with generative AI.

Deployment for production requires research into, and knowledge of, the generative AI ecosystem, which encompasses different aspects including:

- **Models and LLM-as-a-Service**: LLMs and other models either run on-premises or offered as an API on vendor-provided infrastructure.
- **Reasoning heuristics**: Retrieval Augmented Generation (RAG), Tree-of-Thought, and others.
- **Vector databases**: Aid in retrieving contextually relevant information for prompts.
- **Prompt engineering tools**: These facilitate in-context learning without requiring expensive fine-tuning or sensitive data.
- **Pre-training and fine-tuning**: For models specialized for specific tasks or domains.
- **Prompt logging, testing, and analytics**: An emerging sector inspired by the desire to understand and improve the performance of LLMs.
- **Custom LLM stack**: A set of tools for shaping and deploying solutions built on LLMs.

We discussed models in *Chapter 1, What Is Generative AI?* and *Chapter 3, Getting Started with Lang-Chain*, reasoning heuristics in *Chapter 4, Building Capable Assistants - Chapter 7, LLMs for Data Science*, vector databases in *Chapter 5, Building a Chatbot like ChatGPT*, and prompts and fine-tuning in *Chapter 8, Customizing LLMs and Their Output*. In the present chapter, we'll focus on logging, monitoring, and custom tools for deployment.

LLMs are typically utilized using external LLM providers or self-hosted models. With external providers, computational burdens are shouldered by companies such as OpenAI or Anthropic, while LangChain facilitates business logic implementation. However, self-hosting open-source LLMs can significantly decrease costs, latency, and privacy concerns.

Some tools with infrastructure offer the full package. For example, you can deploy LangChain agents with Chainlit, creating ChatGPT-like UIs with Chainlit. Key features include intermediary step visualization, element management and display (images, text, carousel, and others), and cloud deployment. BentoML is a framework that enables the containerization of machine learning applications to use them as microservices running and scaling independently with automatic generation of OpenAPI and gRPC endpoints.

You can also deploy LangChain to different cloud service endpoints, for example, an Azure Machine Learning online endpoint. With Steamship, LangChain developers can rapidly deploy their apps, with features including production-ready endpoints, horizontal scaling across dependencies, persistent storage of app state, and multi-tenancy support.

LangChain AI, the company maintaining LangChain, is developing a new library called LangServe. Built on top of FastAPI and Pydantic, it streamlines documentation and deployment. Deployment is further facilitated through integration with platforms including GCP's Cloud Run and Replit, allowing quick cloning from an existing GitHub repository. Additional deployment instructions for other platforms will follow shortly based on user input.

The following table summarizes the services and frameworks available for deploying LLM applications:

Name	Description	Type
Streamlit	Open-source Python framework for building and deploying web apps	Framework
Gradio	Lets you wrap models in an interface and host on Hugging Face	Framework
Chainlit	Build and deploy conversational ChatGPT-like apps	Framework
Apache Beam	Tool for defining and orchestrating data processing workflows	Framework
Vercel	Platform for deploying and scaling web apps	Cloud service
FastAPI	Python web framework for building APIs	Framework
Fly.io	App hosting platform with autoscaling and global CDN	Cloud service
DigitalOcean App Platform	Platform to build, deploy, and scale apps	Cloud service
Google Cloud	Services such as Cloud Run to host and scale containerized apps	Cloud service

Steamship	ML infrastructure platform for deploying and scaling models	Cloud service
Langchain-Serve	Tool to serve LangChain agents as web APIs	Framework
BentoML	Framework for model serving, packaging, and deployment	Framework
OpenLLM	Provides open APIs to commercial LLMs	Cloud service
Databutton	No-code platform to build and deploy model workflows	Framework
Azure ML	Managed MLOps service on Azure for models	Cloud service
LangServe	Built on top of FastAPI, but specialized for LLM app deployment	Framework

Table 9.1: Services and frameworks for deploying LLM applications

All of these are well documented with different use cases, often directly referencing LLMs. We've already shown examples with Streamlit and Gradio, and we've discussed how to deploy them to the Hugging Face Hub as an example.

There are a few main requirements for running LLM applications:

- Scalable infrastructure to handle computationally intensive models and potential spikes in traffic
- Low latency for real-time serving of model outputs
- Persistent storage for managing long conversations and app state
- APIs for integration into end-user applications
- Monitoring and logging to track metrics and model behavior

Maintaining cost efficiency can be challenging with large volumes of user interactions and the high costs associated with LLM services. Strategies to manage efficiency include self-hosting models, auto-scaling resource allocations based on traffic, using spot instances, independent scaling, and batching requests to better utilize GPU resources.

The choice of tools and the infrastructure determines trade-offs between these requirements. Flexibility and ease is very important, because we want to be able to iterate rapidly, which is vital due to the dynamic nature of ML and LLM landscapes. It's crucial to avoid getting tied to one solution. A flexible, scalable serving layer that accommodates various models is key. Model composition and cloud providers' selection forms part of this flexibility equation.

For the greatest degree of flexibility, **Infrastructure as Code (IaC)** tools such as Terraform, Cloud-Formation, or Kubernetes YAML files can recreate your infrastructure reliably and quickly. More-over, **continuous integration and continuous delivery (CI/CD)** pipelines can automate testing and deployment processes to reduce errors and facilitate quicker feedback and iteration.

Designing a robust LLM application service can be a complex task requiring an understanding of the trade-offs and critical considerations when evaluating serving frameworks. Leveraging one of these solutions for deployment allows developers to focus on developing impactful AI applications rather than infrastructure.

As mentioned, LangChain plays nicely with several open-source projects and frameworks such as Ray Serve, BentoML, OpenLLM, Modal, and Jina. In the next sections, we'll deploy apps using different tools. We'll start with a chat service web server based on FastAPI.

FastAPI web server

FastAPI is a very popular choice for the deployment of web servers. Designed to be fast, easy to use, and efficient, it is a modern, high-performance web framework for building APIs with Python. Lanarky is a small, open-source library for deploying LLM applications that provides convenient wrappers around Flask API as well as Gradio for the deployment of LLM applications. This means you can get a REST API endpoint as well as the in-browser visualization at once and you only need a few lines of code.

A **Representational State Transfer Application Programming Interface (REST API)** is a set of rules and protocols that allows different software applications to communicate with each other over the internet. It follows the principles of REST, which is an architectural style for designing networked applications. A REST API uses HTTP methods (such as GET, POST, PUT, or DELETE) to perform operations on resources, and it typically sends and receives data in a standardized format, such as JSON or XML.

In the library documentation, there are several examples, including a Retrieval QA with Sources Chain, a Conversational Retrieval app, and a Zero Shot agent. Following another example, we'll implement a chatbot web server with Lanarky.

We'll set up a web server using Lanarky that creates a `ConversationChain` instance with an LLM model and settings, and defines routes for handling HTTP requests. The full code for this recipe is available here: `https://github.com/benman1/generative_ai_with_langchain/tree/main/webserver`

First, we'll import the necessary dependencies, including FastAPI for creating the web server and ConversationChain and ChatOpenAI from LangChain for handling LLM conversations, along with some other required modules:

```
from fastapi import FastAPI
from langchain import ConversationChain
from langchain.chat_models import ChatOpenAI

from lanarky import LangchainRouter
from starlette.requests import Request
from starlette.templating import Jinja2Templates
```

Please note that you need to set your environment variables as explained in *Chapter 3, Getting Started with LangChain*. We can do this by importing the setup_environment() method from the config module as we've seen in many other examples before:

```
from config import set_environment
set_environment()
```

Now we create a FastAPI app, which will take care of most of the routing, except for LangChain specific requests that Lanarky will cover as we'll see later:

```
app = FastAPI()
```

We can create an instance of ConversationChain, specifying the LLM model and its settings:

```
chain = ConversationChain(
        llm=ChatOpenAI(
            temperature=0,
            streaming=True,
        ),
        verbose=True,
    )
```

The templates variable gets set to a Jinja2Templates class, specifying the directory where templates are located for rendering. This specifies how the webpage will be shown, allowing all kinds of customization:

```
templates = Jinja2Templates(directory="webserver/templates")
```

An endpoint for handling HTTP GET requests at the root path (/) is defined using the FastAPI decorator @app.get. The function associated with this endpoint returns a template response for rendering the index.html template:

```
@app.get("/")
async def get(request: Request):
    return templates.TemplateResponse("index.html", {"request": request})
```

A router object is created as a LangChainRouter class. This object is responsible for defining and managing the routes associated with the ConversationChain instance. We can add additional routes to the router for handling JSON-based chat that even work with WebSocket requests:

```
langchain_router = LangchainRouter(
    langchain_url="/chat", langchain_object=chain, streaming_mode=1
)
langchain_router.add_langchain_api_route(
    "/chat_json", langchain_object=chain, streaming_mode=2
)
langchain_router.add_langchain_api_websocket_route("/ws", langchain_
object=chain)
app.include_router(langchain_router)
```

Now our application knows how to handle requests made to the specified routes defined within the router, directing them to the appropriate functions or handlers for processing.

We will use Uvicorn to run our application. Uvicorn excels in supporting high-performance, asynchronous frameworks such as FastAPI and Starlette. It is known for its ability to handle a large number of concurrent connections and performs well under heavy loads due to its asynchronous nature.

We can run the web server from the terminal like this:

```
uvicorn webserver.chat:app –reload
```

This command starts a web server, which you can view in your browser, at this local address: http://127.0.0.1:8000

The reload switch (--reload) is particularly handy, because it means the server will be automatically restarted once you've made any changes.

Here's a snapshot of the chatbot application we've just deployed:

Figure 9.3: Chatbot in Flask/Lanarky

I think this looks quite nice for what little work we've put in. It also comes with a few nice features such as a REST API, a web UI, and a WebSocket interface. While Uvicorn itself does not provide built-in load balancing functionality, it can work together with other tools or technologies such as Nginx or HAProxy to achieve load balancing in a deployment setup, which distributes the incoming client requests across multiple worker processes or instances. The use of Uvicorn with load balancers enables horizontal scaling to handle large traffic volumes, improves response times for clients, and enhances fault tolerance. Finally, Lanarky also plays nicely with Gradio, so with a few extra lines we have this webserver running as a Gradio app up and running.

In the next section, we'll see how to build robust and cost-effective generative AI applications with Ray. We'll build a simple search engine using LangChain for text processing and then use Ray for scaling indexing and serving.

Ray

Ray provides a flexible framework to meet the infrastructure challenges of complex neural networks in production by scaling out generative AI workloads across clusters. Ray helps with common deployment needs such as low-latency serving, distributed training, and large-scale batch inference. Ray also makes it easy to spin up on-demand fine-tuning or scale existing workloads from one machine to many. Its capabilities include:

- Scheduling distributed training jobs across GPU clusters using Ray Train
- Deploying pre-trained models at scale for low-latency serving with Ray Serve
- Running large batch inference in parallel across CPUs and GPUs with Ray Data
- Orchestrating end-to-end generative AI workflows combining training, deployment, and batch processing

We'll use LangChain and Ray to build a simple search engine for the Ray documentation following an example implemented by Waleed Kadous for the anyscale Blog and on the `langchain-ray` repository on GitHub. This can be found here: `https://www.anyscale.com/blog/llm-open-source-search-engine-langchain-ray`

You can see this as an extension of the recipe in *Chapter 5, Building a Chatbot like ChatGPT*. You'll also see how to run this as a FastAPI server. The full code for this recipe under semantic search is available here: `https://github.com/benman1/generative_ai_with_langchain/tree/main/search_engine`.

First, we'll ingest and index the Ray docs so we can quickly find relevant passages for a search query:

```python
# Load the Ray docs using the LangChain loader
loader = RecursiveUrlLoader("docs.ray.io/en/master/")
docs = loader.load()


# Split docs into sentences using LangChain splitter
chunks = text_splitter.create_documents(
    [doc.page_content for doc in docs],
    metadatas=[doc.metadata for doc in docs])


# Embed sentences into vectors using transformers
embeddings = LocalHuggingFaceEmbeddings('multi-qa-mpnet-base-dot-v1')
```

```
# Index vectors using FAISS via LangChain
db = FAISS.from_documents(chunks, embeddings)
```

This builds our search index by ingesting the docs, splitting them into chunks, embedding the sentences, and indexing the vectors. Alternatively, we can accelerate the indexing by parallelizing the embedding step:

```
# Define shard processing task
@ray.remote(num_gpus=1)
def process_shard(shard):
  embeddings = LocalHuggingFaceEmbeddings('multi-qa-mpnet-base-dot-v1')
  return FAISS.from_documents(shard, embeddings)

# Split chunks into 8 shards
shards = np.array_split(chunks, 8)

# Process shards in parallel
futures = [process_shard.remote(shard) for shard in shards]
results = ray.get(futures)

# Merge index shards
db = results[0]
for result in results[1:]:
  db.merge_from(result)
```

By running embedding on each shard in parallel, we can significantly reduce the indexing time.

We save the database index to disk:

```
db.save_local(FAISS_INDEX_PATH)
```

`FAISS_INDEX_PATH` is an arbitrary file name. I've set it to `faiss_index.db`.

Next, we'll see how we can serve search queries with Ray Serve:

```
# Load index and embedding
db = FAISS.load_local(FAISS_INDEX_PATH)
embedding = LocalHuggingFaceEmbeddings('multi-qa-mpnet-base-dot-v1')

@serve.deployment
```

```
class SearchDeployment:

  def __init__(self):
    self.db = db
    self.embedding = embedding

  def __call__(self, request):
    query_embed = self.embedding(request.query_params["query"])
    results = self.db.max_marginal_relevance_search(query_embed)
    return format_results(results)

deployment = SearchDeployment.bind()

# Start service
serve.run(deployment)
```

This should load the index we generated and lets us serve search queries as a web endpoint!

If we save this to a file called serve_vector_store.py, we can get the server up and running using the following command from the search_engine directory:

```
PYTHONPATH=../ python serve_vector_store.py
```

Running this command in the terminal gives me this output:

```
Started a local Ray instance.
View the dashboard at 127.0.0.1:8265
```

The message shows us the URL of the dashboard, which we can access in the browser. The search server, however, is running on localhost on port 8080. We can query it from Python:

```
import requests

query = "What are the different components of Ray"
        " and how can they help with large language models (LLMs)?"
response = requests.post("http://localhost:8000/", params={"query":
query})
print(response.text)
```

For me, the server fetches the Ray use cases page at: `https://docs.ray.io/en/latest/ray-overview/use-cases.html`

What I really liked was the monitoring with the Ray Dashboard, which looks like this:

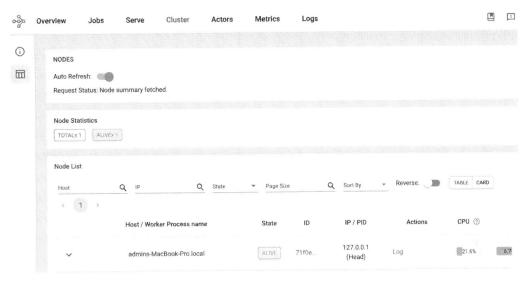

Figure 9.4: Ray Dashboard

This dashboard is very powerful as it can give you a whole bunch of metrics and other information. Collecting metrics is easy, since all you must do is set up and update variables of type `Counter`, `Gauge`, `Histogram`, and others within the deployment object or actor. For time series charts, you should have either Prometheus or the Grafana server installed.

This practical guide has taken you through the key steps of deploying an LLM application locally using LangChain and Ray. We first ingested and indexed documents to power a semantic search engine over the Ray documentation. By leveraging Ray's distributed capabilities, we parallelized the intensive embedding task to accelerate the indexing time. We then served the search application via Ray Serve, which provides a flexible framework for low-latency querying. The Ray dashboard offered helpful monitoring insights into metrics such as request rates, latencies, and errors.

As you can see in the full implementation on GitHub, we can also spin this up as a FastAPI server. This concludes our simple semantic search engine with LangChain and Ray.

As models and LLM apps grow more sophisticated and highly interwoven into the fabric of business applications, observability and monitoring during production become necessary to ensure their accuracy, efficiency, and reliability is ongoing. The next section focuses on the significance of monitoring LLMs and highlights key metrics to track for a comprehensive monitoring strategy.

How to observe LLM apps

The dynamic nature of real-world operations means that the conditions assessed during offline evaluations hardly cover all potential scenarios that LLMs may encounter in production systems. Thus comes the need for observability in production – a more continuous, real-time observation to capture anomalies that offline tests could not anticipate.

We need to implement monitoring tools to track vital metrics regularly. This includes user activity, response times, traffic volumes, financial expenditures, model behavior patterns, and overall satisfaction with the app. Ongoing surveillance allows for the early detection of anomalies such as data drift or unexpected lapses in capabilities.

Observability allows monitoring behaviors and outcomes as the model interacts with actual input data and users in production. It includes logging, tracking, tracing, and alerting mechanisms to ensure healthy system functioning, performance optimization, and catching issues such as model drift early.

Tracking, tracing, and monitoring are three important concepts in the field of software operation and management. While all related to understanding and improving a system's performance, they each have distinct roles. While tracking and tracing are about keeping detailed historical records for analysis and debugging, monitoring is aimed at real-time observation and immediate awareness of issues to ensure optimal system functionality at all times. All three of these concepts fall within the category of observability.

Monitoring is the ongoing process of overseeing the performance of a system or application. This might involve continuously collecting and analyzing metrics related to system health such as memory usage, CPU utilization, network latency, and the overall application/service performance (such as response time). Effective monitoring includes setting up alert systems for anomalies or unexpected behaviors – sending notifications when certain thresholds are exceeded. While tracking and tracing are about keeping detailed historical records for analysis and debugging, monitoring is aimed at real-time observation and immediate awareness of issues to ensure optimal system functionality at all times.

The chief aim for monitoring and observability is to provide insights into LLM app performance and behavior through real-time data. This helps to do the following:

- **Preventing model drift**: LLM performance can degrade over time due to changes in the characteristics of input data or user behavior. Regular monitoring can identify such situations early and apply corrective measures.

- **Performance optimization**: By tracking metrics such as inference times, resource usage, and throughput, you can make adjustments to improve the efficiency and effectiveness of LLM apps in production.

- **A/B testing**: Helps compare how slight differences in models may result in different outcomes, which aids decision-making for model improvements.

- **Debugging issues**: Monitoring helps identify unforeseen problems that can occur during runtime, enabling rapid resolution.

- **Avoiding hallucinations**: We want to ensure the factual accuracy of the response, and – if we are using RAG – retrieved context quality, and sufficient effectiveness in using the context.

- **Ensuring appropriate behavior**: Responses should be relevant, complete, helpful, harmless, conform to the required format, and follow the user's intent.

Since there are so many ways to monitor, it's important to come up with a monitoring strategy. Some things you should consider when coming up with a strategy are:

- **Metrics to monitor**: Define key metrics of interest such as prediction accuracy, latency, throughput, and others based on the desired model performance.

- **Monitoring frequency**: Frequency should be determined based on how critical the model is to operations – a highly critical model may require near real-time monitoring.

- **Logging**: Logs should provide comprehensive details regarding every relevant action performed by the LLM so analysts can track down any anomalies.

- **Alerting mechanism**: The system should raise alerts if it detects anomalous behavior or drastic performance drops.

Monitoring LLMs and LLM apps in production serves multiple purposes, including assessing model performance, detecting abnormalities or issues, optimizing resource utilization, and ensuring consistent and high-quality outputs. By continuously evaluating the behavior and performance of LLM apps via validation, shadow launches, and interpretation along with dependable offline evaluation, organizations can identify and mitigate potential risks, maintain user trust, and provide an optimal experience.

When monitoring LLMs and LLM applications, organizations can rely on a diverse set of metrics to gauge different aspects of performance and user experience. Beyond the crucial metrics of tonality, toxicity, and harmlessness, here is an expanded list that captures a wider range of evaluation areas:

- **Inference latency:** Measures the time it takes for the LLM app to process a request and generate a response. Lower latency ensures a faster and more responsive user experience.

- **Query per Second (QPS):** Calculates the number of queries or requests that the LLM can handle within a given time frame. Monitoring QPS helps assess scalability and capacity planning.

- **Token per Second (TPS):** Tracks the rate at which the LLM app generates tokens. TPS metrics are useful for estimating computational resource requirements and understanding model efficiency.

- **Token usage:** The number of tokens correlates with the resource usage such as hardware utilization, latency, and costs.

- **Error rate:** Monitors the occurrence of errors or failures in LLM app responses, ensuring error rates are kept within acceptable limits to maintain the quality of outputs.

- **Resource utilization:** Measures the consumption of computational resources, such as the CPU, memory, and GPU, to reduce costs and avoid bottlenecks.

- **Model drift:** Detects changes in LLM app behavior over time by comparing its outputs to a baseline or ground truth, ensuring the model remains accurate and aligned with expected outcomes.

- **Out-of-distribution inputs:** Identifies inputs or queries falling outside the intended distribution of the LLM's training data, which can cause unexpected or unreliable responses.

- **User feedback metrics:** Monitors user feedback channels to gather insights on user satisfaction, identify areas for improvement, and validate the effectiveness of the LLM app.

- **User engagement:** We can track how users engage with our app; for example, the frequency and duration of sessions or the usage of specific features.

- **Tool/retrieval usage:** Breakdown of the instances when retrieval and tools are used.

This is just a small selection. This list can easily be extended with many more metrics from **Site Reliability Engineering (SRE)** relating to task performance or the behavior of the LLM app.

Data scientists and machine learning engineers should check for staleness, incorrect learning, and bias using model interpretation tools such as LIME and SHAP. The most predictive features changing suddenly could indicate a data leak.

Offline metrics such as AUC do not always correlate with online impacts on conversion rate, so it is important to find dependable offline metrics that translate to online gains relevant to the business, ideally direct metrics such as clicks and purchases that the system impacts directly.

Effective monitoring enables the successful deployment and utilization of LLMs, boosting confidence in their capabilities and fostering user trust. It should be cautioned, however, that you should study service providers' privacy and data protection policies when relying on cloud service platforms.

The full code for the recipes in this section are available on GitHub in the `monitoring_and_evaluation` directory of the repository corresponding to this book.

In the next section, we'll start our journey into observability by monitoring the trajectory of an agent.

Tracking responses

Tracking in this context refers to recording the full provenance of responses, including the tools, retrievals, the included data, and the LLM used in generating the output. This is key for auditing and reproducibility of responses. We'll use the terms tracking and tracing interchangeably in this section.

Tracking generally refers to the process of recording and managing information about a particular operation or series of operations within an application or system. For example, in machine learning applications or projects, tracking can involve keeping a record of parameters, hyperparameters, metrics, and outcomes across different experiments or runs. It provides a way to document progress and changes over time.

Tracing is a more specialized form of tracking. It involves recording the execution flow through software/systems. Particularly in distributed systems where a single transaction might span multiple services, tracing helps in maintaining an audit or breadcrumb trail, a detailed source of information about that request path through the system. This granular view enables developers to understand the interaction between various microservices and troubleshoot issues such as latency or failures by identifying exactly where they occurred in the transaction path.

Tracking the trajectory of agents can be challenging due to their broad range of actions and generative capabilities. LangChain comes with functionality for trajectory tracking and evaluation, so seeing the traces of an agent via LangChain is really easy! You just have to set the `return_intermediate_steps` parameter to True when initializing an agent or an LLM.

Let's define a tool as a function. It's convenient to re-use the function docstring as a description of the tool. The tool first sends a ping to a website address and returns information about packages transmitted and latency or – in the case of an error – the error message:

```python
import subprocess
from urllib.parse import urlparse
from pydantic import HttpUrl
from langchain.tools import StructuredTool


def ping(url: HttpUrl, return_error: bool) -> str:
    """Ping the fully specified url. Must include https:// in the url."""
    hostname = urlparse(str(url)).netloc
    completed_process = subprocess.run(
        ["ping", "-c", "1", hostname], capture_output=True, text=True
    )
    output = completed_process.stdout
    if return_error and completed_process.returncode != 0:
        return completed_process.stderr
    return output


ping_tool = StructuredTool.from_function(ping)
```

Now we set up an agent that uses this tool with an LLM to make the calls given a prompt:

```python
from langchain.chat_models import ChatOpenAI
from langchain.agents import initialize_agent, AgentType


llm = ChatOpenAI(model="gpt-3.5-turbo-0613", temperature=0)
agent = initialize_agent(
    llm=llm,
    tools=[ping_tool],
    agent=AgentType.OPENAI_MULTI_FUNCTIONS,
    return_intermediate_steps=True, # IMPORTANT!
```

```
)
result = agent("What's the latency like for https://langchain.com?")
```

The agent reports this:

```
The latency for https://langchain.com is 13.773 ms
```

In `results["intermediate_steps"]`, we can see a lot of information about the agent's actions:

```
[(_FunctionsAgentAction(tool='ping', tool_input={'url': 'https://
langchain.com', 'return_error': False}, log="\nInvoking: `ping` with
`{'url': 'https://langchain.com', 'return_error': False}`\n\n\n", message_
log=[AIMessage(content='', additional_kwargs={'function_call': {'name':
'tool_selection', 'arguments': '{\n  "actions": [\n    {\n      "action_
name": "ping",\n      "action": {\n        "url": "https://langchain.
com",\n        "return_error": false\n      }\n    }\n  ]}'}},
example=False)]), 'PING langchain.com (35.71.142.77): 56 data bytes\
n64 bytes from 35.71.142.77: icmp_seq=0 ttl=249 time=13.773 ms\
n\n--- langchain.com ping statistics ---\n1 packets transmitted, 1
packets received, 0.0% packet loss\nround-trip min/avg/max/stddev =
13.773/13.773/13.773/0.000 ms\n')]
```

By providing visibility into the system and aiding in problem identification and optimization efforts, this kind of tracking and evaluation can be very helpful.

The LangChain documentation demonstrates how to use a trajectory evaluator to examine the full sequence of actions and responses they generate and grade an OpenAI functions agent. That's potentially very powerful stuff!

Let's have a look beyond LangChain and see what else is out there for observability!

Observability tools

There are quite a few tools available as integrations in LangChain or through callbacks:

- **Argilla**: Argilla is an open-source data curation platform that can integrate user feedback (human-in-the-loop workflows) with prompts and responses to curate datasets for fine-tuning.
- **Portkey**: Portkey adds essential MLOps capabilities like monitoring detailed metrics, tracing chains, caching, and reliability through automatic retries to LangChain.
- **Comet.ml**: Comet offers robust MLOps capabilities for tracking experiments, comparing models and optimizing AI projects.

- **LLMonitor**: Tracks lots of metrics including cost and usage analytics (user tracking), tracing, and evaluation tools (open-source).

- **DeepEval**: Logs default metrics including relevance, bias, and toxicity. Can also help with testing and monitoring model drift or degradation.

- **Aim**: An open-source visualization and debugging platform for ML models. It logs inputs, outputs, and the serialized state of components, enabling visual inspection of individual LangChain executions and comparing multiple executions side by side.

- **Argilla**: An open-source platform for tracking training data, validation accuracy, parameters, and more across machine learning experiments.

- **Splunk**: Splunk's Machine Learning Toolkit can provide observability into your machine learning models in production.

- **ClearML**: An open-source tool for automating training pipelines, seamlessly moving from research to production.

- **IBM Watson OpenScale**: A platform providing insights into AI health with fast problem identification and resolution to help mitigate risks.

- **DataRobot MLOps**: Monitors and manages models to detect issues before they impact performance.

- **Datadog APM integration**: This integration allows you to capture LangChain requests, parameters, prompt completions, and visualize LangChain operations. You can also capture metrics such as request latency, errors, and token/cost usage.

- **Weights and Biases (W&B) tracing**: We've already shown an example of using W&B to monitor fine-training convergence, but it can also fulfill the roles of tracking other metrics and logging and comparing prompts.

- **Langfuse**: With this open-source tool, we can conveniently monitor detailed information along traces regarding the latency, cost, and scores of our LangChain agents and tools.

- **LangKit**: This extracts signals from prompts and responses to ensure safety and security. It currently focuses on text quality, relevance metrics, and sentiment analysis.

There are more tools out there at different stages of maturation. For example, the AgentOps SDK is aiming to provide an interface to a toolkit for evaluating and developing robust and reliable AI agents, but is still in closed alpha.

Most of these integrations are very easy to integrate into LLM pipelines. For example, for W&B, you can enable tracing by setting the `LANGCHAIN_WANDB_TRACING` environment variable to `True`. Alternatively, you can use a context manager with `wandb_tracing_enabled()` to trace a specific block of code. With Langfuse, we can hand over `langfuse.callback.CallbackHandler()` as an argument to the `chain.run()` call.

Some of these tools are open-source, and what's great about these platforms is that they allow full customization and on-premises deployment for use cases where privacy is important. For example, Langfuse is open-source and provides an option of self-hosting. Choose the option that best suits your needs and follow the instructions provided in the LangChain documentation to enable tracing for your agents. Having been released only recently, I am sure there's much more to come for the platform, but it's already great to see traces of how agents execute, detecting loops and latency issues. It enables sharing traces and stats with collaborators to discuss improvements.

Let's have a look at LangSmith now, which is another companion project of LangChain, developed for observability!

LangSmith

LangSmith is a framework for debugging, testing, evaluating, and monitoring LLM applications developed and maintained by LangChain AI, the organization behind LangChain. LangSmith serves as an effective tool for MLOps, specifically for LLMs, by providing features that cover multiple aspects of the MLOps process. It can help developers take their LLM applications from prototype to production by providing features for debugging, monitoring, and optimizing.

LangSmith allows you to:

- Log traces of runs from your LangChain agents, chains, and other components
- Create datasets to benchmark model performance
- Configure AI-assisted evaluators to grade your models
- View metrics, visualizations, and feedback to iterate and improve your LLMs

On the LangSmith web interface, we can get a large set of graphs for a bunch of statistics that can be useful to optimize latency, hardware efficiency, and cost, as we can see here in the monitoring dashboard:

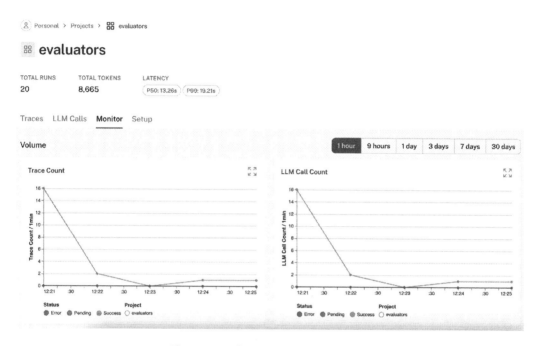

Figure 9.5: Evaluator metrics in LangSmith

The monitoring dashboard includes the following graphs that can be broken down into different time intervals:

Statistics	Category
Trace Count, LLM Call Count, Trace Success Rates, LLM Call Success Rates	Volume
Trace Latency (s), LLM Latency (s), LLM Calls per Trace, Tokens / sec	Latency
Total Tokens, Tokens per Trace, Tokens per LLM Call	Tokens
% Traces w/ Streaming, % LLM Calls w/ Streaming, Trace Time-to-First-Token (ms), LLM Time-to-First-Token (ms)	Streaming

Table 9.2: Statistics in LangSmith

Here's a tracing example in LangSmith for the benchmark dataset run that we saw in the *How to evaluate LLM apps* section:

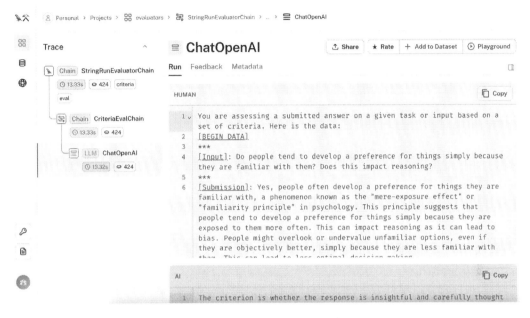

Figure 9.6: Tracing in LangSmith

The platform itself is not open-source, however, LangChain AI, the company behind LangSmith and LangChain, provides some support for self-hosting for organizations with privacy concerns. There are, however, a few alternatives to LangSmith such as Langfuse, Weights and Biases, Datadog APM, Portkey, and PromptWatch, with some overlap in features. We'll focus on LangSmith here because it has a large set of features for evaluation and monitoring, and because it integrates with LangChain.

In the next section, we'll demonstrate the utilization of PromptWatch for prompt tracking of LLMs in production environments.

PromptWatch

PromptWatch records information about response caching, chain execution, prompting and gen-erated output during interactions. The tracing and monitoring can be very useful for debugging and ensuring an audit trail. With PromptWatch.io, you can even track various aspects of LLM chains, actions, retrieved documents, inputs, outputs, execution time, tool details, and more for complete visibility in your system.

Make sure you sign up with PromptWatch.io online and get your API key – you can find it under the account settings.

Let's get the inputs out of the way:

```
from langchain import LLMChain, OpenAI, PromptTemplate
from promptwatch import PromptWatch
```

As discussed in *Chapter 3, Getting Started with LangChain*, I've set all API keys in the environment in the set_environment() function. If you've followed my recommendation, you can follow the imports up with this:

```
from config import set_environment
set_environment()
```

Otherwise, please make sure you set your environment variables in the way you prefer. Next, we need to set up a prompt and a chain:

```
prompt_template = PromptTemplate.from_template("Finish this sentence
{input}")
my_chain = LLMChain(llm=OpenAI(), prompt=prompt_template)
```

Using the PromptTemplate class, the prompt template is configured with one variable, input, indicating where the user input should be placed within the prompt.

We can create a PromptWatch block, where LLMChain is invoked with an input prompt:

```
with PromptWatch() as pw:
    my_chain("The quick brown fox jumped over")
```

This is a simple example of the model generating a response based on the provided prompt. We can see this on PromptWatch.io.

Figure 9.7: Prompt tracking at PromptWatch.io

We can see the prompt together with the LLM's response. We also get a dashboard with a time series of activity, where we can drill down into responses at certain times. This seems quite useful to effectively monitor and analyze prompts, outputs, and costs in real-world scenarios.

The platform allows for in-depth analysis and troubleshooting in the web interface that enables users to identify the root causes of issues and optimize prompt templates. We could have explored more, for example around prompt templates and versioning, but there's only so much we can cover here. `promptwatch.io` can also help with unit testing and versioning prompt templates.

Summary

Taking a trained LLM from research into real-world production involves navigating many complex challenges around aspects such as scalability, monitoring, and unintended behaviors. Responsibly deploying capable, reliable models involves diligent planning around scalability, interpretability, testing, and monitoring. Techniques such as fine-tuning, safety interventions, and defensive design enable us to develop applications that produce helpful, harmless, and readable outputs. With care and preparation, generative AI holds immense potential benefit to industries from medicine to education.

We've delved into deployment and the tools used for deployment. Particularly, we deployed applications with FastAPI and Ray. In earlier chapters, we used Streamlit. There are many more tools we could have explored, for example, the recently emerged LangServe, which is developed with LangChain applications in mind. While it's still relatively fresh, it's definitely worth watching out for more developments in the future.

The evaluation of LLMs is important to assess their performance and quality. LangChain supports comparative evaluation between models, checking outputs against criteria, simple string matching, and semantic similarity metrics. These provide different insights into model quality, accuracy, and appropriate generation. Systematic evaluation is key to ensuring LLMs produce useful, relevant, and sensible outputs.

Monitoring LLMs is a vital aspect of deploying and maintaining these complex systems. With the increasing adoption of LLMs in various applications, ensuring their performance, effectiveness, and reliability is of utmost importance. We've discussed the significance of monitoring LLMs, highlighted key metrics to track for a comprehensive monitoring strategy, and have given examples of how to track metrics in practice.

We've looked at different tools for observability such as PromptWatch and LangSmith. LangSmith provides powerful capabilities to track, benchmark, and optimize LLMs built with LangChain. Its automated evaluators, metrics, and visualizations help accelerate LLM development and validation.

In the next and final chapter, let's discuss what the future of Generative AI will look like.

Questions

Please try and see if you can come up with the answers to these questions from memory. If you are unsure about any of them, you might want to refer to the corresponding section in the chapter:

1. In your opinion, what is the best term for describing the operationalization of language models, LLM apps, or apps that rely on generative models in general?
2. What is a token and why should you know about token usage when querying LLMs?
3. How can we evaluate LLM apps?
4. Which tools can help to evaluate LLM apps?
5. What are the considerations for the production deployment of agents?
6. Name a few tools used for deployment.
7. What are the important metrics for monitoring LLMs in production?
8. How can we monitor LLM applications?
9. What's LangSmith?

Join our community on Discord

Join our community's Discord space for discussions with the authors and other readers:

```
https://packt.link/lang
```

10
The Future of Generative Models

In this book, so far, we have discussed generative models for building applications, and we have implemented a few simple ones – for example, for semantic search, applications for content creation, customer service agents, and assistants for developers and data scientists. We have explored techniques such as tool use, agent strategies, semantic search with retrieval augmented generation, and the conditioning of models with prompts and fine-tuning.

In this chapter, we'll deliberate on where this leaves us and where the future leads us. We'll consider weaknesses and socio-technical challenges of generative models, and strategies for mitigation and improvement. We'll focus on value creation opportunities, where unique customization of foundation models for specific use cases stands out. It remains uncertain which entities – big tech firms, start-ups, or foundation model developers – will capture the most upsides. We'll also evaluate and address concerns such as the extinction threat through AI.

Given the massive potential for increased productivity in various industries, venture funding for generative AI start-ups skyrocketed in 2022 and 2023, and major players like Salesforce and Accenture among many others have made big commitments to generative AI with multibillion-dollar investments. We'll discuss potential effects on jobs in multiple industries, and disruptive changes in creative industries, education, law, manufacturing, medicine, and the military.

We will evaluate and address concerns such as misinformation, cybersecurity, privacy, and fairness, and think about how the changes and disruptions brought about by generative AI should influence regulations and practical implementation.

The main sections of this chapter are:

- The current state of generative AI
- Economic consequences
- Societal implications

Let's start with the current state of models and their capabilities.

The current state of generative AI

As discussed in this book, in recent years, generative AI models have attained new milestones in producing human-like content across modalities including text, images, audio, and video. Leading models like OpenAI's GPT-4 and DALL-E 2, and Anthropic's Claude display impressive fluency in content generation, be it textual or creative visual artistry.

Between 2022 and 2023, models have progressed in strides. If generative models were previously capable of producing barely coherent text or grainy images, now we see high-quality 3D images, videos, and the generation of coherent and contextually relevant prose and dialogue, rivaling or even surpassing the fluency levels of humans. These AI models leverage gargantuan datasets and computational scale, enabling them to capture intricate linguistic patterns, display a nuanced understanding of knowledge about the world, translate texts, summarize content, answer natural language questions, create appealing visual art, and acquire the capability to describe images. Seemingly by magic, the AI-generated outputs mimic human ingenuity – painting original art, writing poetry, producing human-level prose, and even engaging in sophisticated aggregation and synthesis of information from diverse sources.

But let's be a bit more nuanced! Generative models come with weaknesses as well as strengths. Deficiencies persist compared to human cognition, including the frequent generation of plausible yet incorrect or nonsensical statements. Hallucinations show a lack of grounding in reality, given that they are based on patterns in data rather than an understanding of the real world. Further, models exhibit difficulties performing mathematical, logical, or causal reasoning. They are easily confused by complex inferential questions, which could limit their applicability in certain fields of work. The black box problem of lack of explainability for outputs as well as for the models themselves hampers troubleshooting efforts, and controlling model behaviors within desired parameters remains challenging. AI can have serious bias issues because of the prejudiced data they are trained on. This can lead to unfair results and make social inequalities worse.

Here is a table summarizing the key strengths and deficiencies of current generative AI compared to human cognition:

Category	Human Cognition	Generative AI Models
Language Fluency	Contextually relevant, draws meaning from world knowledge	Highly eloquent, reflects linguistic patterns
Knowledge	Conceptual understanding derived from learning and experience	Statistical synthesis lacking grounding
Creativity	Originality reflecting personality and talent	Imaginative but within training distribution
Factual Accuracy	Usually aligns with truth and physical reality	Hallucinations reflecting training data biases
Reasoning	Intuitive yet can apply heuristics after training	Logic is tightly limited to training distribution
Bias	Sometimes recognizes and can override inherent biases	Propagates systemic biases in data
Transparency	Partial, subjective insights from think-aloud techniques	Plausible reasoning from chain-of-thought prompts

Table 10.1: Strengths and deficiencies of LLMs

While LLMs such as GPT-4 showcase language fluency on parity with humans, their lack of grounding, tendency for distortion, opaqueness, and potential for harm underscore deficiencies that temper the promise of generative AI. Progress in domains like logical reasoning and bias mitigation remains at an early stage. As for transparency, while immense complexity poses an immense challenge, determined efforts seek to surface the lineage and mechanisms of reasoning for both humans (advances in the understanding of neurocognition) and AI (interpretability and explainability). Addressing problematic areas is key to developing reliable and trustworthy systems. Throughout the book, we've discussed and implemented potential solutions that address the weaknesses of generative AI.

We should keep in mind, however, that this gap analysis of human versus AI is for highlighting areas of improvement – as we have seen in domains such as Atari games, chess, and Go, AIs can reach superhuman levels if trained properly, and we haven't touched the ceiling yet in many areas. Let's look more broadly at some of the socio-technical challenges involved in unlocking the capabilities of generative AI systems and discuss approaches to overcoming them!

Challenges

The profound potential of generative AI systems indicates an exciting future if development continues at pace. This table shows a summary of a few of the technical and organizational challenges together with approaches to tackle them:

Challenge	Potential Solutions
Knowledge Freshness (+ Concept Drift)	Continuous learning methods like elastic weight consolidation, stream ingestion pipelines, and efficient retraining procedures
Specialized Knowledge	Task-specific demonstrations and prompting, knowledge retrieval and grounding, and context expansion
Downstream Adaptability	Strategic fine-tuning methods, catastrophic forgetting mitigation, and optimized hardware access
Biased Outputs	Bias mitigation algorithms, balanced training data, audits, inclusivity training, and interdisciplinary research
Harmful Content Generation	Moderation systems, interruption and correction, and conditioning methods such as RLHF
Logical Inconsistencies	Hybrid architectures, knowledge bases, and retrieval augmentation
Factual Inaccuracies	Retrieval augmentation, knowledge bases, and consistent knowledge base updating
Lack of Explainability	Model introspection, concept attribution, and interpretable model designs
Privacy Risks	Differential privacy, federated learning, encryption, and anonymization
High Latency and Compute Costs	Model distillation, optimized hardware, and efficient model design
Licensing Limitations	Open/synthetic data, custom data, and fair licensing agreements
Security/Vulnerabilities	Adversarial robustness and cybersecurity best practices

Governance	Compliance frameworks and ethical development governance

Table 10.2: Challenges of generative AI and potential solutions

Challenges of generative AI go beyond just improving content generation—they encompass environmental sustainability, algorithmic equity, and individual privacy. Strategies like employing simplified model architectures, using knowledge distillation, and developing specialized hardware are critical to reducing the carbon footprint of AI in the face of rapid progress. To ensure fair AI, steps such as incorporating balanced datasets, applying bias mitigation algorithms, enforcing fairness through constrained optimization, and promoting inclusivity are essential, despite their complexity.

To counteract potential harm from AI output, such as toxicity or false information (hallucination), techniques like reinforcement learning guided by human feedback and grounding responses in verified knowledge can be employed. Additionally, securing sensitive data through privacy-preserving methods like differential privacy, federated learning, and real-time content correction is fundamental for upholding user dignity.

Finally, staying up to date with the evolving informational landscapes, comprehending specialized domains, and flexibly adapting to emerging needs represent newly visible obstacles as generative models permeate real-world contexts.

Addressing these challenges involves a broad spectrum of responses that must consider the entire life cycle of AI development. Such responses include innovative training objectives focused on consistency, structural knowledge integrations, and design of models for better controllability, as well as software and hardware optimization for infrastructure efficiency.

One of the most effective developments is flexible user control. With concerted effort in research and development, the aim is to steer generative AI toward alignment with societal values. For reasons of computational efficiency and costs, this implies a shift from pretraining to specialized downstream conditioning (particularly, fine-tuning and prompt techniques). This, in turn, will lead to a proliferation of start-ups applying core AI technologies.

Technological innovation together with regulation and transparency of AI development will ensure that generative AI enhances human capability without compromising ethical standards. Looking ahead, generative AI systems are poised to become more powerful and multifaceted.

Let's have a look at some emerging trends in model development!

Trends in model development

The current doubling time in training compute of very large models is about 8 months, outstripping scaling laws such as Moore's Law (transistor density at cost increases at a rate of currently about 18 months) and Rock's Law (costs of hardware like GPUs and TPUs halve every 4 years). This graph illustrates this trend in training compute of large models (source: Epoch, *Parameter, Compute, and Data Trends in Machine Learning*. Retrieved from `https://epochai.org/mlinputs/visualization`):

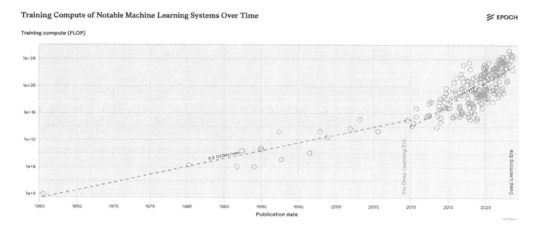

Figure 10.1: Training FLOPs of notable AI systems

The main point from this graph is the increase in compute, which is apparent since the 1960s, and the Cambrian explosion of models of the deep learning era at the top right. As discussed in *Chapter 1, What Is Generative AI?*, parameter sizes for large systems have been increasing at a similar rate as the training compute, which means we could see much larger and more expensive systems if this growth continues.

Empirically derived scaling laws predict the performance of LLMs based on the given training budget, dataset size, and the number of parameters. This could mean that highly powerful systems will be concentrated in the hands of Big Tech.

The **KM scaling** law, proposed by Kaplan and colleagues, derived through empirical analysis and fitting of model performance with varied data sizes, model sizes, and training compute, presents power-law relationships, indicating a strong codependence between model performance and factors such as model size, dataset size, and training compute.

The **Chinchilla scaling law**, developed by the Google DeepMind team, involved experiments with a wider range of model sizes and data sizes and suggests an optimal allocation of compute budget to model size and data size, which can be determined by optimizing a specific loss function under a constraint.

However, future progress may depend more on data efficiency and model quality than sheer size. Though massive models grab headlines, computing power and energy constraints put a limit on unrestrained model growth. It's also unclear if performance will keep up further with the growth in parameters. The future could see the co-existence of massive, general models with smaller and more accessible specialized niche models that provide faster and cheaper training, maintenance, and inference.

It has already been shown that smaller specialized models can prove highly performant. As mentioned in *Chapter 6, Developing Software with Generative AI*, we've recently seen models such as phi-1 (*Textbooks Are All You Need*, 2023, Gunasekar and colleagues), with about 1 billion parameters, that – despite its smaller scale – achieve high accuracy on evaluation benchmarks. The authors suggest that improving data quality can dramatically change the shape of scaling laws.

Further, there is a body of work on simplified model architectures, which have substantially fewer parameters and only modestly drop accuracy (for example, *One Wide Feedforward is All You Need*, Pessoa Pires and others, 2023). Additionally, techniques such as fine-tuning, distillation, and prompting techniques can enable smaller models to leverage the capabilities of large foundations without replicating their costs. To compensate for model limitations, tools like search engines and calculators have been incorporated into agents, and multi-step reasoning strategies, plugins, and extensions may be increasingly used to expand capabilities.

The rapidly decreasing costs of AI model training represent a significant shift in the landscape, enabling broader participation in cutting-edge AI research and development. As noted, several factors are contributing to this trend, including optimization of training regimes, improvements in data quality, and the introduction of novel model architectures. Here is a brief summary of techniques and approaches for making generative AI more accessible and effective:

- **Simplified model architectures**: Streamlining model design for easier management, better interpretability, and lower computational cost.

- **Synthetic data generation**: Creating artificial training data to augment datasets while preserving privacy.

- **Model distillation**: Transferring knowledge from a large model into a smaller, more efficient one for easy deployment.

- **Optimized inference engines**: Software frameworks that increase the speed and efficiency of executing AI models on a given hardware.

- **Dedicated AI hardware accelerators**: Specialized hardware like GPUs and TPUs that dramatically accelerate AI computations.

- **Open-source and synthetic data**: High-quality public datasets enable collaboration and synthetic data enhances privacy and can help reduce bias.

- **Quantization**: Converting models to lower precision by reducing bit sizes of weights and activations, decreasing model size and compute costs.

- **Incorporating knowledge bases**: Grounding model outputs in factual databases reduces hallucinations and improves accuracy.

- **Retrieval augmented generation**: Enhancing text generation by retrieving relevant information from sources.

- **Federated learning**: Training models on decentralized data to improve privacy while benefiting from diverse sources.

Among the technical advancements helping drive down these costs, quantization techniques have emerged as an essential contributor. Open-source datasets and techniques such as synthetic data generation further democratize access to AI training by providing high-quality and data-efficient model development and removing some reliance on vast, proprietary datasets. Open-source initiatives contribute to the trend by providing cost-effective, collaborative platforms for innovation.

These innovations collectively lower barriers that have so far impeded real-world generative AI adoption across various segments:

- Financial barriers are reduced by compressing large model performance into far smaller form factors through quantization and distillation.

- Privacy risks are mitigated via federated and synthetic techniques circumventing exposure.

- The accuracy limitations hampering small models are relieved through grounding generation with external information.

- Specialized hardware exponentially accelerates throughput while optimized software maximizes the existing infrastructure.

- Democratizing access by tackling constraints like cost, security, and reliability unlocks benefits for vastly expanded audiences, steering generative creativity from a narrow concentration toward empowering diverse human talents.

The landscape is shifting from a focus on sheer model size and brute-force compute to clever, nuanced approaches that maximize computational efficiency and model efficacy. With quantization and related techniques lowering barriers, we're poised for a more diverse and dynamic era of AI development where resource wealth is not the only determinant of leadership in AI innovation.

This could mean a democratization of the market, as we'll see now.

Big Tech vs. small enterprises

As for the spread of technology, two primary scenarios exist. In the centralized scenario, generative AI and LLMs are primarily developed and controlled by large tech firms that invest heavily in the necessary computational hardware, data storage, and specialized AI/ML talent. Entities like these benefit from economies of scale and resources that allow them to bear the high costs of training and maintaining these sophisticated systems. They produce general models that are often made accessible to others through cloud services or APIs, but these one-size-fits-all solutions may not perfectly align with the requirements of every user or organization.

Conversely, in the self-service scenario, companies or individuals take on the task of training their own AI models. This approach allows for models that are customized to the specific needs and proprietary data of the user, providing more targeted and relevant functionality. However, this route traditionally requires significant AI expertise, substantial computational resources, and rigorous data privacy safeguards, which can be prohibitively expensive and complex for smaller entities.

The central question is how these scenarios will coexist and evolve. Presently, the centralized approach dominates due to the barriers in cost and expertise required for the self-service model. Yet with the democratization of AI – driven by declining computational costs, more widespread AI training and tools, and innovations that simplify model training – the self-service scenario may become increasingly viable for smaller organizations, local governments, and community groups. These groups could potentially harness tailored AI solutions for highly specific tasks, gaining advantages in agility and privacy preservation.

As these two business models continue to develop, a hybrid landscape may emerge where both approaches fulfill distinct roles based on use cases, resources, expertise, and privacy considerations. Large firms might continue to excel in providing industry-specific models, while smaller entities could increasingly train or fine-tune their own models to meet niche demands. The evolution of this landscape will largely depend on the pace of advancements that make AI more accessible, more cost-effective, and simpler to use without compromising robustness or privacy.

If robust tools emerge to simplify and automate AI development, custom generative models may even be viable for local governments, community groups, and individuals to address hyper-local challenges. While centralized Big Tech firms benefit currently from economies of scale, distributed innovation from smaller entities could unlock generative AI's full potential across all sectors of society.

While large tech firms currently dominate generative AI research and development, smaller entities may ultimately stand to gain the most from these technologies. As costs decline for computing, data storage, and AI talent, custom pre-training of specialized models could become feasible for small and mid-sized companies.

In a timeframe of 3–5 years, constraints around computing and talent availability could ease considerably, eroding the centralized moat created by massive investments. Specifically, if cloud computing costs decline as projected, and AI skills become more widespread through education and automated tools, self-training customized LLMs may become feasible for many companies.

Rather than relying on generic models from Big Tech, tailored generative AI fine-tuned on niche datasets could better serve unique needs. Start-ups and non-profits often excel at rapidly iterating to build cutting-edge solutions for specialized domains. Democratized access through cost reductions could enable such focused players to train performant models exceeding the capabilities of generalized systems.

In the next section, we'll discuss the potential of **Artificial General Intelligence (AGI)** and the threat of extinction by the malicious actions of a superintelligent artificial entity.

Artificial General Intelligence

Not all abilities in LLMs scale predictably with model size. Capabilities such as in-context learning may remain exclusive to particularly large models due to factors beyond raw computational growth. There's speculation that sustained scaling – training vast models on even larger datasets – might lead to broader skill sets and, some suggest, toward the development of AGI with reasoning abilities on par or beyond humans.

Nevertheless, current neuroscientific perspectives and the limitations of existing AI structures provide compelling arguments against an imminent leap to AGI (inspired by the discussion in the article *The feasibility of artificial consciousness through the lens of neuroscience* by Jaan Aru and others; 2023):

- **Lack of embodied, embedded information**: The current generation of LLMs lacks multimodal and embodied experiences, being trained predominantly on textual data. In contrast, human common sense and understanding of the physical world are developed through rich, diverse interactions involving multiple senses.

- **Different architecture from biological brains**: The relatively simple stacked transformer architecture used in models like GPT-4 lacks the complex recurrent and hierarchical structures of the thalamocortical system thought to enable consciousness and general reasoning in humans.

- **Narrow capabilities**: Existing models remain specialized for particular domains like text and fall short in flexibility, causal reasoning, planning, social skills, and general problem-solving intelligence. This could change either with increasing tool use or with fundamental changes to the models.

- **Minimal social abilities or intent**: Current AI systems have no innate motivations, social intelligence, or intent beyond their training objectives. Fears of malicious goals or desire for domination seem unfounded.

- **Limited real-world knowledge**: Despite ingesting huge datasets, the factual knowledge and common sense of large models remain very restricted compared to humans. This impedes applicability in the physical world.

- **Data-driven limitations**: Reliance on pattern recognition from training data rather than structured knowledge makes reliable generalization to novel situations difficult.

As we address pressing AI challenges, the discourse around AI's threat and its potential for societal disruption should not overshadow immediate issues like fairness and privacy.

Given current model limitations and the lack of agency, the notion of today's AI rapidly evolving into a dangerous superintelligence appears highly unlikely. In formulating regulations, we must be vigilant against regulatory capture, where dominant industry players invoke far-fetched scenarios of AI-driven destruction to distract from pressing concerns and to shape rules to fit their interests, potentially marginalizing the concerns of smaller entities and the public. Nonetheless, ongoing attention to safety research and ethical concerns is essential, especially as AI advances.

Let's discuss the broader economy, and – the elephant in the room – jobs!

Economic consequences

Integrating generative AI promises immense productivity gains through automating tasks across sectors – albeit risking workforce disruptions given the pace of change. Assuming computing scales sustainably, projections estimate 30–50% of current work activities will be automatable by 2030, adding $6–8 trillion annually to global GDP. Sectors like customer service, marketing, software engineering, and R&D may see over 75% of use case value. However, past innovations ultimately spawned new occupations, suggesting long-term realignment.

Developed regions are likely to witness faster uptake, displacing administrative, creative, and analytical roles initially. Yet automation extends beyond employment loss – at present, under 20% of US worker tasks seem automatable directly through LLMs. But LLM-enhanced software could transform 50% of tasks, affirming the force multiplication from complementary innovations.

Thus automation's labor impact remains complex – while augmenting productivity, transitional pains persist. Still, the virtuous cycle between AI progress and emerging specializations signals hopes for an uplift over redundancy. And braiding priorities of sustainability, equity, and human dignity throughout this transformation promises optimizing empowerment over exploitation.

In a professional context, generative AI is poised to amplify human creativity and transform traditional workflows across a range of industries. For content creators, such as marketers and journalists, AI can rapidly generate initial drafts, fostering a baseline that human creativity can build upon for more customized outputs. Software developers benefit from AI's ability to produce code snippets, helping to expedite the development process. For scholars and scientists, the ability of AI to distill complex research into comprehensive summaries can catalyze scholarly progress and innovation.

Here are some key predictions about how jobs may be impacted by advances in language models and generative AI:

- Routine legal work like draft preparation will be increasingly automated, changing job roles for junior lawyers and paralegals.

- Software engineering will see a rise in AI coding assistants handling mundane tasks, enabling developers to focus on complex problem-solving.

- Data scientists will spend more time refining AI systems rather than building predictive models from scratch.

- Demand for specialized roles like prompt engineering will continue to rise.

- Teachers will utilize AI for course preparation and personalized student support.

- Journalists, paralegals, and graphic designers will employ generative AI to enhance content creation, raising concerns about job impacts.

- Demand will grow for experts in AI ethics, regulations, and security to oversee responsible development.

- Musicians and artists will collaborate with AI, boosting creative expression and accessibility.

- Striking an optimal balance between AI capabilities and human judgment will be vital across sectors.

- The common thread is that while routine tasks face increasing automation, human expertise to steer AI directions and ensure responsible outcomes will remain indispensable.

While certain jobs may be displaced by AI in the near term, especially routine cognitive tasks, it may automate certain activities rather than eliminate entire occupations. Technical experts like data scientists and programmers will remain key to developing AI tools and realizing their full business potential. By automating rote tasks, models may free up human time for higher-value work, boosting economic output.

Concerns have emerged about saturation as generative AI tools are relatively easy to build using foundation models. Customization of models and tools will allow value creation, but it's unclear who will capture the most upsides and how powerful these applications can be. While current market hype is high, investors are tempering decisions given lower valuations and skepticism following the 2021 AI boom/bust cycle. The long-term market impact and the winning generative AI business models have yet to unfold.

The **2021 AI boom/bust cycle** refers to a rapid acceleration in investment and growth in the AI start-up space followed by a market cooldown and stabilization in 2022 as projections failed to materialize and valuations declined.

Here's a quick summary:

- **Boom phase (2020-2021):** There was huge interest and skyrocketing investment in AI start-ups offering innovative capabilities like computer vision, natural language processing, robotics, and machine learning platforms. Total funding for AI start-ups hit record levels in 2021, with over $73 billion invested globally according to Pitchbook. Hundreds of AI start-ups were founded and funded during this period.

- **Bust phase (2022):** In 2022, the market underwent a correction, with valuations of AI start-ups falling significantly from their 2021 highs. Several high-profile AI start-ups like Anthropic and Cohere faced valuation markdowns. Many investors became more cautious and selective with funding AI start-ups. Market corrections in the broader tech sector also contributed to the bust.

- **Key factors:** Excessive hype, unrealistic growth projections, historically high valuations in 2021, and broader economic conditions all contributed to the boom-bust cycle. The cycle followed a classic pattern seen previously in sectors like dot-com and blockchain.

As AI models become more sophisticated and economical to operate, we can anticipate a substantial proliferation of generative AI and LLM applications into novel domains. Beyond just the plummeting hardware expenses that have historically followed Moore's Law, there are additional economies of scale affecting AI systems.

In *Chapter 1, What Is Generative AI?*, we discussed the pertinent trend in the AI industry that encompasses gains in efficiency stemming from the iterative refinement of code, the development of sophisticated tools, and the enhancement of techniques. The improved efficiency because of new techniques and approaches, combined with the declining hardware costs, fosters a virtuous cycle: as costs diminish, AI adoption widens, in turn spurring further cost reductions and efficiency improvements. What emerges is a feedback loop where each iteration of efficiency catalyzes increased usage, which in itself leads to even greater efficiency – a dynamic poised to dramatically advance the frontier of AI capabilities.

Let's look at various sectors where generative models will have profound near-term impacts, starting with creative endeavors.

Creative industries and advertising

The gaming and entertainment industries are leveraging generative AI to craft uniquely immersive user experiences. Major efficiency gains from automating creative tasks could increase leisure time spent online. Generative AI can enable machines to generate new and original content, such as art, music, and literature, by learning from patterns and examples. This has implications for creative industries, as it can enhance the creative process and potentially create new revenue streams. It also unlocks new scales of personalized, dynamic content creation for media, film, and advertising.

For media, film, and advertising, AI unlocks new scales of personalized, dynamic content creation. In journalism, automated article generation using massive datasets can free up reporters to focus on more complex investigative stories. **AI-Generated Content (AIGC)** is playing a growing role in transforming media production and delivery by enhancing efficiency and diversity. In journalism, text generation tools automate writing tasks traditionally done by human reporters, significantly boosting productivity while maintaining timeliness. Media outlets like the Associated Press generate thousands of stories per year using AIGC. Robot reporters like the Los Angeles Times Quakebot can swiftly produce articles on breaking news.

Other applications include Bloomberg News' Bulletin service where chatbots create personalized one-sentence news summaries. AIGC also enables AI news anchors that co-present broadcasts with real anchors by mimicking human appearance and speech from text input. Chinese news agency Xinhua's virtual presenter Xin Xiaowei is an example, presenting broadcasts from different angles for an immersive effect.

AIGC is transforming movie creation from screenwriting to post-production. AI screenwriting tools analyze data to generate optimized scripts. Visual effects teams blend AI-enhanced digital environments and de-aging with live footage for immersive visuals. Deep fake technology recreates or revives characters convincingly.

AI also powers automated subtitle generation, even predicting dialogue in silent films by training models on extensive audio samples. This expands accessibility via subtitles and recreates voice-overs synchronized to scenes. In post-production, AI color grading and editing tools like Colourlab AI and Descript simplify processes like color correction using algorithms.

In advertising, AIGC unlocks new potential for efficient, customized advertising creativity and personalization. AI-generated content allows advertisers to create personalized, engaging ads tailored to individual consumers at scale. Platforms like **Creative Advertising System (CAS)** and **Smart Generation System Personalized Advertising Copy (SGS-PAC)** leverage data to automatically generate ads with messaging targeted to specific user needs and interests.

AI also assists in advertising creativity and design – tools like Vinci produce customized attractive posters from product images and slogans, while companies like Brandmark.io generate logo variations based on user preferences. GAN technologies automate product listing generation with keywords for effective peer-to-peer marketing. Synthetic ad production is also on the rise, enabling highly personalized, scalable campaigns that save time.

In music, tools like Google's Magenta, IBM's Watson Beat, and Sony CSL's Flow Machine can generate original melodies and compositions. AIVA similarly creates unique compositions from parameters tuned by users. LANDR's AI mastering uses machine learning to process and improve digital audio quality for musicians.

In visual arts, MidJourney uses neural networks to generate inspirational images that can kickstart painting projects. Artists have used its outputs to create prize-winning works. DeepDream's algorithm imposes patterns on images, creating psychedelic art. GANs can generate abstract paintings converging on a desired style. AI painting conservation analyzes artwork to digitally repair damage and restore pieces.

Animation tools like Adobe's Character Animator and Anthropic's Claude can help with the generation of customized characters, scenes, and motion sequences, opening animation potential for non-professionals. ControlNet adds constraints to steer diffusion models, increasing output variability.

For all these applications, advanced AI expands creative possibilities through both generative content and data-driven insights. In all cases, quality control and properly attributing the contributions of human artists, developers, and training data remains an ongoing challenge as adoption spreads.

Education

One potential near-future scenario is that the rise of personalized AI tutors and mentors could democratize access to education for high-demand skills aligned with an AI-driven economy. In the education sector, generative AI is already transforming how we teach and learn. Tools like ChatGPT can be used to automatically generate personalized lessons and customized content for individual students. This reduces instructor workloads substantially by automating repetitive teaching tasks. AI tutors provide real-time feedback on student writing assignments, freeing up teachers to focus on more complex skills. Virtual simulations powered by generative AI can also create engaging, tailored learning experiences adapted to different learners' needs and interests.

However, risks around perpetuating biases and spreading misinformation need to be studied further as these technologies evolve. The accelerating pace of knowledge and the obsolescence of scientific findings mean that training children's curiosity-driven learning should focus on developing the cognitive mechanisms involved in initiating and sustaining curiosity, such as awareness of knowledge gaps and the use of appropriate strategies to resolve them.

While AI tutors tailored to each student could enhance outcomes and engagement, poorer schools may be left behind, worsening inequality. Governments should promote equal access to prevent generative AI from becoming a privilege of the affluent. Democratizing opportunity for all students remains vital.

If implemented thoughtfully, personalized AI-powered education could make crucial skills acquisition accessible to anyone motivated to learn. Interactive AI assistants that adapt courses to students' strengths, needs, and interests could make learning efficient, engaging, and equitable. However, challenges around access, biases, and socialization need addressing.

Law

Generative models like LLMs can automate routine legal tasks such as contract review, documentation generation, and brief preparation. They also enable faster, comprehensive legal research and analysis. Additional applications include explaining complex legal concepts in plain language and predicting litigation outcomes using case data. However, responsible and ethical use remains critical given considerations around transparency, fairness, and accountability. Overall, properly implemented AI tools promise to boost legal productivity and access to justice while requiring ongoing scrutiny regarding reliability and ethics.

Manufacturing

In the automotive sector, generative models are employed to generate 3D environments for simulations and aid in the development of cars. Additionally, generative AI is utilized for road-testing autonomous vehicles using synthetic data. These models can also process object information to comprehend the surrounding environment, understand human intent through dialogues, generate natural language responses to human input, and create manipulation plans to assist humans in various tasks.

Medicine

A model that can accurately predict physical properties from gene sequences would represent a major breakthrough in medicine and could have profound impacts on society. It could further accelerate drug discovery and precision medicine, enable earlier disease prediction and prevention, provide a deeper understanding of complex diseases, and improve gene therapies. However, it also raises major ethical concerns around genetic engineering and could exacerbate social inequalities.

New techniques with neural networks are already employed to lower long-read DNA sequencing error rates (Baid and colleagues; *DeepConsensus improves the accuracy of sequences with a gap-aware sequence transformer*, September 2022), and, according to a report by ARK Investment Management (2023), in the short term, technology like this can make it already possible to deliver the first high-quality, whole long-read genome for less than $1,000. This means that large-scale gene-to-expression models might not be far away either.

Military

Militaries worldwide are investing in research to develop **Lethal Autonomous Weapons Systems (LAWS)**. Robots and drones can identify targets and deploy lethal force without any human supervision. Machines can process information and react faster than humans, removing emotion from lethal decisions. However, this raises significant moral questions. Allowing machines to determine whether lives should be taken crosses a troubling threshold. Even with sophisticated AI, complex factors in war like proportionality and distinction between civilians and combatants require human judgment.

If deployed, completely autonomous lethal weapons would represent an alarming step toward relinquishing control over life-and-death decisions. They could violate international humanitarian law or be used by despotic regimes to terrorize populations. Once unleashed fully independently, the actions of autonomous killer robots would be impossible to predict or restrain.

The advent of highly capable generative AI will likely transform many aspects of society in the coming years beyond the economics and the disruption of certain jobs. Let's think a bit more broadly about the societal impact!

Societal implications

As generative models continue to develop and add value to businesses and creative projects, generative AI will shape the future of technology and human interaction across domains. While their widespread adoption brings forth numerous benefits and opportunities for businesses and individuals, it is crucial to address the ethical and societal concerns that arise from increasing reliance on AI models in various fields.

Generative AI offers immense potential benefits across personal, societal, and industrial realms if deployed thoughtfully. At a personal level, these models can enhance creativity and productivity, and increase accessibility to services like healthcare, education, and finance. By democratizing access to knowledge resources, they can help students learn or aid professionals in making decisions by synthesizing expertise. As virtual assistants, they provide instant, customized information to facilitate routine tasks.

From a consumer standpoint, generative AI has the potential to deliver unprecedented personalization. Recommendation systems can fine-tune their outputs to individual preferences. Marketing efforts can be adapted to specific customer segments and local tastes while maintaining consistency and scale.

The rise of generative AI represents a significant milestone within a broader societal trend of how creative content is being generated and consumed. The internet has already nurtured a culture of remixing, where derivative works and co-creation are the norms. Generative AI fits naturally within this paradigm by creating new content through the recombination of existing digital materials, promoting the ethos of shared, iterative creation.

However, the capacity of generative AI to synthesize and remix copyrighted materials at scale presents intricate legal and ethical challenges. The training of these models on extensive corpora that encompass literature, articles, images, and other copyrighted works creates a tangled web for attribution and compensation. Existing tools struggle to identify content generated by AI, which complicates efforts to apply traditional copyright and authorship principles. This dilemma underscores the urgent need for legal frameworks that can keep pace with technological advances and navigate the complex interplay between rights-holders and AI-generated content.

One of the major problems that I can see is misinformation, either in the interest of political interest groups, foreign actors, or large corporations. Let's discuss this threat!

Misinformation and cybersecurity

AI presents a dual-edged sword against disinformation. While it enables scalable detection, automation makes it easier to spread sophisticated, personalized propaganda. AI could help or harm security depending on whether it is used responsibly. It increases vulnerabilities to misinformation along with cyberattacks using generative hacking and social engineering.

There are significant threats associated with AI techniques like micro-targeting and deepfakes. Powerful AI can profile users psychologically to deliver personalized disinformation that facilitates concealed manipulation, escaping broad examination. Big Data and AI could be leveraged to exploit psychological vulnerabilities and infiltrate online forums to attack and spread conspiracy theories.

Disinformation has transformed into a multifaceted phenomenon, involving biased information, manipulation, propaganda, and intent to influence political behavior. For example, during the COVID-19 pandemic, the spread of misinformation and infodemics has been a major challenge. AI can influence public opinion and sway elections.

It can also generate fake audio/video content to damage reputations and sow confusion. State and non-state actors are weaponizing these capabilities for propaganda to damage reputations and sow confusion. AI can be used by political parties, governments, criminal groups, and even the legal system to launch lawsuits and/or extract money.

This likely will have far-reaching consequences in various domains. A significant portion of internet users may be obtaining the information they need without accessing external websites. There is a danger of large corporations being the gatekeepers of information and controlling public opinion, effectively being able to restrict certain actions or viewpoints.

Careful governance and digital literacy are essential to build resilience. Though no single fix exists, collective efforts promoting responsible AI development can help democratic societies address emerging threats.

Let's talk more about regulations!

Regulations and implementation challenges

Realizing the potential of generative AI in a responsible manner involves addressing a number of practical legal, ethical, and regulatory issues:

- **Legal**: Copyright laws remain ambiguous regarding AI-generated content. Who owns the output – the model creator, training data contributors, or end users? Replicating copyrighted data in training also raises fair use debates that need clarification.

- **Data protection**: Collecting, processing, and storing the massive datasets required to train advanced models creates data privacy and security risks. Governance models ensuring consent, anonymity, and safe access are vital.

- **Oversight and regulations**: Calls are mounting for oversight to ensure non-discrimination, accuracy, and accountability from advanced AI systems. However, flexible policies balancing innovation and risk are needed rather than burdensome bureaucracy.

- **Ethics**: Frameworks guiding development toward beneficial outcomes are indispensable. Integrating ethics through design practices focused on transparency, explicability, and human oversight helps build trust.

Overall, proactive collaboration between policymakers, researchers, and civil society is essential to settle unresolved issues around rights, ethics, and governance. With pragmatic guardrails in place, generative models can fulfill their promise while mitigating harm.

There is a growing demand for algorithmic transparency. This means that tech companies and developers should reveal the source code and inner workings of their systems. However, there is resistance from these companies and developers, who argue that disclosing proprietary information would harm their competitive advantage. Open-source models will continue to thrive, and local legislation in the EU and other countries will push for transparent use of AI.

The consequence of AI bias includes potential harm to individuals or groups due to biased decisions made by AI systems. Incorporating ethics training into computer science curricula can help reduce biases in AI code. By teaching developers how to build applications that are ethical by design, the probability of biases being embedded into the code can be minimized. To stay on the right path, organizations need to prioritize transparency, accountability, and guardrails to prevent bias in their AI systems. AI bias prevention is a long-term priority for many organizations; however, without legislation driving it, it can take time to be introduced. Local legislation in EU countries, for example, such as the European Commission's proposal for harmonized rules on AI regulation, will drive more ethical use of language and imagery.

A current German law on fake news, which imposes a 24-hour timeframe for platforms to remove fake news and hate speech, is impractical for both large and small platforms. Additionally, the limited resources of smaller platforms make it unrealistic for them to police all content. Further, online platforms should not have the sole authority to determine what is considered truth, as this could lead to excessive censorship. More nuanced policies are needed that balance free speech, accountability, and feasibility for a diversity of technology platforms to comply. Relying solely on private companies to regulate online content raises concerns about a lack of oversight and due process. Broader collaboration between government, civil society, academics, and industry can develop more effective frameworks to counter misinformation while protecting rights.

To maximize benefits, companies need to ensure human oversight, diversity, and transparency in development. Policymakers may need to implement guardrails preventing misuse while providing workers with support to transition as activities shift. With responsible implementation, generative AI could propel growth, creativity, and accessibility in a more prosperous society. Addressing potential risks early on and ensuring a just distribution of benefits designed to serve public welfare will cultivate a sense of trust among stakeholders, such as:

- **The dynamics of progress**: Fine-tuning the pace of transformation is critical to avoid any undesired repercussions. Moreover, excessively slow developments could stifle innovation, suggesting that determining an ideal pace through encompassing public discourse is crucial.

- **The human-AI symbiosis**: Rather than striving for outright automation, more advantageous systems would integrate and complement the creative prowess of humans with the productive efficiency of AI. Such a hybrid model will ensure optimal oversight.

- **Promoting access and inclusion**: Equitable access to resources, relevant education, and myriad opportunities concerning AI is key to negating the amplification of disparities. Representativeness and diversity should be prioritized.

- **Preventive measures and risk management**: Constant evaluation of freshly emerging capabilities via interdisciplinary insights is necessary to evade future dangers. Excessive apprehensions, however, should not impede potential progress.

- **Upholding democratic norms**: Collaborative discussions, communal efforts, and reaching a compromise will inevitably prove more constructive in defining the future course of AI, as compared to unilateral decrees imposed by a solitary entity. Public interest must take precedence.

Let's conclude this chapter!

The road ahead

The forthcoming era of generative AI models offers a plethora of intriguing opportunities and unparalleled progression, yet it is interspersed with numerous uncertainties. As discussed in this book, many breakthroughs have been accomplished in recent months, but successive challenges continue to linger, mainly pertaining to precision, reasoning ability, controllability, and entrenched bias within these models. While grandiose claims of superintelligent AI on the horizon may seem hyperbolic, consistent trends predict sophisticated capabilities sprouting within a few decades.

On a technical level, generative models like ChatGPT often function as black boxes, with limited transparency into their decision-making processes. A lack of model interpretability makes it difficult to fully understand model behavior or to control outputs. There are also concerns about potential biases that could emerge from imperfect training data. On a practical level, generative models require extensive computational resources for training and deployment; however, we discussed developments and trends that change that.

On the positive side, AI can democratize skills, allowing amateurs to produce professional quality output in design, writing, and other areas. Businesses can benefit from faster, cheaper, on-demand work. However, there are major concerns about job losses, especially for specialized middle-class roles like graphic designers, lawyers, and doctors. Their work is being automated while low-skilled workers learn to leverage AI as a superpower.

However, the proliferation of generative content raises valid concerns about misinformation, plagiarism in academia, and impersonation in online spaces. As these models become more adept at mimicking human expression, people may have difficulty discerning what is human-generated versus AI-generated, enabling new forms of deception. Deepfakes produced in real-time will proliferate scams and erode trust. Most ominously, AI could be weaponized by militaries, terrorists, criminals, and governments for propaganda and influence. There are also fears about generative models exacerbating social media addiction due to their ability to produce endless customized content.

The sheer pace of advancement creates unease surrounding human obsolescence and job displacement, which could further divide economic classes. Unlike physical automation of the past, generative AI threatens cognitive job categories previously considered safe from automation. Managing this workforce transition ethically and equitably will require foresight and planning. There are also philosophical debates around whether AI should be creating art, literature, or music that has historically reflected the human condition.

For corporations, effective governance frameworks have yet to be established around acceptable use cases. Generative models amplify risks of misuse, ranging from creating misinformation such as deepfakes to generating unsafe medical advice. Legal questions around content licensing and intellectual property arise. While generative models can enhance business productivity, quality control and bias mitigation incur costs.

Looking decades ahead, perhaps the deepest challenges are ethical. As AI is entrusted with more consequential decisions, alignment with human values becomes critical. While accuracy, reasoning ability, controllability, and mitigating bias remain technical priorities, other priorities should include fortifying model robustness, promoting transparency, and ensuring alignment with human values.

While future capabilities remain uncertain, proactive governance and democratization of access are essential to direct these technologies toward equitable, benevolent outcomes. Collaboration between researchers, policymakers, and civil society around issues of transparency, accountability, and ethics can help align emerging innovations with shared human values. The goal should be to empower human potential, not mere technological advancement.

Join our community on Discord

Join our community's Discord space for discussions with the authors and other readers:

`https://packt.link/lang`

packt.com

Subscribe to our online digital library for full access to over 7,000 books and videos, as well as industry leading tools to help you plan your personal development and advance your career. For more information, please visit our website.

Why subscribe?

- Spend less time learning and more time coding with practical eBooks and Videos from over 4,000 industry professionals

- Improve your learning with Skill Plans built especially for you

- Get a free eBook or video every month

- Fully searchable for easy access to vital information

- Copy and paste, print, and bookmark content

At www.packt.com, you can also read a collection of free technical articles, sign up for a range of free newsletters, and receive exclusive discounts and offers on Packt books and eBooks.

Other Books You May Enjoy

If you enjoyed this book, you may be interested in these other books by Packt:

Transformers for Natural Language Processing and Computer Vision

Denis Rothman

ISBN: 9781805128724

- Master the art of fine-tuning models and engineering effective prompts
- Tackle examples of LLM risks by delving into strategies to mitigate them
- Learn about the potential functional AGI capabilities of foundation models
- Visualize transformer model activity for deeper insights using BertViz, LIME, and SHAP
- Create and implement cross-platform chained models, such as HuggingGPT
- Skyrocket your productivity with an automated generative ideation process
- Go in-depth into vision transformers with CLIP, DALL-E 2, DALL-E 3, and GPT-4V

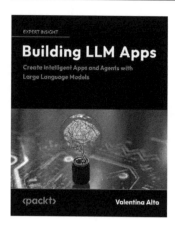

Building LLM Apps

Valentina Alto

ISBN: 9781835462317

- Core components of LLMs' architecture, including encoder-decoders blocks, embedding and so on
- Get well-versed with unique features of LLMs like GPT-3.5/4, Llama 2, and Falcon LLM
- Use AI orchestrators like LangChain, and Streamlit as frontend
- Get familiar with LLMs components such as memory, prompts and tools
- Learn non-parametric knowledge, embeddings and vector databases
- Understand the implications of LFMs for AI research, and industry applications
- Customize your LLMs with fine tuning
- Learn the ethical implications of LLM-powered applications

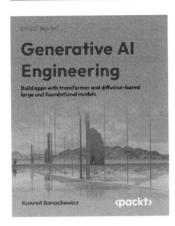

Generative AI Engineering

Konrad Banachewicz

ISBN: 9781805120513

- Get to grips with the fundamentals of generative AI and its applications
- Familiarize yourself with different types of generative models and when to use them
- Train and Finetune generative models using PyTorch
- Evaluate the performance of your models and fine-tune them for optimal results
- Find best practices for deploying and scaling generative AI models in production environments

Packt is searching for authors like you

If you're interested in becoming an author for Packt, please visit authors.packtpub.com and apply today. We have worked with thousands of developers and tech professionals, just like you, to help them share their insight with the global tech community. You can make a general application, apply for a specific hot topic that we are recruiting an author for, or submit your own idea.

Share your thoughts

Now you've finished *Generative AI with LangChain*, we'd love to hear your thoughts! Scan the QR code below to go straight to the Amazon review page for this book and share your feedback or leave a review on the site that you purchased it from.

https://packt.link/r/1835083463

Your review is important to us and the tech community and will help us make sure we're delivering excellent quality content.

Index

Download a free PDF copy of this book

Thanks for purchasing this book!

Do you like to read on the go but are unable to carry your print books everywhere? Is your eBook purchase not compatible with the device of your choice?

Don't worry, now with every Packt book you get a DRM-free PDF version of that book at no cost.

Read anywhere, any place, on any device. Search, copy, and paste code from your favorite technical books directly into your application.

The perks don't stop there, you can get exclusive access to discounts, newsletters, and great free content in your inbox daily

Follow these simple steps to get the benefits:

1. Scan the QR code or visit the link below

https://packt.link/free-ebook/9781835083468

2. Submit your proof of purchase
3. That's it! We'll send your free PDF and other benefits to your email directly